P9-CCP-908

INSIDE TEACHING

INSIDE TEACHING

How

Classroom

Life

Undermines

Reform

MARY KENNEDY

Harvard University Press
Cambridge, Massachusetts
London, England
2005

For Tom

Library of Congress Cataloging-in-Publication Data
Kennedy, Mary M.
  Inside teaching : how classroom life undermines reform / Mary Kennedy.
    p.   cm.
  Includes bibliographical references and index.
  ISBN 0-674-01723-4 (alk. paper)
  1. Classroom environment—United States.   2. Educational change—United
States.   I. Title.

LC210.5.K46 2005
371.1—dc22   2004060570

Acknowledgments

I am grateful to the Pew Charitable Trusts for providing financial support for this study. Their generosity paid for research assistants, for videotaping equipment, for transcribing expenses, and for time, the most valuable of commodities in research.

Throughout this book I rely on the rhetorical convention of using "we" whenever writing about anything a researcher saw in a classroom or anything a researcher asked a teacher in an interview, even though no more than one person directly witnessed any classroom or interviewed any teacher. These observations and interviews were conducted not only by me but also by my colleagues Rachel Lander, Paula Lane, and Brenda Neumann. They not only gathered data but also contributed in numerous ways to the design of the study, the sample selection, the interview guides, and the analytic strategies.

Teachers demonstrated a generous willingness to participate. Because we not only interviewed them but also entered their classrooms and videotaped their lessons, the study was much more invasive than most research projects. Some teachers were accustomed to being videotaped, but many had never seen themselves on tape, including one teacher who had taught for 30 years. The prevailing norms of privacy in teaching make it all the more impressive that these teachers were willing to allow a stranger to enter, videotape, and then interrogate them about their teaching practices. I am indebted to them all.

Once teachers were interviewed, audiotapes came streaming into Michigan State's College of Education, where an extremely organized person, Kathy Lessard, trained and coordinated a pool of transcribers who converted the tapes to transcripts. Although I don't know the names of all the transcribers, I thank them and Kathy for their contributions.

Richard Elmore, Paula Lane, Brenda Neumann, and Alan Shoenfeld critiqued earlier versions of this book. Their comments were enormously helpful in moving my thinking and in helping me find better ways to present my ideas. Adam Gamoran commented on one section and provided helpful insights. I am grateful to them all.

Earlier versions of parts of Chapter 2 appeared as "Reform Ideals and Teachers' Practical Intentions," in *Education Policy Analysis Archives* 13, no. 13 (April 7, 2004). Earlier versions of parts of Chapter 7 appeared as "Knowledge and Teaching," in *Teachers and Teaching: Theory and Practice* 8, no. 3–4 (2002), copyright © 2002 by Taylor and Francis Ltd.

Contents

1. The Mysterious Gap between Reform Ideals and Everyday Teaching

I never understood the phrase "knowing everything and knowing nothing" until I examined my knowledge of teaching. Like most educated adults, I knew everything, and yet nothing, about teaching. The "everything" part of our knowledge has to do with what teaching *looks like*. As children, we spent many days sitting before teachers. As adults, many of us have visited our own children's classrooms. From these experiences, we have a sense of the variety of ways in which teaching occurs, and we have a sense of what counts as good teaching or bad teaching. Some of us also have strong views about what teaching *should* look like, and some of us become education reformers, devoting substantial energy to trying to improve teaching.

But reforms typically fail, forcing us to acknowledge that although we know a lot about what teaching looks like, we know almost nothing about *why* it looks like this. We don't understand why teaching seems so intractable to reform efforts, why teachers seem to ignore the guidance offered to them by so many concerned groups. Most American teachers are highly educated and highly dedicated. They are members of professional associations, receive various kinds of continuing professional development, and have access to textbooks and other materials. They care about their students and work long hours preparing their lessons and reading their students' work. The question we have to ask is this: How can it be that people who are well educated and committed to their work engage in practices that receive so much criticism?

This book aims to fill in these large knowledge gaps—to go as deeply as possible into classrooms, and into teachers' heads, to learn why teaching looks the way it does and in particular to learn why teachers appear to be immune to reform efforts. The study I describe shows how classroom events appear to teachers and how routine conditions of classroom life often dictate teaching practices. It reveals that teachers are not unaware of reform ideals, and indeed are sympathetic with them. But they also have to attend to many other things, simultaneously orchestrating time, materials, students, and ideas. They must finish a lesson by 11:33 so that students can be in the cafeteria at 11:35. They must make sure that all students are on the same page, digesting the same ideas, gaining the same understandings. They must make sure that the right diagram, chart, or globe is readily accessible to show to students at exactly the right moment, and that the handouts students will need are also nearby. They must be prepared to respond to individual confusions, misunderstandings, and tangential observations without distracting or boring the rest of the class.

They must also be prepared to have the entire plan disrupted or defeated by some unforeseen event. Someone from down the hall may enter the room and interrupt the lesson midstream. A student may poke another student or ask a question that other students don't understand or don't care about. The projector may break, or there may not be enough copies of a handout to go around. Though such distractions appear everywhere, schools seem more susceptible to them than other organizations. Perhaps because schools are teeming with children, they are subject to much higher levels of distraction than most other organizations. And in schools, distractions are not merely temporary setbacks; they are obstacles to intellectual progress. They get in the way of good teaching. All these interruptions and complications can distract teachers from the thread of their own thought and make it harder for them to present coherent lessons. Ironically, schools are places where sustained thought is rare.

These difficulties provide an explanation for our long history of failed reform efforts in education. Reform movements have come and gone for decades without much visible impact on teaching practices. The problem is so widely recognized that historians are now chronicling these movements (e.g., Cuban, 1984, 1990; Gold, 1999; Tyack and Cuban, 1995). Yet reformers continue to try, and others continue to generate hypotheses to account for the failures. Perhaps teachers need more knowledge or better guidance; perhaps we need to change their values or their dispositions. The sad fact is that most reforms don't acknowledge the realities of classroom teaching, where both God and the devil are in the details.

What Do Reformers Want?

Teachers in the United States have remarkable flexibility in what they teach and how they teach it. Virtually all other countries have national curricula, which can significantly influence practice. For example, in a comparison of American, Chinese, and Japanese schools, Stevenson and Stigler (1992) found that in the Asian schools, which had national curricula and prescribed texts, the lessons in all classrooms were virtually the same from one day to the next. And while American teachers are all provided with textbooks and other materials, they can and do skip sections they think are irrelevant and add material not covered by the text (Porter et al., 1989).

Teachers also design their own classroom settings, including what is on the walls, how the furniture is arranged, whether student activities are structured or unstructured, and whether students work alone or in groups. They often create their own demonstrations, their own problems for students, their own homework assignments.

Meanwhile numerous groups try to influence teachers' local decisions. Textbook publishers, professional associations, parent associations, religious groups, and business alliances all enter the education arena. Some compete with state and local policies, some try to change them, and some reinforce them. The education policy landscape is routinely crowded with competing, often conflicting, ideas about what is the most important thing for teachers to accomplish in their classrooms. Teachers may encounter educational ideas and arguments in state or district pronouncements, specific textbooks or tests, workshops, professional newsletters or conferences, parents, neighbors, or their daily newspapers. Teachers may seek some of these ideas themselves, but others may be pushed toward them by bureaucrats, parents, businessmen, or other interested groups.

Despite their apparent instructional autonomy, and despite the many ideas available to them, teachers have very little time to digest these proposals and to make decisions about what to do in their classrooms. Again relying on international comparisons, we find that American teachers have less time away from their students than teachers in many other countries, and thus less time to plan their instructional activities or to gain access to ideas about how to teach specific content. Stevenson and Stigler (1992), for instance, found that Asian teachers are typically at school for nine hours a day, but are directly teaching students for only three or four hours a day. The American teacher has a shorter school day, but she teaches almost the entire day, frequently having only one "free" period.[1] A recent study comparing teachers in nine industrialized countries found similar ratios of instructional time to total time: the amount of total time spent teaching ranged from 65 percent to nearly 100, and the U.S. average was 81 percent (Stoel and Thant, 2002).

The practices teachers devise in this environment are often criticized, with different reformers focusing on different problems. Some reformers perceive the process of learning as dull and dreary, some perceive classroom life as stultifying, some perceive the knowledge acquired in schools as uninteresting, unimportant, or thin. One source characterized the American curriculum as "a mile wide and an inch deep" (Schmidt, McKnight, and Raizen, 1997). These general perceptions have been reinforced by researchers throughout the twentieth century. For instance, in 1932 Willard Waller noted that school subject matter was boring and irrelevant to life outside schools. Decades later, Hoetker and Ahlbrand (1969) reviewed a series of studies stretching back almost to the beginning of the twentieth century, in which researchers observed that teachers relied heavily on recitations—rapid-fire questions requiring rapid-fire responses—that focused on trivial facts and denied students the opportunity to think much about the content. Another review done at around the same time (Gall, 1970) also noted that teachers focused primarily on factual recall.

In the 1980s a spate of studies examined school content and found it wanting. Walter Doyle (1986) found that teachers transformed academic content into academic tasks, and that this transformation frequently destroyed the original significance of the content. Linda McNeil (1985) found that teachers reduced complex ideas to labels and lists, sacrificed depth for breadth, glossed over difficult topics, and omitted controversial ones. Both Doyle and McNeil attributed these practices to teachers' need to maintain control over their students. Doyle argued that routine tasks were easier to manage, and McNeil argued that as teachers became more concerned about control, they were more likely to trivialize knowledge, and their students were less likely to be engaged.

Many reformers have referred to such observations to justify their goals. For instance, Mary Campbell Gallagher rationalized the 1960s curriculum reform with the assertion: "Disgusted with the dull and inaccurate lessons in commercial school textbooks in science and mathematics, a handful of scientists, mathematicians and educators . . . [decided to develop] new precollege curricula" (Gallagher, 2001, p. 283). And in its 1983 report, *A Nation at Risk,* the National Commission on Excellence in Education offered this dramatic statement: "We report to the American people that while we can take justifiable pride in what our schools and colleges have historically accomplished and contributed to the United States and the well-being of its people, the educational foundations of our society are presently being eroded by a rising tide of mediocrity that threatens our very future as a Nation and a people. What was unimaginable a generation ago has begun to occur—others are matching and surpassing our educational attainments" (p. 5).

These perceptions, whether correct or not, frequently motivate reform movements. Though reformers disagree on what is needed, their proposals can be grouped into three broad ideals: more rigorous and important content, more intellectual engagement with content, and universal access to knowledge.[2]

More Rigorous and Important Content

The first persistent reform ideal is sometimes expressed in a call for "more demanding" or "more challenging" content or for "central ideas." But there are many different views about what makes content important. One group of reformers focuses on meanings. Thus they want students not only to learn the relevant names and dates of the Civil War but also to understand the causes and consequences of that war; not only to read or recite passages from Shakespeare but also to understand the significance of these passages; not only to learn computational procedures but also to understand how those procedures work; not only to learn a body of scientific details but also to understand how those details were ascertained and why they are thought to be true. Most of these reformers also want students to learn the intellectual habits and values of these fields of study.

Another group of reformers wants to give students the knowledge and skills they will need to function in our society. They want students to acquire the ideas and values that define our culture and to be prepared for constantly changing technology and for an increasingly complex economy. They fear that too much attention to the liberal arts will interfere with these goals. For these reformers, the most important ideas are those that are most culturally and technologically relevant.

The reform proposal developed by the American Association for the Advancement of Science (1989) emphasized the first set of ideas. It advocated that students learn not just specific scientific facts but also ideas related to the essential nature of science—that science assumes that the world is understandable, that science demands evidence, and that scientific knowledge is durable, for instance. The proposal also emphasized the importance of large organizing ideas such as the nature of the universe and the structure of matter. Similarly, the National Council of Teachers of Mathematics focused on central mathematical ideas: "School mathematics curricula should focus on mathematics content and processes that are worth the time and attention of students. Mathematics topics can be considered important for different reasons, such as their utility in developing other mathematical ideas, in linking different areas of mathematics, or in deepening students' appreciation of mathematics as a discipline and as a human creation. Ideas may also merit curricular focus because they are useful in representing and solving problems within or outside mathematics" (2000, p. 12).

In contrast, the National Commission on Excellence in Education stressed the importance of practical knowledge: "The people of the United States need to know that individuals in our society who do not possess the levels of skill, literacy, and training essential to this new era will be effectively disenfranchised, not simply from the material rewards that accompany competent performance, but also from the chance to participate fully in our national life. A high level of shared education is essential to a free, democratic society and to the fostering of a common culture, especially in a country that prides itself on pluralism and individual freedom" (1983, p. 7).

Despite their different agendas, these groups share a perception that the content currently offered in classrooms is either not very important or not very demanding, and that the task of reform is to correct that situation.

More Intellectual Engagement

The second persistent reform ideal focuses on how students interact with school subject matter. Reformers want teachers to increase students' interest, capture their imagination, or pique their curiosity. They want students to be actively engaged with important ideas. The notion of intellectual engagement is often associated with progressive education, where the emphasis is on physical activity as well as mental activity. One of the earliest examples of a progressive reform is William Heard Kilpatrick's (1918) proposal for projects. Kilpatrick argued that the *purposeful act* was the central feature of life in general, and that it should also be the central feature of school life. He wanted classroom lessons to be organized around projects that students wanted to do, whether they involved building a boat, putting on a play, or trying to solve an intellectual problem of some sort. All of these would be more meaningful and engaging to students than the sort of learning activities that teachers normally assigned.

These twin ideas of meaningfulness and engagement reappeared in the 1960s reform movement, which relied heavily on a pedagogy called discovery learning. Discovery learning was intended to ensure that students acquired the most important ideas and that they thought hard about those ideas. It assumed that students would find those ideas meaningful and engaging because of the way they interacted with them. Numerous curricula were developed during this period, most of them in mathematics and the sciences, and nearly all relied on complicated classroom activities that were designed to promote students' intellectual engagement with content. Jerome Bruner, a central figure in the discovery learning movement, defended the proposal for discovery learning again in 1996, when he summarized his original reasoning as follows: "Acquired knowledge is most useful to a learner when it is 'discovered' through the learner's own cognitive efforts, for it is then related to and used in reference to what one has known before. Such acts of discovery are enormously facilitated by the structure of knowledge itself, for however complicated any domain of knowledge may be, it can be represented in ways that make it accessible through less complex elaborated processes" (p. xii).

The importance of meaningfulness and intellectual engagement resurfaced yet again in the 1990s standards-based reform. Here is how the National Council of Teachers of Mathematics laid out the meaning-and-engagement theme:

> In effective teaching, worthwhile mathematical tasks are used to introduce important mathematical ideas and to engage and challenge students intellectually. Well-chosen tasks can pique students' curiosity and draw them into mathematics. The tasks may be connected to the real-world experiences of students, or they may arise in contexts that are purely mathematical. Regardless of the context, worthwhile tasks should be intriguing, with a level of challenge that invites speculation and hard work. Such tasks often can be approached in more than one way, such as using an arithmetic counting approach, drawing a geometric diagram and enumerating possibilities, or using algebraic equations, which makes the tasks accessible to students with varied prior knowledge and experience.   (2000, p. 18)

This interest in real-world activities is held by a subset of reformers, referred to broadly as "progressives," who assume that the inherent interest of the instructional task is an essential tool for motivating students and engaging them in learning. Other reformers believe that an overemphasis on activities can suffocate rigorous content. They worry that activities lead to hands-on learning but not to minds-on learning.

Still, even nonprogressive reformers must acknowledge the importance of intellectual engagement, for learning cannot occur without it. The debatable question is whether learning requires the kind of activities that progressive reformers tend to seek. There may be ways to engage students intellectually that don't involve complicated activities. These disputes about the strategy for achieving intellectual engagement need not concern us. The central issue is intellectual engagement, not whether this engagement must be achieved through particular kinds of learning activities.

Universal Access to Knowledge

The third persistent reform ideal reflects a commitment to making school knowledge accessible to the full range of students attending

American schools, not just those who are gifted or who are college-bound. When Cronbach and Suppes wrote their book on disciplined inquiry in education in 1969, they put the issue this way:

> The older form of education—transmitting facts and rules of thumb, and issuing a lifetime certificate of professional competence—has no validity in a world where social goals, communication patterns, and even scientific theories are changing constantly. At the other end of the spectrum, the school is asked to instruct the children from homes where there is no educational tradition and no preparation for responsible intellectual effort. The nation, speaking through its local and national leadership, is calling for the invention of new educational methods that will wipe out the cultural depression of the inner city. . . . Yet the reforms have not truly succeeded. An International Study that compared the mathematical achievements of adolescents in various countries showed that American students have a proper understanding of mathematics as a growing field of knowledge, but find mathematics more alien and uninteresting that students in several other nations.   (Pp. 2–3)

In her reminiscence about the 1960s curriculum reform movement, Gallagher also stressed the importance of universal access: "I must emphasize that while the Curriculum Reform movement benefited from national interest in keeping up with Russia's scientists, the Reformers themselves believed so passionately in their subjects that they wanted to teach *all* students, not just aspiring scientists and mathematicians. Phylis Morrison told me, A thing that we saw again and again . . . is that if you treat science as an open-ended exploration, *all* the students learn science" (2001, p. 286).

Following the curriculum reform of the 1960s, the nation went through a spate of federal legislation designed to increase educational opportunities to students who had historically been underserved. Congress passed legislation creating the Head Start program, and the Elementary and Secondary Education Act, both of which included a large entitlement for disadvantaged students. These were followed by the creation of programs for students with limited

English and for special education students. In each case, a central purpose of the legislation was to provide greater access to education for a broader range of students.

In 1983, when the National Commission on Excellence in Education wrote its now famous *A Nation at Risk*, it said: "All, regardless of race or class or economic status, are entitled to a fair chance and to the tools for developing their individual powers of mind and spirit to the utmost. This promise means that all children by virtue of their own efforts, competently guided, can hope to attain the mature and informed judgment needed to secure gainful employment, and to manage their own lives, thereby serving not only their own interests but also the progress of society itself" (p. 8).

This third reform ideal is probably less contentious today than ever before. Nearly all reformers, nearly all citizens, and nearly all teachers agree on the importance of giving all students access to school content. However, there are still vigorous debates about how to achieve that ideal, with one side wanting to maintain a focus on important content and a rigorous curriculum and the other wanting to focus on meaningful and engaging activities. In his history of efforts to "popularize" education, Cremin (1990) noted that this debate goes back at least to the 1830s, with one side pushing to expand educational opportunities and the other worrying that expansion would mean diluting the curriculum. It is not clear that these two ideals must be mutually exclusive, but advocates frequently pit them against each other, forcing a complicated issue into a simple dichotomy. Chall (2000), for instance, pitches "teacher-centered" instruction against "student-centered," and Ravitch (2000) pits "progressive" education against "traditional" education. These dichotomies do not address the fundamental nature of instruction, which is that it cannot occur without *both* important content *and* intellectually engaged students. Teachers must think about both things at once.

My goal here is not to settle any of these disputes, but to use these broad ideals as a way to evaluate teaching practices. Throughout this book I refer to this general constellation of ideas as *the reform ideals*. The question that motivates this study is this: Given that reformers have tried repeatedly to achieve these three ideals, why have they failed to persuade teachers to be as ambitious as they themselves are?

Hypotheses about the Failure of Reform

The four most widely mentioned reasons given for the failure of reform are:

Teachers need more knowledge or guidance in order to alter their practices.

Teachers hold beliefs and values that differ from reformers' and that justify their current practices.

Teachers have dispositions that interfere with their ability to implement reforms.

The circumstances of teaching prevent teachers from altering their practices.

There is a fifth hypothesis that also needs to be considered, for if there is merit to any of the others, there is also merit to this:

The reform ideals themselves may be unattainable or may actually impede practice.

Reformers rarely consider this hypothesis, but the history of reform requires us to consider it.

Teachers Lack Sufficient Knowledge or Guidance

The first hypothesis is that teachers cannot teach in the way reformers want because they lack some important body of knowledge or some important guidance (for a review of this literature, see Borko and Putnam, 1996). The missing knowledge may have to do with content, student learning, pedagogy or some other area, but the most frequently proffered version is that teachers lack subject matter knowledge. Several studies have documented areas in which teachers' content knowledge tends to be thin, and there is some evidence that teachers' understanding of the content influences the strategies they use to teach that content (see, e.g., Ball, 1991; Carlsen, 1987, 1997).

Another popular version of the knowledge hypothesis is that reform calls for a kind of pedagogy that is unfamiliar to most teachers; therefore, change will require substantial professional development to help teachers learn the new approaches (Cohen and Ball, 1998; Elmore and Burney, 1999; McLaughlin and Oberman, 1996). Yet another version is that teachers could improve their teaching if states provided clearer and more coherent direction to teachers through their curriculum guidelines, student assessments, and other guidelines (e.g., Rowan, 1996; Porter, 1989).

Each version of this hypothesis has some supporting evidence, but the history of reform itself provides strong evidence against it. Nearly all reform efforts have provided knowledge or guidance to teachers, yet most have failed to produce consistent or persistent changes in practice. Often, in fact, teachers claim that their practice has changed substantially as a result of professional development, but observers are unable to see the differences (Applebee, 1991; Cohen, 1990; Spillane, 1999). From such findings one could conclude that knowledge and guidance are *not* the best avenues for altering teaching practices, but most analysts conclude instead that past efforts to provide additional knowledge and guidance have been insufficient.

Teachers Hold Beliefs and Values That Differ from Reformers'

Teachers hold a number of important beliefs that are relevant to teaching—beliefs about the nature of school subjects and what is important to learn about them, about how students learn and what motivates them, about how teachers influence students, and so forth. Researchers who have studied teachers' beliefs (Kagan, 1992; Kennedy, 1991; Pajares, 1992) have identified their relevant features: they tend to be very durable and resistant to change; they are part of internally consistent networks of ideas, a factor that also makes them resistant to change; and they are used to filter and interpret new experiences in a way that reinforces the beliefs instead of challenging them.

Like people in other walks of life, teachers form their ideas about teaching when they themselves are children in school, as their childhood selves respond to their teachers. Lortie (1975) has called this early experience an *apprenticeship of observation,* and he notes that teaching differs from most other occupations in the amount of time youngsters spend observing practitioners. Yet children are not privy to the whole of teaching. They are unaware of the decisions teachers make, the plans they make, and the work they do outside class. Moreover, they are emotionally dependent upon teachers, so their interpretation is not likely to be based on a close analysis of events. Yet from these naive experiences, many durable values are formed about the nature of school subjects, how teachers and students should behave in classrooms, and what constitutes "good" teaching.

Notice that all of us share these early experiences, so the ideals that drive reformers can derive from their personal responses to their teachers, just as teachers' ideas derive from their personal responses to their teachers. In each case, a complex set of beliefs and values about the nature of classroom life—both how it is and how it should be—continues to influence people's thinking even into adulthood, and in the case of teachers it may continue to influence their thinking as they develop their own practices.

Teachers Have Dispositions That Interfere with Their Ability to Implement Reforms

The third hypothesis suggests that teachers may possess dispositions or attitudes that interfere with their ability to create ideal practices. There have always been some who argue that teachers simply don't care, that they don't like children, or that they are merely marking time until retirement. This is a cynical hypothesis, suggesting that teachers themselves are cynical. Though there undoubtedly are some teachers like this, they probably appear in the same proportions that might be found in any other line of work. Every field has some members who are disgruntled or emotionally disabled to the point where they are unable to function well. But this hypothesis does not plausibly explain *widespread* resistance to reform ideals.

The Circumstances of Teaching Prohibit Teachers from Changing Their Practices

The fourth hypothesis moves away from teachers and suggests that the problem may lie in the teaching situation itself. The argument is that circumstances place so many constraints on teachers that they cannot rise above these circumstances to create the kind of practices that reformers want to see. There are at least two versions of this hypothesis, one that refers to specific daily details of work and one that refers more broadly to the structure of the job itself.

With respect to the daily details of teaching, instruction can be interrupted by public address systems, office personnel bringing questions or messages, classroom telephones, and students entering or leaving for special-purpose classes. Less frequently, instruction is interrupted or temporarily postponed for tests and examinations, fire drills, assemblies, holiday celebrations, field trips, parent-teacher conferences, and so forth. In her examination of instructional time in Chicago, Smith (2000) estimated that sanctioned noninstructional events such as these occurred about 35 days per academic year, and that teachers lost anywhere from 20 percent to 100 percent of their instructional time on these days.

The academic calendar itself also imposes constraints. Teachers schedule their units of instruction to fit into uninterrupted segments of the year, taking account of scheduled breaks for Thanksgiving, Christmas, and spring vacations, when students may lose the thread of a unit.

School governance also creates difficulties for teachers. Johnson (1990) enumerates a wide range of difficulties teachers face in trying to do their jobs—complicated bureaucracies that make it difficult to order supplies or make the supplies arrive too late, leaky ceilings, electric outlets that don't work, and so forth. Johnson argues that the bureaucratic processes themselves can interfere with thoughtful teaching. Ingersoll (2003) found that secondary teachers felt that they could influence the particulars of their own classroom practices but that they had little influence over other matters that were highly pertinent to their teaching, including their own teaching assignments, the evaluation of teachers in their schools, and even discipline policies in the schools, which they were required to enforce.

There are also circumstances inherent in the teaching profession, apart from daily annoyances, that can deeply affect teachers. Lortie (1975) noted, for example, that the work itself does not change much throughout one's career. The responsibilities of a 30-year veteran are virtually the same as those of a first-year novice. There is also little reward or recognition for extra effort. Moreover, it is relatively easy to leave the profession temporarily and to return at will. These circumstances encourage teachers to think about their work as an avocation rather than a vocation, as something that does not require substantial intellectual or emotional investment.

Lortie also pointed out that there is very little induction into teaching: teachers normally convert in just a few months from being full-time college students to being full-time teachers with complete responsibility for their classrooms and their students. The transition is usually abrupt, and the teacher is expected to create her entire practice on her own. This approach to induction encourages teachers to rely on their own prior beliefs and values for guidance and to think of their practice as a highly personal and idiosyncratic endeavor.

Several observers, including Lortie, have also noted that teachers are almost entirely dependent on their students for evidence of their own successes or failures. If students appear to be bored, this is evidence that the teacher has failed. Teachers need student cooperation in order to do anything in their classrooms, and they often obtain that cooperation through tacit bargaining. These bargains usually take the form of offering a more predictable and routine curriculum or a curriculum with fewer serious intellectual challenges in exchange for a more docile and pliant student body (Cusick, 1983; Doyle, 1986; Metz, 1993; Sedlak, Wheeler, Pullin, and Cusick, 1986). Thus student pressures to reduce complexity and reduce intellectual burdens are an important part of the circumstances in which teachers must teach.

David Labaree (2000) has also weighed in on this hypothesis, noting that, in addition to the problems found by Lortie and others, teachers must manage emotions as well as children and academic ideas, and that their task is made more difficult by the facts that they "serve" a compulsory clientele and that they are isolated from other adults most of the time.

Notice that these circumstances have to do with teaching itself, not with the institutions or organizational structures in which teachers and students function. Sociologists have long sought an organizational theory that could account for the caliber of teaching that occurs in schools and have been unable to show systematic relationships between most organizational features and the quality of teaching practices (Gamoran, Secada, and Marrett, 2000). The results of the study detailed in the following pages indicate that circumstances inherent in the practice of teaching itself combine to make rigorous, intellectual teaching difficult even for highly knowledgeable and committed teachers.

The Reform Ideals Are Not Realistic

The hypotheses surveyed above have received far more attention than one that, in a sense, follows from all the others: that if teachers in general lack needed knowledge and guidance *and* hold different beliefs and values from those of reformers *and* work in entropic circumstances, then indeed reformers are asking too much. But even apart from all these problems, there are reasons to be skeptical about the reformers' ideals. The ideals assume, for example, that it is possible to teach rigorous and demanding content to all students, and that it is possible for all students to become intellectually engaged with this content. These assumptions may not apply to, say, students whose parents have instilled anti-intellectual attitudes in them, or they may not apply when classrooms contain an exceptional array of students, or they may not apply when there are gang rivalries among students that dominate all interactions and render serious intellectual discourse impossible. Rarely do reformers think seriously about the array of real students and situations that teachers face in their classrooms.

For the most part, the reform ideals also don't address the nitty-gritty problem of how to organize and manage learning in large groups, where managing the group can interfere with managing the ideas. And reformers tend not to think about ways in which, in real schools, their ideals may conflict with one another. For instance, the ideal of universal access to knowledge implies that some classrooms will contain severely handicapped children, yet the presence of such children may hinder the teaching of rigorous and important content to other children. Moreover, the ideal of intellectual engagement does not address the question of how students with widely differing backgrounds and interests can take an intellectual interest in the same content. Reformers also don't address the problem of how teachers are to respond to parents who disagree with their curricular goals, sometimes wanting *less* demanding curricula for their children.

Finally, there is some evidence that reforms are exhausting for teachers. Even though teachers can get swept up in reform movements, the time and effort required by reform eventually wear them out. In their review of the eight-year study, Tyack and Cuban (1995) noted that participating teachers gradually returned to their traditional practices at the end of the study because they were depleted by the demands of the reform.[3] Given that most teachers have just one planning period per day, reformers may be asking too much when they expect every lesson in every subject to be intellectually spirited, rigorous, engaging, and accessible to all students.

The Study

This book poses three questions. First, it asks *what teachers are actually doing,* in an effort to evaluate the accuracy of reformers' perceptions and to see if their dissatisfactions are justified. For this part of the work, it adopts the reformer's critical eye, preferring to critique teaching practices rather than merely describing them. Second, it asks *how teachers account for these practices*, in an effort to see if and how teachers' intentions and values differ from those of reformers. For this task, it tries to take the teachers' point of view rather than the reformers' and to learn as much as possible about how teachers think about their work and what they are trying to accomplish. Third, it asks *where teachers got the ideas that motivated their practices*, in an effort to learn more about when and how teachers are influenced by outside sources such as professional development or policy guidelines, sources frequently used by reformers to convey their ideas.

Pursuing these questions required several procedural decisions: what kinds of practices to study, what schools, teachers, and lessons to study, and how to talk to teachers about their practices.

What Teaching Practices to Study

Over the past century, researchers have tried dozens of strategies for documenting teaching practices. Some characterize classroom atmosphere on dimensions such as businesslike versus warm (e.g., Ryans, 1960), while others tally the frequency with which very tiny bits of behavior occur. The former approach is criticized for failing to define what teachers actually do, and the latter is criticized for reducing teaching practices to units that are so small that their educational meaning is not apparent. In the past couple of decades researchers have begun to focus on more meaningful segments of lessons. For instance, Doyle (Doyle, 1983, 1986; Doyle and Carter, 1984) focused on what he called the academic task; Stodolsky (1988) divided lessons into segments such as uniform seatwork, recitation, and individualized seatwork; and Leinhardt, Weidman, and Hammond (1987) sorted out "activity structures" that include things like homework review, monitored practice, and transitions. All these researchers were seeking segments of practice that are discrete enough to analyze, yet still large enough to be educationally meaningful.

In devising this study, I sought segments of practice of that sort: segments that were analytically distinct enough that they could be examined independently, yet substantively rich enough to have educational meaning. The study capitalizes on lessons as the fundamental unit of instruction because they are themselves discrete and coherent. They typically have a beginning, a middle, and an end, and distinct parts within them. Two features of interest are how they construct their lessons and how they manage a handful of tasks that are essential to each lesson. These essential tasks are outlined below.

Developing the Day's Agenda

Three tasks that must occur in every lesson are establishing learning outcomes, portraying content to students, and constructing learning activities.

1. Establishing learning outcomes. While institutional policies may outline an official body of content, teachers define its larger meaning, and they often have an epistemological stance on the character and quality of the content itself. If we want to see whether and how teachers respond to reform ideals, we need to examine their decisions about learning outcomes, for it is here that teachers translate official curriculum topics into issues, themes, morals to the story, and emphases. It is here that teachers decide, for instance, whether the Earth's atmosphere will be presented as an ecosystem or as a list of layers with labels and ingredients, and whether the American Revolution will be presented as a collection of names and dates, as a dramatic narrative, or as an event involving difficult political issues.

2. Portraying content to students. Teachers portray content in a number of ways. The most direct approach is simply to tell students about it, perhaps through lectures alone or perhaps with physical props such as illustrations, diagrams, pictures, or physical demonstrations. Sometimes they portray content by presenting a puzzle or a dilemma, by raising questions or posing problems for students to think about. Portrayals can vary considerably, and much of the variation reflects different ideas about learning outcomes. If the official content is the Civil War, for instance, teachers may portray the war as a political, economic, military, or social event. If the content is division with fractions, teachers may portray this content as procedural (that is, how to do it), conceptual (that is, what it means to do it), or integrative (e.g., how this process relates to division with decimals). Reformers often take strong positions about the kind of portrayals they believe are most appropriate. Certainly if we want to see whether or how teachers respond to reformers' ideals, we want to see how they present and represent content to students, for it is through these portrayals that they tell students, in effect, what matters about this content.

3. Constructing learning activities for students. Teachers also provoke students into interacting with the content, to enable them to assimilate it. They may ask students to read texts, write papers, solve problems, conduct experiments, or engage in other activities. It is through these learning activities that students become acquainted with the new content, grasp its nuances and complexities, gain facility with it, and, in general, come to *know* it.

With respect to reform ideals, some advocates prefer the kind of learning activities that might be called "traditional," such as reading texts, listening to lectures, writing, or solving a set of assigned problems; others prefer more progressive activities such as participating in debates, conducting laboratory experiments, or engaging in open-ended explorations. Regardless of one's position on this matter, the fact remains that *some kind* of learning activity is likely to occur. What is of interest here is how and why teachers construct their learning activities as they do.

Managing Conversations about Content

Questions and answers are essential to instruction, as both teachers and students need to clarify ideas and sort out important distinctions. On one side are questions teachers ask, which may be used to guide students or to assess their understanding; on the other side, teachers respond to the questions and comments offered by students. Both are important to instruction.

1. Q&A routines. Most teachers have routine ways of organizing their questions. One teacher might begin each day with a series of questions designed to see what students recall from the previous day, while another might put forward a series of questions after introducing something new, to see where student confusions might lie. A third might use questions to orient students to new content or to push their thinking in a particular direction. These varied uses of questions share one important feature: all allow the teacher to ask students about content and to see what they understand or don't understand about that content. I will refer to these question-and-answer sequences as *Q&A routines*. These routines offer an excellent opportunity to learn whether or how teachers respond to reformers' ideals, for their approaches to Q&A routines can direct students toward larger or smaller ideas, can encourage or discourage intellectual engagement, and can encourage participation from everyone in the class or from a select few.

2. Responding to unexpected student comments. Just as teachers may pose questions to guide learning, students may introduce ideas of their own, either by offering ideas about the content or by asking questions about that content. Through their questions and comments, students convey to teachers, either intentionally or inadvertently, their own interpretation of the content or of what the class as a whole is doing. Many such comments and questions follow the substantive direction the teacher has set, but sometimes students veer into entirely new terrain, and their ideas have the potential, if seriously addressed, to take the entire class in a different direction. Teachers must therefore develop strategies for responding to students' comments and questions.

The practice of responding to unexpected student ideas differs from other practices in two important ways. First, these responses cannot be planned ahead. Teachers may design entire lessons so that they include elements such as portrayals, learning activities, and Q&A routines, but they cannot anticipate the ideas that students may introduce on their own. So their responses must be constructed on the spot. And even though these exchanges may be brief, they can influence the overall coherence and integrity of the lesson. How teachers manage these situations may give us important insights into their responses to reformers' ideals.

Establishing a Tranquil Learning Environment

Teachers try to make their classrooms orderly and tranquil in many ways. They want intellectual tranquility—a lack of distractions—so that students can concentrate on their work. They want social tranquility—courteous interactions among students—so that students learn to adopt social and cultural norms. And they want emotional tranquility—lack of stress and distress—so that students will be more willing to participate in their lessons. To further all these ends, teachers establish a wide variety of classroom rules, routines, and social norms. Rules about poking and teasing, taking turns, listening, and generally being respectful to one another help establish social norms. Operating procedures such as where students should store their book bags or when they may move about the room make classroom life more efficient. Some routines, such as greeting each child at the beginning of the day or calling students by their names rather than simply pointing to them, make the learning environment more friendly to students and thereby increase their willingness to participate. Classroom routines create the ambiance that leads us to view classrooms as being organized or disorganized, friendly or cold, exciting or boring. Classroom norms and rituals are rarely discussed when reformers describe their ideals, so an important question we need to ask is whether or how these routines may hinder or facilitate teachers' ability to respond to those ideals.

Each of these essential teaching tasks has a clear function and meaning in the context of the lesson as a whole, yet the tasks themselves are analytically distinct. Notice, too, that this method of parsing the lesson does not prescribe the sequence in which these various parts are used. Different teachers may arrange these events in different sequences, using Q&A routines at the beginning of a lesson to orient students to new ideas or at the end to review ideas that have already been examined. One teacher might organize an entire lesson around a single learning activity while another might use several different learning activities.

Which Schools, Which Teachers, Which Lessons?

In a nation as large and varied as the United States, finding schools and teachers to study is no simple task. There are too many variations, too many options, and too many considerations. As a result, every researcher must make important limiting decisions. In my case, these decisions had to do with which reform contexts, grade levels, and subjects to study.

Reform Contexts

Since one major goal of this study is to learn more about why *ordinary* teachers do the things they do, it seemed important to study schools that were ordinary—not renowned for their reform activities. At the same time, I wanted to ensure that teachers had been at least exposed to reform ideas, so that I could see how they responded to those ideas. My solution was to seek schools that lay within the catchment areas of significant reform initiatives but were not particularly notable for their own local reform efforts. I hoped that such schools would represent the kinds of places that reform initiatives often hope to influence but rarely do.[4] I also reasoned that a mix of schools, exposed to a mix of reform messages, would yield a collection that roughly represented the variety of ideas currently reaching teachers. The reform ideas encompassed in this sample include two that emphasized content, one that emphasized intellectual engagement, and one that emphasized all three reform ideals. The appendix provides details about these sites.

Grade Levels and School Subjects

I sought teaching situations that might maximize my ability to test the various hypotheses listed above, and settled on upper elementary classrooms, for several reasons. First, concerns about teachers' knowledge, particularly of their subject matter, are most acute in the upper elementary grades, where teachers tend to hold elementary teaching certificates, perhaps with no subject matter major in college, and yet are expected to teach all school subjects. Moreover, in the upper elementary grades the curricula in these different subjects can be relatively complex and demanding. At the same time, we might expect these grade levels to reveal more variation in teachers' beliefs and values. Whereas secondary teachers tend to focus more tightly on their discipline, and early elementary teachers to focus more on nurturing their children, we might expect upper elementary teachers to struggle with the competing ideals of nurturing students who are still young and emotionally immature, of managing students who are nevertheless old enough to be more brazen and boisterous, and of helping them learn important academic content. Finally, we might also expect the influence of teaching circumstances to be more apparent in upper elementary classrooms. For the most part, students in elementary schools are too young to drop out of school, and they are not tracked by ability levels, so teachers may confront substantial variation among students in a single classroom. At the same time, schools do offer several special-purpose classes for students who need remedial assistance, language assistance, or other kinds of help, so students in elementary schools are often pulled from their regular classrooms to attend special classes.

Finally, these grade levels are included in nearly all reform initiatives. Student assessments nearly always include at least one upper elementary grade, and data from the Third International Mathematics and Science Study (TIMSS) suggest that the upper elementary grades are where a great deal of U.S. achievement decline occurs relative to other countries. These grade levels have been the focus of many national and international assessments and of a great deal of classroom research and observation. They are high enough to permit some attention to academic content, and yet low enough that teachers are expected to teach all content areas and to nurture students as well.

With respect to the particular lessons that would be examined, my colleagues and I left this decision up to the teachers. The research process was more invasive than most teachers are accustomed to (we videotaped each lesson and then interviewed teachers about it), and we wanted them to be as comfortable as possible with our visit. The appendix furnishes more detail about how these decisions were reached.

To solicit teacher participation, we generally presented the study to the entire school staff and invited participation from all attending teachers. About half of those who were asked to participate agreed to do so. This is a lower response rate than I have experienced in other research projects, and I suspect that it reflects, at least in part, the invasive nature of the research.

Talking to Teachers about Their Practices
The original idea for these interviews was to ask each teacher about at least one routine, at least one learning outcome, one portrayal of content, one learning activity, one Q&A routine, and one response to an unexpected student idea. However, teaching practices don't present themselves with labels, and sometimes teachers categorized their practices differently from the observer. For instance, when we observed Mr. Awles introducing a new unit on the ocean, we saw him ask students to open their science journals and to write down two facts and three opinions about the ocean. We asked about that practice, assuming that the "facts and opinions" writing assignment constituted an instructional routine.[5] However, Mr. Awles explained that he had introduced the distinction between facts and opinions earlier in the day in his language arts lesson. He then used his science lesson to give students more opportunities to work with this distinction.

Because teaching practices are necessarily embedded in a continuing stream of activity, the interviews dealt with entire episodes rather than the teacher's practices per se. Teachers generally described what preceded their actions, what they saw or were concerned about, and what they did and why. On average a given interview addressed about 11 episodes from the teacher's observed lesson, with episodes varying in length from very brief exchanges between teacher and students to long and detailed learning activities or Q&A routines. Altogether, the 45 teachers who participated in this study discussed 499 episodes of teaching practice. Table 1 summarizes the distribution of these episodes.

Table 1   Number of episodes examined representing each type of teaching task

Number of mentions	Teaching task	Total no.	Percent
	Constructing the day's agenda	111	22
60	Establishing learning outcomes		
56	Portraying content (demonstrations, definitions, visuals, etc.)		
75	Constructing learning activities (experiments, dice games, writing, problem solving)		
	Managing conversations about content	189	38
59	Q&A routines (question and answer patterns)		
102	Responding to unexpected student ideas		
28	Responding to student misbehaviors		
	Creating a tranquil environment	191	38
38	Instructional routines (journals, homework assignments, etc.)		
27	Participation routines (grouping practices, systems for calling on students)		
36	Behavior control routines (attention-getters, reminders, seating assignments, etc.)		
10	Other misc. routines (beginning the hour, students finishing early, etc.)		
	Responding to unexpected events	8	2
	Total practices examined	499	100

For the most part, these 499 episodes constitute the material of this study. They do not reflect everything that occurred in these lessons, just those that were talked about. The distinction is important, particularly with regard to two categories: responding to student behaviors and responding to unexpected events. We made a policy of asking teachers about most of the categories of practice listed in Table 1, but we didn't ask about student misbehaviors unless they were particularly egregious. We also tended not to ask about other interruptions, such as an interloper entering the classroom or a telephone ringing, because these fell outside our list of core teaching practices. Thus, the small number of episodes tabulated as interruptions reflects an a priori decision about what to ask about, and not the actual frequency of these events.

Overview of the Book

The remaining chapters describe the findings from this study. Chapter 2 provides an overview of the way teachers generally accounted for their practices. It describes a line of reasoning that appeared frequently in the interviews. It also describe teachers' intentions and the main areas of concern that appear to drive them. Of interest here is the extent to which teachers appear to be guided by reform ideals, as opposed to other possible areas of concern they may have. More than other chapters, this one tests the hypothesis that teachers may hold different values and beliefs from those of reformers. One important finding reported here is that teachers' intentions address far more areas of concern than reformers tend to think about. In addition to concerns about content, intellectual engagement, and universal access to knowledge, teachers think about how to foster student learning, the kind of classroom community they want to create, how to maintain lesson momentum, and how to satisfy their own personal needs for order and calm. When these different areas of concern conflict, teachers most often lean toward maintaining the momentum of the lesson, a tendency that can, ironically, reduce their attention to fostering student learning.

Chapter 3 describes the strategies teachers use to create tranquil learning environments. Since every classroom contains a large number of energetic and easily distracted youngsters, teachers devise a host of classroom norms and routines that make their lives more stable, more predictable, and more calm. Chapter 3 shows how these routines work, the extent to which they contribute to reform ideals, and the lines of reasoning that teachers use to account for their routines. More than other chapters, this one tests the hypothesis that the circumstances of teaching create the teaching practices we often see. One finding presented here is that teachers are frequently motivated by a fear of distractions and that this fear sometimes motivates them to suppress intellectual engagement. Chapter 3 also shows that many of the distractions teachers experience are caused by local institutional policies and organizational norms. We saw distractions from public address systems, students entering and leaving the classroom, telephones ringing in the classrooms, and other teachers entering to ask irrelevant questions. When these disruptions occurred, students distracted both teachers and one another.

Chapter 4 describes two kinds of conversational practices: the habitual Q&A routines that teachers rely on, and their responses to student ideas. Again the goal is to ascertain the extent to which teachers' practices reflect reformers' ideals and also to learn the lines of thinking that lead teachers to construct these particular practices. The most important finding revealed in this chapter is that intellectual engagement can significantly *add* to teachers' difficulties, and that as a result teachers frequently discourage intellectual engagement. Just as students who are disengaged can disrupt lessons by misbehaving, so can students who are engaged disrupt a lesson by enthusiastically offering ideas that move the lesson away from the direction teachers are aiming for. Student enthusiasm can substantially complicate classroom discussions about content.

Chapter 5 describes three practices essential to acquainting students with academic content: the establishment of learning outcomes, portrayals of content, and learning activities. This chapter shows the variety of learning outcomes, portrayals, and learning activities that teachers construct and shows how these practices can heighten or suppress content and intellectual engagement. One important finding from this chapter is that the extent to which learning activities succeed in intellectually engaging students depends in large part on teachers' own theories of learning, a set of beliefs that are rarely considered by reformers. Chapter 5 also shows that logistical problems associated with complicated presentations and learning activities frequently reduce students' access to content.

Chapters 6 through 8 synthesize the results to provide insight into how reformers might better help teachers improve their practices. Chapter 6 examines problems in teachers' lessons—both the kinds of things that went wrong and why they went wrong—from three points of view: things that teachers mentioned as problems, things that reformers would be likely to mention as problems, and things that a parent might notice as interfering with the progress of the lesson. It outlines three main sources of these problems. First, students themselves create problems for teachers. Because they are novices, their thinking frequently doesn't go in directions teachers expect. Second, local institutional policies and norms introduce complications and interruptions into lessons. Third, teachers' own beliefs, values, dispositions, and attitudes can create problems for teachers.

Chapter 7 examines practices that teachers believe have improved over time and the sources of the ideas that appear to have motivated these improvements. It contrasts three main sources of ideas: knowledge vendors such as colleges, universities, and professional developers; experience and other informal sources for ideas; and institutions, which provide teachers with guidelines and policies, usually about curriculum content and learning outcomes. All three sources make important contributions to improvements in practice, and each also has important drawbacks. Ultimately teachers need all three, and the burden on policymakers is to coordinate them for maximum benefit.

Finally, Chapter 8 summarizes the book's overall argument. It reviews each of the hypotheses frequently used to explain reform failures and summarizes the evidence for each. All hypotheses have at least some supporting evidence. Two that demand more attention from reformers, however, are the hypothesis that the very circumstances of teaching thwart reform and the hypothesis that reform ideals are inherently unattainable.

2. How Teachers Think about Their Practices

One of the hypotheses advanced to explain the intractability of teaching is that teachers' beliefs and values differ from those of reformers. Perhaps, the hypothesis suggests, teachers are trying to achieve different goals from the reformers'. This chapter examines the content of teachers' thoughts and intentions, with an eye to where they resemble and differ from reformers' ideas.

One reason disparities may occur between teachers and reformers is that everyone, including teachers and reformers, holds multiple and sometimes conflicting ideals for our schools. As a society, we want our youngsters to learn specific content, but we also want them to be nurtured, to be developed into good citizens, and to be motivated to participate productively in society. We want teachers to be role models for moral and ethical behavior and to create positive climates for learning in their classrooms, but we also want them to be efficient and goal-oriented. We believe that all students deserve equal treatment and resources, but sometimes we think that particular students should receive more. We are divided on whether children should be controlled by external rules with consequences or whether, instead, they should be taught to regulate themselves. We want to socialize students to accommodate the prevailing cultural

norms, yet we want them to be critical thinkers; we want to culti-
vate cooperation yet enable them to compete in later life; and so
forth. These different ideas wax and wane in social popularity and
strain the education system. Several writers have struggled to understand and to explicate the various dimensions of these tensions (e.g.,
Cremin, 1990; Egan, 1997, 2001; Berlak and Berlak, 1981; Tyack and
Cuban, 1995).

Another reason we might expect to see disparities is that, both individually and as a society, we all espouse ideas that are more idealis-
tic and pure than the ideas that actually guide our everyday practice.
Argyris and Schön (1996) refer to these two sets of ideas as our *espoused theories* and our *theories in use*. We may espouse, say, a principle of honesty, but in specific situations we may violate that ideal. We
do so for apparently good reasons, of course, and these reasons constitute our theory-in-use. In education, we know that teachers' practices often differ from the ones they espouse, and that they frequently
describe their own practices as more consistent with reform ideals
than outside observers believe to be the case (e.g., Applebee, 1991;
Cohen, 1990; Oliver, 1953). It is not clear, when such disparities surface, whether teachers misunderstand the reform concepts and really
believe they are doing the things reformers advocate, or whether
they subscribe to the same ideals as reformers but their practices involve so many exceptions to the rule that observers can't see the rule
itself. In either case, the practices teachers actually engage in differ
from those reformers espouse and often also from those the teachers
themselves espouse.

Many contemporary authors (e.g., Brophy, 1989; Richardson, 1996;
Stigler and Hiebert, 1999) suggest that teachers' beliefs about such
things as the nature of the subject matter, how students learn, and
the role of the teacher in promoting learning are central to explaining teaching practices. But the role of teachers' beliefs is difficult to
separate from the role of the circumstances of teaching, for beliefs
are influenced by these circumstances. The two hypotheses together
lead to questions about how teachers interpret their situations
and how these interpretations influence their practice. Van den Berg

(2002) refers to these interpretations as teachers' *meanings*—that is, the meanings that teachers ascribe to the events they see in their classrooms. If the practices that teachers construct depend on these meanings, then it is important to learn more about how teachers interpret and respond to their situations.

Our interviews with teachers covered a tremendous range of episodes, including numerous examples of each of the essential practices laid out in Chapter 1, constructed in different grade levels, different subjects, and different contexts. Two important patterns are apparent in these interviews. First, teachers talked about their practices in ways that appeared to reflect their *lines of thinking* about those practices. These lines of thinking may be an artifact of the way in which the interview was conducted,[1] but they were sufficiently widespread and powerful to warrant attention. Second, teachers mentioned a plethora of *intentions* for the things they did, and these intentions spanned a much wider range of concerns than reformers tend to think about.

Lines of Thinking

The first pattern has to do with how teachers laid out their ideas in the interviews. They generally started discussing an episode by describing either what they intended to do or what they saw in the situation. For instance, when Ms. Pass (grade 3 language arts, 25 years' experience) brought up an episode that she wanted to discuss, she told us what she saw in the situation: "I noted a bunch of different things. One was that I realized at one point in the tape that a child had his hand up, and almost gave up on me coming to him because I didn't see him very quickly. It probably wasn't a great length of time; but for this particular child who isn't down as having an attention deficit—but I feel he does to some degree anyway. And I thought I'd kept better track of making sure I was in closer contact with him. And I found that at one point he had his hand up for maybe 30 to 40 seconds, and he was about to give up on me when I happened to—"

Ms. Pass's perception of this situation includes far more than the fact that she failed to see a child's hand raised. She also noted that the child has difficulty learning and that she apparently failed to make sure she was in close contact with him, even though she had intended to be. So part of what she saw was that she was not achieving one of her intentions.

Once teachers offered their immediate impressions and intentions, we often asked them to elaborate, and their responses revealed another layer of thought, consisting of *accumulated principles and strategies*—rules of thumb about how to achieve certain goals, how to respond to certain situations, what to expect from students in particular situations, typical patterns of student behavior, and typical patterns of relationships between what teachers do and how students respond. For instance, after Ms. Pass noticed that she hadn't responded to the student whose hand was raised, the conversation proceeded as follows:

> [Do you feel it's important to address all students with their hands raised right away, or is it mostly just this child?] No. I feel pretty much that way for all children. Their question needs to be answered. And that's another reason why I have them not sit with their hand up while they're waiting for me, because lots of times they even lose the question by the time I get to them. But if they take their hand back down because I'm engaged with another student, sometimes they work out whatever the question was anyway. So I don't know that I feel that it's absolutely vital that I get to every child. And if they put their hand back down, then it's probably one of two things: the question didn't really pertain to what we were doing, or they really weren't stuck, and maybe they just wanted me to see something. Or, you know, these kids who tend to be stuck and definitely need my help will put it back up again when I go back.

Here Pass has laid out a rather detailed account of what happens in general when students raise their hands, and how students' problems should be resolved. Her general intention is to ensure that the question gets answered, but the question need not be answered immediately or by Pass herself. Her *principle of practice* for situations like this is that students should put their hand down while waiting for her to get to them. Her reasoning is that if they do this, they may work out the answers for themselves or the question may become moot.

Principles of practice codify patterns of student behavior, patterns of teacher behavior, the myriad relationships between what teachers do and what students do, and some rules of thumb about how to respond to particular types of situations. They represent teachers' understanding of how the system of teaching and learning works in their classroom settings. Sometimes teachers also refer to principles that they have acquired elsewhere, such as from a professional development program or from a state policy. For instance, a teacher may refer to a principle of practice having to do with student motivation, and say that she acquired this idea at a workshop, or she may refer to a policy relating to grading practices. These references will be important later, when we try to ascertain the extent to which teachers' practices appear to be influenced by reform initiatives under way in their regions.

Another layer of ideas extends even deeper. Underlying teachers' accumulated principles of practice is a set of *standing beliefs and values* that they may have held since childhood, or at least have held for many years, about such fundamental things as how students learn, what motivates them, and what the teacher's role should be in the classroom.

In our interviews, teachers generally started by describing their intentions or what they saw in the particular situation; they then moved to their principles of practice, and then to their standing beliefs and values. But the sense of the conversation was that the ideas themselves developed in the opposite direction. Each newly revealed layer was somewhat deeper and more long-standing than the one discussed before. The way these ideas were introduced suggests that the line of thinking actually began with the teachers' most deeply held, most long-standing, and most general ideas about teaching and learning, and ended with interpretations of specific situations and with specific actions.

Three important points need to be made about these lines of

thinking. First, with only a few exceptions, they are internally consistent both within an episode and between episodes. That is, we seldom found conflicting ideas within a given line of thinking or even within a given interview. For instance, in one of her lines of thinking, Ms. Defoe (grade 5 science, 3 years' experience) mentioned a standing belief that the teacher's role in the classroom is *always to remain calm and in control*. An examination of her entire interview reveals that every episode she nominated for discussion was an instance in which she perceived a situation that could get out of control, but that she was able to stop before it did. And in every case, she nominated the episode because she was pleased with her own performance in preventing minor student infractions from escalating into major lesson distractions.

Second, prior ideas are likely to influence later ideas. Teachers whose standing beliefs are progressive will accumulate principles of practice that are consistent with those beliefs, while those whose standing beliefs lead them to value direct instruction will accumulate principles consistent with that idea. And of course, once teachers accumulate a set of principles of practice, these principles serve to reinforce, through instantiation, their standing beliefs and values, so that the entire system is a continuously developing set of ideas that can be drawn upon to interpret specific situations and to construct specific practices in response to those situations.

However, it is also possible for new experiences to alter teachers' principles of practice and even their long-standing beliefs. For example, Ms. Toklisch (grade 6 math, 10 years' experience) told us that her practice had radically changed about six years earlier. She described both her current beliefs and her prior beliefs, although all her principles of practice were consistent with her new belief system. Even teachers who hadn't undergone such big changes said things like: "I used to think that students needed more flexibility and freedom, but I now see that they work much better with more structure." So standing beliefs and accumulated principles can influence teachers' interpretations of events, but interpretations of events can also alter standing beliefs and accumulated principles of practice.

The third important point about these lines of reasoning is that they nearly always include more than one intention for a given practice. That is, when teachers explained what they were concerned about, they mentioned more than one intention, and each of their intentions could have a complicated set of beliefs, values, principles, strategies, and interpretations standing behind it.

There are also, of course, some important limitations to teachers' accounts of their thinking. They may not be complete or accurate accounts of what teachers were actually thinking in the moment. They reflect ideas that teachers were aware of, thought were salient to their decision, and perhaps believed were most socially acceptable.[2]

One thing that needs further examination is *inconsistency* within lines of thinking. Most lines of thinking are thematically consistent, a feature that may make it harder for teachers to alter their practices in response to reform initiatives. But some are inconsistent, and the inconsistencies seem to appear when teachers have been exposed to a set of ideas that contradicts their own, or to a set of conditions that contradicts their own prior assumptions. Understanding the nature of these internal contradictions may also help us understand how teaching practices are formed and how they are changed.

Ms. Buford's line of thinking. Consider Ms. Buford. Ms. Buford is a fifth-grade math teacher with 25 years' experience who has a difficult class, mainly because it includes a boy named Juan, who is highly volatile and prone to violence. Juan acts out a lot, has temper tantrums, and gets into fights with other children. Buford wants to keep him in class as much as possible, because she does not want to deny him the opportunity to learn (she values the third reform ideal, universal access to knowledge) and because she wants him to learn how to behave in social settings. But in fact she expels him frequently because he causes so many disturbances and disrupts learning for other children. In addition, she perceives the other children in her class as easily distracted and excited, a situation that complicates the problem of Juan.

Ms. Buford has decided to maintain a very calm demeanor and a very calm classroom, with no joking or extraneous comments at all, in the hope that she can prevent both Juan and other children from getting overly excited and rambunctious. As a result she herself needs to be very calm and to avoid any actions that might incite Juan or the class as a whole. The "action" in this case, then, is a calm, deliberate, even boring, persona. A close look at Buford's line of thinking reveals conflicting ideas. She has one set of ideas that represents her notion of an ideal classroom, and another that reflects her understanding of this particular classroom. Her long-standing beliefs incline her to be enthusiastic about her teaching. She believes that students should participate in a variety of activities and that they should share ideas. These ideas suggest that she wants high intellectual engagement, a reform ideal. Also consistent with this theme is a principle of practice that she acquired from a recent workshop that encouraged teachers to promote children's internal motivations and to reduce their dependence on external consequences as a way to motivate students.

The second theme in her thinking relates to being on task. Her accumulated principles of practice include the observations that students get easily distracted and that it is very difficult to bring them back once this happens. Associated with these observations is a belief that teachers should serve as role models for being on task. When discussing the lesson we observed, Ms. Buford indicated that she sometimes curtailed discussions and that she particularly discouraged any comments that might lead a discussion off task. This strategy contrasts with the ostensible value she places on children sharing ideas, but is still consistent with her belief that the teacher must serve as a role model for how to behave in class and how to remain on task.

In constructing any specific practice, Buford must use these conflicting ideas to interpret her situation and decide what to do. She perceived the class we observed as a particularly difficult one. She saw many students who fell quickly off task, got silly, and lost the thread of the lesson. And in particular, she had Juan, who was especially volatile, often violent, and who had repeatedly incited other students. She wanted to increase Juan's internal motivations for participating. But she also wanted to manage Juan's behavior while also keeping everyone else thinking about mathematics. She noted that this class "wears me out."[3] The combination of her prior ideas and her interpretation of this situation, then, led to her decision to maintain a very calm, deliberate persona, one that soothed the group and kept the entire class on an emotionally even keel. She concluded that she could not be the enthusiastic teacher she wanted to be. On the contrary, she gave herself a number of specific prescriptions for her own behavior: no joking, no informal asides, no "pizzazz." This was not a pleasant outcome for Buford, who noted with disappointment, when observing the videotape, that the class was slow and even boring, but who also argued that this was a necessary climate for this particular group of students. In effect, Buford traded one reform ideal—intellectual engagement—for another reform ideal: providing all her children, including Juan, access to knowledge.

Buford's line of thinking illustrates the number and variety of concerns that can influence teachers' practices, but it also shows that these ideas can contradict one another. In Buford's case, she had a conflict between her standing value of holding discussions that are enthusiastic and lively, and her perception of this particular class as being too volatile to respond appropriately to such a climate. She decided, reluctantly, to adopt a persona that verges on boring. In spite of this, or perhaps because of it, the class wore her out. Buford's situation reveals a complex interplay of beliefs and values, accumulated principles and strategies, and the circumstances of practice itself. If Buford were our only case, we would conclude that the current situation had greater control over her practice than did her long-standing beliefs and values, many of which are consistent with reform ideals, and her knowledge of specific reform initiatives.

Intentions

The second important pattern that was apparent as teachers talked about their practices was the number and variety of intentions that they mentioned. For instance, here is how Ms. Temple (grade 5 language arts, 15 years' experience) responded to a question about one of her practices during a phonics lesson:

[You said something along the lines of "I see some different ways of doing it." What was going on there?] When you have an *a-n* together it changes the sound. It's "uhn," not "an." So we call that . . . a welded sound. What I'm looking for is for kids to recognize that; I have it up on my board, they have it on their cookie sheets [The children are arranging magnetic letters on cookie sheets. They have separate magnets for *a* and *n*, but they also have a magnet with a blended "an" symbol.], so I'm hoping that they recognize these welded sounds, because it changes the sound of the actual letter. That they use that so that they are thinking about what they're spelling.

Almost immediately after this, she offered two other intentions: "[What was going through your mind?] I was trying to look at who it was that recognized the *an* as the welded sound. And I was also making sure that they split the word in the right place, by the syllables."

Thus, when Ms. Temple said to her students, "I see some different ways of doing it," a relatively simple move in her lesson, her behavior derived from three separate intentions: she wanted to get students to recognize the "an" combination as a welded sound; she wanted to see which particular students had in fact used the welded sound when they spelled the word; and she was also looking around to make sure that the students separated their syllables correctly. Such references to multiple intentions were very common in these interviews.

It should not be surprising that teachers hold numerous intentions for their practices. Moreover, it should not be surprising to find contradictions among those intentions. The number and variety of things that teachers care about, and the number and variety of intentions they have for their practices, virtually ensure that some of these intentions will conflict with others (Fenwick, 1998; Hammer, 1997; Lampert, 1985; Schwab, 1978). Sometimes internal contradictions can create "knots" in teachers' thinking. For instance, a teacher may feel that she must stop being such a boring lecturer, yet she can't change her approach without appearing to be a phony, yet she must change, yet she can't . . . (Wagner, 1987). Wagner notes that when teachers get such knots in their thinking, they experience tension, and the tension, in turn, can lead them to be more rigid and less spontaneous.

But some understanding of the terrain of these intentions might also help reformers. The apparent resilience of teaching practices in the face of continual reform initiatives raises the question of where reform ideas fit in the entire landscape of ideas that guide teachers' practices. Perhaps a map of their intentions can help us understand why teachers appear to attend less to reform ideals than to other ideas.

In our interviews about specific practices, teachers volunteered numerous intentions for doing the things that they did. From these 45 lessons and 499 specific episodes within them, we eventually heard nearly 1,000 references to intentions. This is an average of slightly over 20 intentions per lesson.[4] Understanding these intentions, then, is an important step in understanding the origins of teaching practices. Teachers' intentions varied in both *form* (how they were expressed) and *content* (what areas of concerns were addressed).

Forms of Expression

Readers may wonder why I use the term "intentions" rather than the more common term "goals." My choice of terms reflects the fact that only a fraction of the things teachers were interested in were expressed as goals. Another fraction referred to things teachers wanted to *avoid*, such as lesson disruptions. If goals represent teachers' hopes, then classroom disruptions and the like represent teachers' fears. The difference is important, for hopes and fears are accompanied by different senses of urgency. Psychologists have been aware for some time that people are "risk averse." In financial tests, such as gambling and investing, for instance, people are more motivated to avoid losses than to achieve gains (Kahneman and Tversky, 1986). Teachers, too, may feel a greater sense of urgency to avoid those things they fear than to accomplish the things they hope for.

Moreover, teachers' intentions include more than just goals and avoidances. A third set of intentions may be called *aspirations*. These are things teachers want to *be,* such as kind, sensitive, and fair. Yet another set of intentions pertains to *obligations.* Teachers feel obligated or responsible to their students, to their colleagues, and/or to society as a whole. Thus a teacher may intend to promote intellectual engagement simply because this is something she wants to accomplish, or because she feels obligated to students or their parents. The content of the intention remains constant, but its importance and emotional valence vary. A fifth and final set of intentions encompasses *personal needs* that teachers want to satisfy, such as a need to reduce confusion or to reduce emotional strain.

So of all the things that teachers said they wanted to do, only some were expressed as goals, or as things teachers wanted to accomplish. Others were expressed as fears, aspirations, obligations, or personal needs. The differences in how intentions were expressed indicate the kind and degree of commitment that teachers had to their various intentions. For example, when we asked teachers what would happen if they failed to meet an *obligation,* they usually indicated that they would feel *guilty,* whereas if we asked what would happen if they failed to *avoid* something, they usually indicated a strong sense of urgency that they *not fail.* The phrases that teachers used to express their intentions revealed what they felt was at stake if they succeeded or failed, including how much of their own ego was invested in the outcomes. These feelings were most apparent when teachers talked about the things they wanted to avoid; at these times they often described anxieties over real or imagined outcomes, and some even described their reaction to particular events with words like "panic." Most of these emotions came up when teachers feared that they might lose students' full attention or lose control of the classroom, and when they articulated their strong need to avoid these outcomes.

Content of Intentions

Several writers have attempted to devise taxonomies of the things teachers or other educators should think about as they are teaching. For instance, Joseph Schwab (1978) maintained that curriculum developers must accommodate the four "commonplaces of teaching":

students, teachers, subject matter, and milieu; and the National Academy of Sciences (Bransford, Brown, and Cocking, 1999) stated that an effective learning environment must attend to four aspects of teaching: learners, knowledge, community, and assessment to support learning. Notice that there are differences among these taxonomies. The National Academy did not consider teachers' needs or interests relevant to the learning environment, and Schwab did not consider assessment relevant to curriculum. Neither taxonomy addresses the momentum of lessons themselves, in particular the avoidance of distractions, which were of great interest to teachers in this study.

Taxonomies such as these are usually based on idealized conceptions, not on empirical examinations, so it should not be surprising to learn that the intentions described by these 45 teachers did not fit into these ready-made taxonomies. However, they did sort into a few general groupings, which I call *areas of concern*. Two of these areas of concern had to do with the problem of acquainting students with new knowledge: defining learning outcomes and fostering student learning. Two others had to do with moving students through the work: maintaining lesson momentum and fostering student willingness to participate. The last two had to do with personal and social issues: establishing the classroom as a community and attending to personal needs.

Defining Learning Outcomes
When teachers talked about content, their language tended toward a sense of obligation—not to their states, their districts, or their administrators, but to other teachers and to students. These teachers seemed very aware that they were part of larger, coordinated systems of instruction, and in particular that the teachers who received their students the following year would expect the students to have learned specific content. They didn't want to disappoint their colleagues. With respect to their obligations to students, they wanted to ensure that their students would be able to handle state tests and the next year's curriculum. For instance, Ms. Abundo (grade 3 science,

2 years' experience) indicated an obligation to her students in this comment: "[Are you doing it just because it's there? I mean could you just decide "I'm not interested, so I'm not going to do this?"] You could do that. You could do that. It's up to the person I guess. But then that would be in your conscience, because if you don't do it, you're making the kids lose out." Similarly, Ms. Joiner (grade 6 writing, 3 years' experience) indicated an obligation to next year's teacher: "[So you could probably teach whatever you wanted.] But then I'd be doing a disservice to the seventh-grade teachers who want to do their job too. Then they wouldn't have anything to build on. If everyone below me taught what they were supposed to, heck, it'd be a lot easier to teach them."

Within this area of concern there is an important difference between content coverage and desirable learning outcomes. Even when content coverage is held constant, teachers may formulate very different learning outcomes for that content. Here are three upper-grade mathematics teachers' descriptions of what they hope students will learn from their lessons. One teacher wants students to learn the symbolic language of mathematics, another wants only to expose her students to this content, and the third wants students to be able to reason about mathematical problems well enough that they don't have to take someone else's word for a solution.

> [Math] is a whole different language. It's got its own language, and its own set of symbols. . . . And in Vermont anyway, there's a major emphasis on using math language and accurately applying math language. [Mr. James, grade 6 math, 6 years' experience]

> They really have not completely mastered metrics, as far as I'm concerned, in any year that we've done it. They've gotten it enough to surface-satisfy the requirements and move on. Hopefully they'll master it at some other point. But this is really the first year they get into metrics and I, I really don't go for mastery at this level. [Ms. Todd, grade 5 math, 20 years' experience]

> I wanted them to realize whether what [one student] was saying made mathematical sense or not, and if I say, "That's a good

idea," then everybody is going to think, "Yep, yep, so she's right, and let's just do what she does." Because that happens a lot. So I try really hard, especially since they're older, for them to be the judge. That's why I asked them, "Does that make sense to you" or "Does that seem like a reasonable way to think about how we could find area?" That's what I always try to do. [Ms. Toklisch, grade 6 math, 10 years' experience]

Similar variety was apparent in all school subjects. Within each subject, teachers defined learning outcomes that addressed many different aspects of the content.

Teachers' discussions of content as an area of concern reveal several important features. One is that their intentions with regard to content were often based on a sense of obligation to their students and colleagues to cover the content that was designated for their grade level. Another is that they had their own ideas about what was important to learn about the designated content, and the values they placed on different aspects of content were remarkably various. Yet another is that they rarely denied the importance of any content or learning outcome. In our interviews, we often asked teachers why they did *not* teach some other content. The most frequent response was that the other content was also important, or that it would be sought in some other situation, but that in this situation—for these particular students at this particular time—this particular content was more important.

Fostering Student Learning

The second main area of concern reflected in teachers' intentions is fostering student learning. This is a concern distinct from concerns about the content itself, and has to do not with *what* to teach, but rather with *how* to teach. Intentions that reflected this area of concern tended to focus on finding the best ways to stimulate, motivate, assess, and so forth.

Teachers' intentions regarding fostering student learning are probably closest to what most outsiders assume teachers think about. They indicate an interest in keeping track of what students are learning and thinking, and making sure students are responding in the way teachers hoped for.

As an area of concern, fostering student learning is particularly important for teachers. Intentions in this area justify many of the strategies, techniques, and devices that teachers may draw upon to move students toward a learning outcome. Reforms that concentrate on content itself, rather than on how to foster student learning of that content, leave this important problem entirely to the teachers. Chapter 5, which examines teachers' choices of learning outcomes, portrayals of content, and learning activities, shows how teachers actually try to foster student learning.

Maintaining Lesson Momentum

As an area of concern, lesson momentum gets almost no attention from reformers. Yet in our conversations with teachers, we heard numerous references to the importance of keeping things moving along, avoiding distractions, making sure everyone was on the same page, and so forth. Maintaining momentum was clearly a very important area of concern for teachers.

The most prominent specific intention within this area was *avoiding distractions*. Almost to a person, teachers indicated a strong desire to avoid distractions while they were teaching. They said that small distractions tended to escalate into larger ones and that such escalation could cause them to lose control of the lesson, lose the momentum of the lesson, or lose students' attention, and that these disruptions often meant that they needed to go back and start all over because students forgot everything that had happened before the distraction. They worried that the classroom would dissolve into chaos. Much of the discussion about maintaining momentum used the language of avoidance and included a strong sense of urgency, suggesting that the need to move through the planned events in an orderly and stable way was urgently important to teachers, not just because disruptions took time away from learning, but also because they created emotional distress for the teachers themselves.

It might be easy to assume that concerns of this sort plague mostly novice teachers, and that they would not appear in interviews with experienced teachers, but that is not the case. Almost all teachers seemed to believe that the *potential* for a major disruption was *always present*, and that they had to be ever-vigilant to avert these disruptions. Moreover, the fear of losing control was articulated even among teachers who *appeared* to be quite composed. Often the things they saw that triggered this concern were not visible to me on the tape even after numerous replays. Yet these small aberrations were signals to the teacher that a potentially disastrous situation could occur if action weren't taken immediately. Here are some examples of how this concern was expressed. Notice that not all these comments come from novice teachers.

[What would it mean to lose a kid here?] Well, in the small group, it wouldn't be a big issue, because I'm in very close proximity to all of them, and all I have to do is reach over and touch somebody's hand, and I bring them back in immediately. But, in a large group, you lose somebody in row 2, pretty soon they'd have their neighbor gone, and they're playing with pencils or something. And it's not a huge issue, because you lose kids all the time. All the time. I'm not going to be able to keep everybody's interest all the time. But there is a general thing where you don't want to go off on a tangent, just lose everybody. [Ms. Dawes, grade 4–5 reading, 13 years' experience]

[So you lose a lot of momentum in the lesson if you have to stop and diddle around?] Yes, we do. At least I do, because it's like we're doing one thing after another after another. So those few minutes or so, I could lose everybody. I could lose one or two kids, or I could lose the whole class in concentration. [Ms. Abundo, grade 3 science, 2 years' experience]

[So you said when you put them in groups they were out of control. What do you mean by out of control?] Very difficult to get them to listen, because they were sitting, you know, in groups of four at a table. Even like during times when they were supposed to be silent reading, then they're playing with one another, and they're fiddling at each other's desks, and they're talking even when I was talking. It was just real difficult to stop. It was real difficult for them to stop talking and listen when they were in groups. They feed off one another, and if it gets started—. They would get rude and crude and nasty and mean, and those were the kinds of things that were happening. [Ms. Awkler, grade 5 math, 9 years' experience]

[So what's the trade-off here?] Well, timing definitely is the trade-off, and keeping them engaged, because when I write [on the board], well, the kids have to wait till I am done writing. When you are writing, then the kids tend to goof off, you know. They start losing their interest and, um, or forget what the conversation is. [Mr. Awles, grade 3–4 science, 9 years' experience]

Many teachers seemed to believe that preventing disruptions and maintaining momentum were important in achieving their learning outcomes. How can students learn, after all, if they don't get through the lesson? It is not simply a matter of covering the content; it is a matter of getting students through the learning activities, discussions, and so forth that are designed to foster learning of the content. Yet one criticism of American lessons is that they cover too much content, and that students don't have an opportunity to engage with it intellectually. Many of our discussions with teachers revealed a severe tension between the desire to foster student learning and the desire to maintain lesson momentum. This tension is discussed in later chapters.

Fostering Student Willingness to Participate
The fourth area of concern reflected in teachers' intentions was student willingness to participate. Teachers tended to care about student willingness to participate for two very different reasons. On one side, they understood that students could not learn if they didn't want to. On the other side they also knew that they could not entice 100 percent of their students 100 percent of the time to engage with the content. Children are too various in their interests and too easily dis-

tracted. So they frequently hoped for a lesser goal—that their students would *at least cooperate* with the lesson and learning activities and would not disrupt the rest of the class. The strongest desire for student willingness to participate extended well beyond the desire to avoid disturbances: many intentions addressed students' attitude toward classroom life in general or toward their own ability to participate successfully. In fact the most prevalent specific intention mentioned in this area of concern was that teachers wanted to *respond positively to students.* There was a widespread belief among these teachers that students would respond positively to the teacher if the teacher responded positively to them. The notion that self-confidence or self-esteem was a prerequisite to learning came up far more often than the notion that *interest* in the content or a desire to learn might be a prerequisite to learning. Here are some examples of teachers' ideas about self-concept.

> I think every child needs to feel equally important in the classroom. And that's why I shake their hands at the end of the day. I want to make sure there's a connection. I greet them at the beginning of the day and make sure that I acknowledge all of them. [Ms. Mines, grade 6 language arts, 26 years' experience]

> There's a lot of kids that, once they get shot down, they stay down. So I didn't want to just deflate anyone's bubble by saying "No, that's not what we were doing . . ." [Mr. Waffner, grade 4 history, 25 years' experience]

> I try not to do anything that would be critical, even when they make a suggestion or do something that's clearly not in the right direction. . . . If I say, "That's wrong," it's not okay. I don't think you should tell that to a child. I don't think you should say, "That's wrong. That won't work." [Ms. Buford, grade 5 math, 25 years' experience]

> [Why have you decided to not correct it?] I wanted to make him feel that he was making a connection. . . . So I was hoping to kind of ease him and make him feel better about what he had done. [Why is that important?] I really feel that their confidence is go-

ing to be better and they're not going to be shy about answering questions. Every time they raise their hand in class, they're taking a risk. And if they always take the risk and fail, I am afraid that starts to diminish their enthusiasm to participate. So, I always try, even if the child gives a wrong answer, I try to say, "That's really close, but let's look at it this way." [Ms. Mueller, grade 6 science, 3 years' experience]

[And what is it that you hope to accomplish with this project as a whole?] That they have pride in their work. That when they put it up, they can be proud of themselves that "Gee, I did that." You know, that they'll say to their mom, "Take a look at my 5." So I think you have to do those polishing kinds of things at the end to show that it's nice and it's important and that they can be proud of the work they accomplish. [Ms. Pass, grade 3 writing, 25 years' experience]

Another theme running through these comments was that fostering students' self-esteem was an independent learning outcome apparently distinct from other learning outcomes. Teachers wanted to encourage students, to affirm them, and to make them feel good about themselves and about their capabilities. These passages reveal an important tension between the desire to affirm students, on one side, and the desire to foster student learning, on the other. Several references to the importance of affirming students came up in the context of a wrong answer. Because of their desire to encourage students, teachers find wrong answers to be especially troublesome. Almost to a person, teachers abhorred the idea of telling a child that he or she was wrong. Yet, since students are novices at the subjects they are learning, they are likely to often be wrong, thus placing teachers on the horns of an agonizing dilemma.

Establishing the Classroom as a Community
The fifth area of concern relates to the social atmosphere in the classroom. Teachers wanted to create a particular kind of social climate in their classroom, in which students would learn to interact with the teacher and with one another in specific ways. For instance, they

wanted order, cooperation, politeness, turn-taking, deference, and so forth. To this end, teachers mentioned one group of intentions that had to do with their own persona and the importance of providing a role model for students, and another group of intentions that had to do with norms of behavior for students. Among these many ideas, the most frequently mentioned intentions related to their own persona. A variety of specific intentions for persona were mentioned, and they were sometimes contradictory. One teacher wanted students to respect her authority, another wanted to befriend students and diminish the distance between teacher and student. One teacher wanted to be calm and quiet, another to be enthusiastic and lively. Despite this variety, a common assumption running through these intentions was that the teacher's persona influenced both classroom norms and student willingness to participate. Consequently, teachers tried to control their own movements, voices, and interactions with students in ways they believed would promote a more civilized classroom and a more stable learning environment. Ms. Buford's attempt to maintain a calm and boring persona is an example of such an intention.

Attending to Personal Needs

The final area of concern that arose in these interviews related to teachers' personal needs. This is another area of concern that is rarely discussed in reform literature, or even in hortatory literature; but it is important to teachers, for they are unlikely to remain in this line of work if they can't find ways to make classroom life agreeable. Although personal needs were mentioned less frequently than other areas of concern, they were important to teachers. Half the teachers participating in this study mentioned a need to reduce either intellectual or emotional strains associated with teaching. Both of these needs appeared to derive from feeling overwhelmed or confused by the number of different things they were trying to monitor. Here are some examples of their comments.

> [Where did you get the idea of using a timer?] Well, I have a timer because we do timed tasks for arithmetic. But actually I'm

using it for their work time, because that way I don't have to pay attention to the clock. That way I can just focus on what they're doing, and the clock is just running itself. [Ms. Sesnerson, grade 3 science, 5 years' experience]

It's very hard [teaching in this school] because I've never had to go home holding things on my shoulders as I have here. It's a terrible weight to have on your shoulders all night, wondering if that kid is going to come back to school tomorrow. [Ms. Damon, grade 3 Spanish, 8 years' experience]

Today they were helping each other with story problems. [One student asked] "Can I help" [I answered:] "Oh, please go help! I'm one person! Please help them!" [Ms. Bowes, grade 5 math, 30 years' experience]

In a sense, these references to personal needs follow from the number and variety of other things teachers were trying to do. It is not surprising that teachers felt overwhelmed, given the variety of intentions outlined above. Teachers wanted to cover important content, foster student learning, maintain lesson momentum, increase student willingness to participate, be ethical and even-handed with their students, and encourage their students to interact with one another in a civilized way and to participate equally in classroom activities.

Summary of Intentions

Table 2 shows how frequently teachers mentioned intentions in each of these six areas of concern. The first thing that Table 2 reveals is that teachers mentioned more intentions related to *fostering student learning* and with *maintaining lesson momentum* than to any other areas of concern. The third most frequently mentioned area was student willingness to participate. However, as teachers discussed this area of concern, it was clear that they believed student willingness to participate depended more on self-esteem than on interest in the content. Notice, too, that all three areas of concern have to do, in one

Table 2   Number of intentions mentioned within each area of concern

Number of mentions	Area of concern
127	*Defining learning outcomes,* including: Obligatory content coverage, specific required content, need to cover all chapters in the text Desirable learning outcomes such as acquiring factual content, learning to reason, developing appropriate attitudes toward the material, learning terminology, getting the big picture
215	*Fostering student learning,* including: Defining appropriate content for students, adapting content to student interests or capabilities, modeling thought processes and language usage, and monitoring and assessing student learning Intermediate learning goals, such as helping students learn to manage their time, to focus, and to write notes or use other study strategies
204	*Maintaining lesson momentum,* including making sure materials are ready and available, making sure students understand what they are supposed to be doing, monitoring behavior, preventing disturbances, adjusting procedures to accommodate readiness and understanding, and making sure everyone is on the same page
165	*Fostering student willingness to participate,* including keeping students focused, nurturing and affirming students, challenging and motivating students, and accommodating individual differences
123	*Establishing the classroom as a community,* including concerns about: The teacher's maintenance of a persona as kind, fair, receptive, encouraging, honest, strict Student participation and interactions, including ensuring full participation, ensuring equal opportunity to participate, taking turns speaking, cooperating, and demonstrating mutual respect
103	*Attending to personal needs,* including reducing emotional strain, reducing cognitive strain, promoting order, quiet, sense of accomplishment, and looking good to colleagues
937	Intentions mentioned across all six areas of concern

way or another, with manipulating students: how to maintain lesson momentum, how to get students to cooperate, and how to get them to actually learn. Since teachers usually have from 20 to 25 students in their rooms, it should not be a surprise that they are very concerned about how to maneuver them all through their lessons.

Table 2 is also important for what it tells us about the reform ideals. Two differences between teachers' intentions and reform ideals are apparent. One is that teachers' intentions cover a much wider swath. Even if all three reform ideals were present exactly as reformers would express them, these ideals would be a small fraction of all the things teachers aim to do. The second important difference is that teachers do not express their intentions in the same way reformers that express their ideals. The differences bear examination.

One difference is that no teacher indicated a specific intention to ensure that the content they taught was *inherently* important. Instead, for teachers, content was important because it would be on a test, because it was in curriculum guidelines, or because the teacher at the next grade level would expect students to know it. Teachers seemed very aware that their instruction fitted into a larger system, and the importance of any given content was defined in terms of how well it fitted into that larger system.

Similarly, no teacher specifically mentioned intellectual engagement, but many talked of the importance of engagement in general, without referring specifically to intellectual engagement. The difference is slight, but it means that teachers may sometimes seek learning activities that will be fun, rather than intellectually stimulating, in order to promote engagement.

Finally, teachers did not discuss universal access to knowledge, but they frequently discussed universal participation in their lessons. Again, this difference is slight but could make a significant difference in how teaching decisions are made.

Further Notes on Intentions

The number and variety of things teachers care about and intend to do complicates our understanding of teaching in several ways. Before moving on to examine specific teaching practices, these complicating factors need to be articulated. They are as follows:

1. Teachers routinely account for their actions by outlining more than one intention. Classroom practices do not derive from a single intention—a single hope, fear, aspiration, obligation, or need. Instead, they derive from a complicated process of weighing numerous ideas and ideals to determine a course of action. Thus it is not easy to attach a single intention to any particular practice, for most practices were intended to accomplish multiple things simultaneously.

2. Areas of concern fit together differently in teachers' overall lines of reasoning. Teachers hold a variety of theories about how success in one area of concern contributes to success in another. One teacher, for instance, may view student willingness to participate as important because it helps the teacher maintain lesson momentum, while another may see lesson momentum as important because it helps foster student willingness to participate. Many teachers agree with both of these propositions.

3. Different areas of concern have different emotional valences. Intentions reflecting different areas of concern tend to be discussed with different kinds of language; some areas of concern are dominated by needs, others by obligations, and still others by fears. The way in which teachers expressed different intentions suggested that different areas of concern may have different emotional potency for them. For example, they often used the language of avoidance to discuss lesson momentum; they were afraid that they would lose control, that the lesson would devolve into chaos. There was a sense of fear in these discussions, and a sense of urgency. On the other hand, when they talked about content coverage, they tended to use the language of obligations and its emotional counterpart, guilt. So even though these various areas of concern do contribute to one another, and even though each area is a real concern of virtually every teacher, each area of concern has its own rationale and its own emotional valences, and these may ultimately determine which intentions have most influence on practices.

4. Multiple intentions can lead to confusion and frustration. Many teachers had trouble keeping track of all the things they wanted to do. Given the 937 intentions articulated in the 45 interview transcripts, an average of over 20 intentions per lesson, it should not be surprising that teachers were sometimes overwhelmed by all things they tried to keep track of. Again, these expressions were not limited to novice teachers. For instance, Ms. Bowes, who has been teaching for 30 years, had this to say about her work:

> I think that's part of a teacher thing; you learn to carry lots of things in your head—where the lesson's going, what you're going to say next, who is paying attention to you, there's a problem here. You're carrying lots of things—I've got to watch the clock because at ten o'clock we have an assembly—I think that's just part of becoming a teacher is being able to do that. You have all these thoughts going on—I think sometimes it affects how I speak to people because it comes out disjointed when I'm having a conversation, because another thought comes in, and it rushes out, and there're all these thoughts bombarding all the time. I think that's part of being a teacher, because you have to carry all this stuff in your head. You can write out nice little note cards and have things all organized, but then there's always something—the assembly is 10 minutes late because they were late getting—all these things, so you learn how to adjust and be flexible and how to carry these things around, partly through practice, I guess.

5. *Teachers face trade-offs among competing intentions.* Because different intentions and different areas of concern can conflict with one another, teachers frequently had to make decisions about which intentions to pursue. Many of the practices teachers discussed with us were constructed after weighing trade-offs or reconciling dilemmas among conflicting intentions, and teachers often described their thoughts using "on the one hand . . . on the other hand" to explain their reasoning in specific situations. The problem introduced by this plethora of intentions is not simply their number, for even if

they were cut by two-thirds, teachers would have difficulty balancing them all if they addressed every area of concern. For example, imagine a teacher who focused on only the single most prevalent intention mentioned within each area of concern, thus reducing her cognitive burden from 20 intentions to 6. This teacher would be trying to do the following:

Avoid distractions and ensure lesson momentum

Cover content that prepares students for the next grade level

Use teaching strategies that foster student learning

Affirm all students at all times to ensure their willingness to participate

Maintain a persona that will promote an appropriate classroom community

Reduce the personal emotional strain that results from trying to do all the above

Even this abbreviated list would be difficult to manage, for these six broad intentions address very different areas of concern and do not always yield the same decisions. Here is a particularly telling example. Ms. Chalmers (K–2 science, 22 years' experience) was teaching her students about light and shadow. At one point, she mentioned that we couldn't have a shadow unless we had a source of light, at which point a student responded that indeed we could, because she had a kitten named Shadow. This comment created an instant conflict within Chalmers because she wanted to respond positively to all her students and she also wanted to maintain the momentum of the lesson and didn't want the discussion derailed by this comment.

> I was thinking, yeah, it was sort of off the topic, and I was trying to acknowledge the fact that a cat could be named Shadow, but what we were talking about was something else. Um, I guess I was trying to expand what she was saying, to move on to what we

were actually talking about, rather than to have it digress into something else, and to see what the kids knew, what their understanding was. . . . I guess my thought process was that I was acknowledging and thinking that Shadow was a good name for a cat, and that we were talking about shadow in a different context. To sort of move it to that and not say, "Oh, that was a silly thing to say, or that doesn't have anything to do with— . . . At that time, we were in a little bit of a transition time there, and I did have a little bit of time, and I could give her that attention. But it starts to be the kind of thing where everybody is telling a story.

It is by weighing the *momentary* importance of their many intentions that teachers construct their practices. At any given moment, one intention may become a more prominent concern in the teacher's reasoning. Across different situations, different patterns of intentions will emerge, and across time, different intentions may become more or less important in general. Often teachers criticized their decisions upon viewing the videotape, for the viewing allowed them to see things differently than they had appeared at the time. For instance, Ms. Eckhard (grade 4 language arts, 6 years' experience) criticized her use of time as follows: "I think that if I was really sticking to my guns, I wouldn't have wasted five minutes of time when I could have been helping another student. That's when I think I realized it. When I looked at the video, and I took five minutes to deal with those two kids who were arguing, when there was a student right next to you who needs complete assistance to read or write. And I should have been back there working with him instead of up there dealing with a petty issue, such as stealing a pencil, or whatever it was." Teachers frequently face conflicting intentions, so that they are forced to choose which will take precedence in a given situation. The most frequently mentioned trade-offs were these:

Keeping the group on task versus responding to one student's confusion. Many teachers discussed the ambivalence they felt when it became clear that one student wasn't following the discussion. They feared that if they took the time to help that one student get back on track, they would lose the rest of the group. On the other side, they didn't want to lose the one student either.

Maintaining consistent rules versus responding to individual needs. Many teachers placed a high value on being fair and consistent in their application of rules, rewards, and punishments. At the same time, they also valued accommodating individual differences and individual needs and allowing that there are often extenuating circumstances involved in a transgression.

Disciplining students versus affirming them.

Allowing students to figure things out for themselves versus giving them an answer. The dilemma here is that teachers tended to believe that students need to work things through for themselves, but they often feared that if they allowed the time needed to do that, the momentum of the lesson would be lost or some content would never be taught.

Pursuing an idea that interests students versus moving on. Sometimes students become too interested in a particular idea, and the teacher faces a trade-off between allowing students to pursue an idea versus maintaining lesson momentum.

6. *When areas of concern compete, lesson momentum usually takes priority.* A closer examination of these trade-offs also suggests that teachers tended to resolve their trade-offs by focusing more on maintaining lesson momentum than on other areas of concern. Here are some examples of teachers' choosing momentum over other concerns.

> But even then if one group's completely and totally finished and another group's almost finished and I have a group over here, at one point I have to say, "You need to hurry it up a little bit here." I think [the student in question] was working for accuracy, but if

I had waited for him it would—you know, recess would have been over. [Ms. Knutsen, grade 4–5 science, 4 years' experience]

I was starting to give them that [answer]. I was giving it to them, which is always an action that you don't do. You know you don't give it to them; you teach it to them, but you don't give it to them. So I was trying to again rush the lesson. [Ms. Masters, grade 6 science, 29 years' experience]

[A student remark] was totally off the topic, after I just explained what we were going to do today, which is not uncommon to happen . . . Sometimes I wonder if it's okay to answer it immediately and then go on, or if you should say, "Hey, does that have anything to do with, relate to, what we're talking about right now? If not, can you talk to me about it later?" [Ms. Damon, grade 3 Spanish, 8 years' experience]

Implications for Reform

This examination of teachers' thinking supports the hypothesis that teachers' beliefs and values differ from those of reformers. Whereas reformers' ideals can be captured in three main ideas, teachers' intentions reflect at least six areas of concern. Moreover, teachers hold numerous intentions within each of these areas. Not only are teachers' intentions numerous and diverse, but they often contradict one another, so that it is never possible for teachers actually to achieve all their intentions.

Teachers' intentions also have strong emotional valences. Teachers *need* a living environment that is stable and pleasant for themselves, they are *obligated* to ensure that students learn the content in the curriculum that is assigned to them, they *fear* distractions and disruptions that will get their lessons off course and perhaps cause it to disintegrate altogether, and they *hope* to enlist students' willingness to participate and ultimately to foster student learning. These emotional attachments to various intentions suggest that different intentions are likely to have different impacts on practice. For example, the fear of distractions appears to be so strong that it is likely to override other areas of concern whenever an unexpected event occurs, and these events occur frequently.

Reform ideals are also generally present in teachers' thoughts, but they are barely visible in the complex landscape of competing intentions and the multiple areas of concerns that are important to teachers. Moreover, teachers' intentions are expressed slightly differently than reformers'. For example, teachers were often unable to reject alternative content, and instead responded to our queries by saying that all content was important, and that the content they chose to teach just happened to be most important at this particular moment. Their acceptance of all potential content may suggest that they have little or no basis for sorting content or for ascertaining which is relatively more or less inherently important or is substantively more central to the subject. Instead, for teachers, important content is content that fits within the larger system of instruction.

Similarly, teachers embraced the idea of engagement, though they thought much less about *intellectual* engagement. In fact, even as they sought engagement, they also feared that too much engagement could hinder lesson momentum and could prevent them from finishing lessons on time. This tension between intellectual engagement and the pressure of time is something that reformers rarely address but that teachers must address. Teachers indicated that intellectual engagement was not an easy thing to manage in a classroom with 25 children, any one of whom might derail a conversation by misinterpreting an idea or getting confused or, conversely, by "getting it" immediately and losing interest while waiting for others to get it.

The reform ideal that was most widely mentioned in teachers' thinking was the ideal of universal access to knowledge, expressed by teachers in terms of universal *participation* in classroom activities. Virtually all teachers in this study expressed intentions to include all their students, to encourage all their students, and to be fair in their treatment of all their students. Even still, as we saw in the case of Ms. Buford, this intention did not translate unilaterally into a practice that reformers would necessarily admire. For Buford, universal participation meant that classroom discourse had to be staid and dull so that a particularly volatile student would remain calm. It is unlikely that many reformers have envisioned a situation such as Ms. Buford's or have thought about how to resolve problems that arise when their ideals conflict.

3. Creating a Tranquil Environment

One hypothesis seeking to account for why teachers are unable to achieve reform ideals is that the circumstances of teaching militate against them. There are both subtle and overt versions of this hypothesis. The subtle version suggests that even the beliefs and values that teachers embrace may derive from the situation, not from their own biographies. The more overt version suggests that the circumstances of classroom life impinge to the point that any intellectual thread can get lost. The 45 lessons observed in this study revealed plenty of evidence that the details of classroom life, as a condition of teaching, constrained teachers' ability to teach.

For good teaching to occur, teachers need an environment in which they and students can think about ideas. Tranquil environments not only help students concentrate; they also help teachers, who are trying to keep track of many things simultaneously. Tranquility involves freedom from distractions, but it also involves freedom from stress. To create a tranquil environment, teachers develop rules, routines, and norms that they hope will reduce confusions and distractions and increase the chances that students can concentrate on the matter at hand. Teachers also rely heavily on routines to create the kind of classroom community that they want—one in which students are respectful of one another, where they take turns, share, defer, wait their turn, and so forth. By creating a social climate that is conducive to learning, teachers also hope to increase student willingness to participate and thereby prevent distractions from students who misbehave.

Despite their best efforts, though, classrooms are routinely disrupted, and students routinely turn their attention to other things. The first half of this chapter describes the kinds of distractions—threats to tranquility—that occurred in the 45 lessons we observed and how teachers responded to them. The second half describes their efforts to create routines and norms that reduce distractions and stress, and increase tranquility and student willingness to participate.

Threats to Tranquility

It has been almost four decades since Philip Jackson published his important study, *Life in Classrooms* (Jackson, 1968). In it Jackson pointed out that classrooms are crowded, and that the teachers and students in them must learn to constrain themselves and to live with distractions. Jackson's observation is as true today as it was then. The remarkable number and variety of distractions we observed makes me suspect that classrooms—or at least American classrooms—are inherently unstable entities. Even when events appear to be peaceful and orderly, the threat of disorder, distraction, and loss of control is always present. Understanding the number and variety of distractions that routinely occur affords an insight into why teachers so frequently mention a strong need to avoid distractions and to maintain the momentum of their lessons.

Several researchers who study teaching have noted that teachers' plans resemble scripts (see, e.g., Shavelson, 1983). That is, planning for instruction is not so much a matter of outlining a set of curricular goals as a matter of *envisioning* a sequence of instructional events: what will be said, where students will be, how they will respond, and what will happen next. Envisioning enables teachers to "see" how a lesson will go, how they will maintain lesson momentum, how students will interact, how teachers will respond to the students and model the kind of behavior they expect from everyone. The lessons themselves, then, are enactments of scripts that teachers have worked out in their minds ahead of time.

What teachers seem to envision is not as precise as a script, of course, but it is something like the enactment of a play, in which events unfold in a particular way and lead to a particular conclusion. Both teacher and students have parts in the play, and each character has a role to play. Teachers often say "we" when describing their plans: "We would talk about this, and that would lead to a discussion of that. Then *we* would . . ." If the play unfolds as the teacher hopes, students will increase their understanding of atmosphere, fractions, explorers, or haiku. But if the plan goes awry, if the story line doesn't unfold as anticipated, the whole point of the lesson can be lost. The problem presented by distractions involves more than merely losing a few minutes of time to the distraction, and more than merely losing a few more minutes trying to pull students back into the play again. For many teachers, the threat is that they might have to start all over again because students will have lost the entire thread of the story. This is why teachers often perceive even small distractions as serious threats.

One reason teachers worried about these threats is that they were operating under a variety of schedule constraints so that efficiency became especially important. About half the teachers we interviewed mentioned some form of scheduling constraint that affected their plans: students had to be in the cafeteria at 11:30 or at an assembly by 10:00, a visitor was scheduled to arrive at 2:00, or the class had to get through the material by Friday because midterms began on Monday. Given all these pressures, it is little wonder that teachers try to envision scripts that will move students efficiently through the content and maximize the likelihood that they will remain attentive throughout the lesson.

Three kinds of distractions occurred frequently. They varied in size and significance, but each posed a threat in that each presented the possibility that the teacher would lose her tenuous hold on the coherence of her story line. These were:

Interruptions caused by students or other teachers walking into the room unexpectedly

Implementation problems caused by missing or inadequate materials

Off-task behaviors among students

Before examining these distractions, a caveat: Chapter 1 lists 499 episodes of practice that were discussed in our interviews with teachers. Many of the distractions I describe here were not discussed in interviews. In the interview, because both teachers and researchers were most interested in things the teacher intended to do, neither party brought up interruptions. Only 8 of the 499 episodes discussed in interviews involved distractions of any kind. Yet disruptions occurred routinely. Much of the analysis presented in this chapter, therefore, refers to observed, but not discussed, events—that is, to things that were visible in classrooms and on the videotapes but were rarely discussed in the interviews.

Distractions Caused by Interruptions

Interruptions occurred in over a third of the lessons. Students arrived late and entered the classroom at will, colleagues entered classrooms in midlesson to ask minor clerical questions, telephones rang and teachers answered them, and public announcements blared over loudspeakers, often with extensive messages. Many of these interruptions were motivated by special situations. For example, in one school a student had died from a long and protracted illness, and counselors were sent into each classroom to tell the students about this event. So a lesson we observed was cut short to accommodate the counselors. In another school, two instances of head lice were discovered, and it was decided that the nurse should inspect everyone in the building. So one lesson we observed was cut short to suit the nurse's schedule.

Other distractions were caused by established school policies or customs. One school principal gave daily announcements through a public-address system that interrupted everyone during the first period. Teachers appeared to have no control over the volume of the speakers in their rooms or over the timing of the announcements. This is what we observed in Ms. Buford's fifth-grade math class:[1]

Buford: So, there's a process of elimination, like yesterday? Okay. All right. Anyone else use a different strategy besides the process of elimination? Drew?

Drew: I just looked on the board for one that wasn't there.

Buford: Okay, there was one that wasn't up there. Mark?

Mark: You can see the only day you couldn't see was Saturday.

Buford: Okay. Now, many of you are saying that because Saturday is the only day not listed up here, it has to be Saturday.

P. A.: Good morning. Just a reminder that this is a busy day here at Oak Street school. We have several things that are going on. First of all, we have the fourth-grade open-ended. The fourth-grade open-ended tests are this morning. Those teachers will of course have their phones off the hook, but I need to remind people that they need to be very very quiet out in the hall, in the halls, it's the fourth-grade open-ended assessment. Ms. Smith and Ms. Jones will be testing their fourth-graders, therefore those other children will go out from those classes because they will be testing those children.

The second announcement is that we do have the vision screening and the dental screening today. Ms. Green and Ms. Brown are here. Please be on time. You have signed up in the office. We will be doing both of those procedures in the lunch room. Now, for efficiency's sake, those of you who are having your vision screening will go in the double doors next to the gymnasium. Those of you who are having your dental screening will go in a single door next to, um, the outside play area. That will help them keep themselves separated and be efficient. I want you monitors, besides being on time, to try and keep the kids very orderly, because the teachers particularly need to hear what the children are saying when she is doing their vision check.

And the third reminder is Ms. Marvin is also testing, and I apologize for omitting that in my earlier deal. Ms. Marvin, Ms. Smith, and Ms. Brown are all testing.

The final announcement concerns, as we go into dialogue groups, every morning at 8:15, boys and girls in second and third grade, I've been very disappointed at how you do when you get out of your classroom. Remember, our school rule is we go single file on the right, and a single file on the right lost focus, so we are trying to renew that today. So, we are having dialogue, but you need to be very careful about how you go back and forth to classes and particularly be very attentive to your noise near the fourth-grade classes.

Thank you very much.

Buford: You mentioned Saturday, and Drew, you said it was the only one not there. Process of elimination. Did you go back and check?

Drew: Yes.

Buford had apparently learned to live with this particular kind of interruption, as it occurred every morning at roughly the same time. She directed her lesson as if the announcement had never happened; when it was over, Buford and her students picked up their discussion exactly where it had left off. In fact Buford didn't bring up this interruption in the interview as a noteworthy episode. But Ms. Taswell, with 14 years' experience, who taught sixth-grade math in the same school, brought it up in her interview to explain why her class was so slow to begin:

I knew you wanted me to pick out interesting things, but I was figuring probably you wondered why it took so long to begin. I watched how many minutes the tape went before I even started. And I knew [the principal] would do announcements. I knew the tardy bell didn't ring until about five after. [And then there was] the homecoming breakfast, and then when you start, car riders and that sort of thing, they're all coming in at different times. And if I start, then they come in and they wonder, "Where are we? What are we doing?" And it's just as much an interruption as it is to just go ahead and wait and try to begin at about 8:15 usually. And I try to give them that thing, like on the overhead, the morning math, so that they have something to keep them busy, or getting started in a math mode when they first get in.

Most teachers in this school started their day with some sort of "warm-up" activity, something that would fill the gap between the official start of the school day and the time when everyone was actually settled and all the interruptions finished.

Surprisingly, many interruptions were side effects of reform initiatives. For instance, one school we visited had devised an in-house suspension policy that allowed teachers to remove disruptive children from their own classrooms and take them into another teacher's classroom. The policy solved an important problem and was useful for any teacher who had a misbehaving student. But it disturbed the neighboring teacher who received the child midlesson. This happened to Ms. Keeblefrau (grade 2 math, 2 years' experience) when we were in her classroom. Another teacher suddenly appeared midlesson with a child in tow and asked Keeblefrau to take this child in. The episode caused consternation for Ms. Keeblefrau because she already had a visitor with a camera and tripod in her classroom, and there was no remaining space for the child. Moreover, she had already begun her lesson and feared she would lose momentum as a result of the interruption.

Yet another school prided itself on the number of "specials" it offered students. The school served a relatively poor, rural population and so was eligible for a variety of special funds. The principal actively sought funds for special programs in physical education, foreign languages, arts, music, and so forth. These programs enhanced the curriculum and made a much richer array of content available to students. Students could choose to participate in any of these they wanted. However, the schedules for their participation were determined by the person coordinating the special program, not by the regular classroom teacher. So in this school, teachers had to become accustomed to their own students coming and going at odd times to participate in their particular "specials." We frequently saw children entering or leaving these classrooms in midlesson.

We saw side effects from another reform initiative in Ms. Chalmers' K–2 science classroom. Among her students was a severely handicapped child who was confined to a wheelchair and unable to communicate. Placing such a student in regular classrooms is called "inclusion" and is assumed to benefit the child by giving him or her a more normal school experience. This child had an attendant who took care of him, so he made no nursing demands on Chalmers or on other students. But he made loud crying noises throughout the lesson, sounding like a child who had just fallen off the swings or been hit by a baseball. Chalmers and the other students had to speak up to in order to hear one another over this boy's cries.

Distractions Caused by Implementation Failures

The second kind of distraction occurred when teachers encountered problems implementing the lesson as originally envisioned. The combination of implementation problems and interruptions yielded a 50-50 chance that one or the other kind of distraction would occur in a given lesson. Many of these implementation problems were brought up by the teachers themselves as episodes they wanted to discuss. Table 3 provides examples of these problems.

I had the impression from reading the interviews that these problems arose because teachers had very little time to think, and were barely on top of their work. For example, one teacher had hall duty in the morning, which meant that she had to monitor the hallways as students arrived and moved to their classrooms. By the time she was able to return to her own classroom, she was already behind schedule and had no time to compose herself, move into her role in the forthcoming script about the metric system, or organize her thoughts about the metric system before leaping into the lesson. Other implementation problems occurred because teachers forgot to bring something with them to class or because they discovered that a

Table 3 Examples of implementation problems

Missing materials

Ms. Snyder (grade 4–5 art, 32 years' experience) left materials at home on the kitchen counter.

Ms. Lafayette (grade 5–6 language arts, 28 years' experience) left handouts in another teacher's room.

Ms. Abundo (grade 3 science, 2 years' experience) lacked enough copies of a handout.

Mr. Kimberly (grade 6 science, 21 years' experience) lacked enough copies of a handout, student refused to share.

Mr. Awles (grade 3–4 science, 9 years' experience) threw away a wall poster, so cannot use it now.

Spontaneous curriculum changes

Ms. Masters (grade 6 science, 29 years' experience) abandoned a unit in the middle to do another project, was dismayed to see how little students remembered when she returned to it.

Ms. Chalmers (K–2 science, 22 years' experience) decided at the last minute to add a demonstration of the Earth's orbit, but it confused the students.

Ms. Sesnersen (grade 3 science, 5 years' experience) realized today that she had forgotten to do a lesson that would have prepared her students for today's lesson.

Ms. Todd (grade 5 math, 20 years' experience) skipped several chapters that covered dividing by decimals, only to discover later that students needed this content to understand the metric system.

Inadequate materials

Mr. James (grade 6 math, 6 years' experience) realized while reading a handout to students that it was worded awkwardly, tried to translate it quickly.

Ms. Knutsen (grade 4–5 science, 4 years' experience) realized that a handout was "kind of cutesy" and wasn't very clear, but it was too late to revise it now.

---

unit they had skipped over weeks earlier turned out to be relevant to today's content.

Some implementation problems arose when teachers were overly ambitious. This was the case with Ms. Masters, who had been teaching for nearly 30 years and continued to enthusiastically seek out new learning opportunities for her students. In this case, she found an opportunity for her sixth-graders to participate in an internationally coordinated science project in which students all over the world would test soil and water samples and submit their data over the Internet to a central site. Masters saw this as a terrific science opportunity for her students and decided to redirect her science curriculum toward this project. The problem was, Masters couldn't insert this unit into her curriculum at her own convenience, but instead had to schedule it at the time it was offered. So she dropped the science unit she had been working on and turned her students' attention to this new project. When we visited her classroom, she was returning to her original curriculum—the one she had abandoned two months earlier to pursue this special project—because she realized that it was nearly time for midterm exams and her students needed to know the original curriculum content. She was surprised and disturbed at how little her students recalled of their earlier work. Throughout the lesson, students were repeatedly unable to respond to her queries, and Ms. Masters seemed unable to adjust her instruction to accommodate their lack of recall. In the interview, Masters expressed frustration and annoyance at her students for their failure to recall the material, but indicated no reservations about the wisdom of her own curricular decision making.

Notice that Ms. Masters' problems were also a side effect of a reform initiative. One important feature of the education landscape in the United States is that reformers can appear both within and outside the official education system. In this case, a well-intentioned private foundation wanted to contribute to education reform by introducing its own curricular unit. Masters found the offer intriguing, but the digression into this unit proved to be a distraction for both her and her students, and students lost track of the original curriculum content.

Masters' lack of awareness of her own role in her students' difficulties is similar to that of other teachers whose errors we observed. Most teachers seemed either oblivious to their own oversights or relatively forgiving of them. There was a matter-of-fact attitude across most of these discussions, as if teachers understood that it was simply not possible to anticipate everything that needed to be anticipated, and that, therefore, failures of this sort were to be expected.

In fact none of these teachers indicated that they had learned any lessons from these episodes. Ms. Masters didn't conclude that she should focus on one unit at a time rather than jumping between units; teachers who had skipped over preliminary content didn't indicate that they now realized the importance of that content in preparing students for current material, and teachers who had forgotten to bring needed materials didn't comment on a need to become better organized.

In fact teachers were just as resigned to their own implementation and planning failures as they were to the interruptions described above. Rather than seeking to prevent either type of distraction, teachers accepted both as part of classroom life. They forgave others who interrupted their lessons and forgave themselves for their own planning failures. This resignation appears to reflect a certain feeling of helplessness. Teachers have so much to do and so little time to plan it all out that they don't really expect to be fully prepared or fully in control of their lessons.

Distractions Caused by Students

The third major group of distractions consisted of off-task behavior by students. Even in the best of classroom worlds—one with no outside interruptions, no planning failures, and plenty of supporting classroom routines—tranquility is continually threatened by students moving off-task. Distractions caused by off-task students are difficult to tally because classrooms are routinely abuzz with activity. Students scrape their chairs, drop their pencils, wiggle, giggle, talk to each other, and tease each other. That such activity is commonplace means that each teacher must define her own level of tolerance for commotion. We never asked teachers about student misbehaviors unless the behavior was acute, as was one incident in which two Asian boys and a black boy traded racial epithets throughout a lesson. But teachers brought up off-task behaviors they saw when watching the tape, some of which they had failed to see during class, and some of which they had noticed during class, had responded to, and wanted to talk about. Twenty-eight such episodes were cited in these interviews. The types of student violations that teachers mentioned form no particular pattern, but instead consist of a potpourri of unallowed movements and side-bar conversations among students. Often the behaviors that triggered responses from teachers were not visible to us from the back of the classroom but were salient to teachers because they signaled a possible beginning of a major setback. Apart from those brought up by teachers, it would be impossible to tally all the student acts that could have counted as disruptive. Students are constantly moving, jiggling, and fidgeting, so that what counts as a "disruption" depends heavily on the teacher's judgment.

Student disruptions represent a particularly perplexing problem with respect to student opportunities for intellectual engagement. For teachers, student disruptions threaten classroom tranquility and lesson momentum. Teachers can lose their students' attention, and students can lose the thread of the lesson. On the other hand, their efforts to suppress these behaviors can also discourage students from intellectually engaging with content. A particularly painful example of such a response occurred in Ms. Defoe's fifth-grade science lesson. Defoe was nearing the end of a unit on physical fitness that included attention to the nature of scientific evidence, and to what made one claim or another "believable." In the lesson we observed, she wanted her students to write advertisements for physical fitness products that were believable. When she explained their task to them, Defoe discussed at length the problem of grandiose claims by advertisers, and pointed to ads for miracle drinks that were not believable because fitness could derive only from effortful work and not from elixirs. She reminded her students of a sample ad in the textbook for something called "Multiple Powers" and reminded her students that they shouldn't believe ads like that because the ads made unbelievable claims. As she concluded this discussion and summarized the assignment, one student, Andy, raised his hand and told Defoe about an ad he had recently seen for an empowering drink that he found believable. The conversation went like this:

> Defoe: Okay, I'm going around and I'm listening and I'm hearing some people who aren't quite understanding what I'm

asking. I don't want you to make up your own product. I don't want you to create a drink that's called, um, SlimDown. I want you to use an actual product that's out there, and how you are going to use that actual product to help someone become fit. Don't make up a product like SlimDown and say it's a drink that you drink every morning and then you don't have to exercise, because that's not a believable ad. That's not going to make me want to go out and buy that ad [she misspeaks herself here]. And don't take something that already exists like Slimfast, because that's not necessarily a believable product either. I want you to take something that's a believable fitness product or fitness service, and I want you to write an ad for it.

Andy: I saw a drink ad that said it gave you energy . . .

Defoe: Okay, but is that something that, if you were to see that in an ad, that you would believe that automatically and without doubt, that that claim would be true and that there was evidence to support that claim? You wouldn't be skeptical? You wouldn't be a skeptical scientist if you saw that ad? [Andy shakes head no.] Okay, well, we'll talk about that later, okay? William, can you share what you're going to make your fitness ad about?

Defoe tried more than once to hint to Andy that the ad he had read didn't meet her criteria for believability, but she finally gave up on helping Andy and simply said, "We'll talk about that later." This is a clear case of avoiding an important substantive question, but Defoe was not thinking about Andy's dilemma at the moment. She was thinking about yet another student, William. Here is her account of the episode:

Defoe: Okay. There was an instance at 12:31 [minutes into the lesson]. William was fooling around, so in order to get him back on track I said "Well, why don't you share with us what you're gonna make your ad about?" and the reason I did this was because if he was fooling around, then he was not only distracting himself from learning; he was distracting everyone in his group from learning. Whereas if I just said, "William, could you share your idea?" I wasn't pointing out that he was making a bad choice, and I wasn't stopping the class, and I wasn't getting off track; I was just bringing him back into the learning situation, so that was neat.

[And how did you decide at that moment to ask him to share? What was going through your mind?] I think because I saw it escalating the way it normally does, where William just giggles a little bit and is just fooling around a little bit, and then it gets out of hand where "Ooh, he was doing this" or "They were doing that," so I think that it's experience. It's that I've worked with him and I know him and I know what it's gonna lead to, so I saw it and I said, "Okay, let's have him share," so just insight from working with him for so long.

Defoe was proud that she had found a subtle way of bringing William back to the group discussion and preventing him from disturbing other students. But in her haste to bring William back, she had also abandoned Andy, who apparently was still confused on the issue of "believable" claims. As we continued to interrogate Defoe about this episode, she continued to be pleased with the way she had managed it, and never mentioned anything about Andy. She appeared to be more concerned about William's misbehavior than about Andy's confusion. Her strong desire to prevent a potential disturbance was particularly painful to watch because it also prevented her from responding to another student who was having conceptual difficulties with the content.

Ms. Defoe's line of thinking. Ms. Defoe's line of thinking about this episode is instructive. She began with the beliefs that students need to be attentive at all times and that the teacher needs to be always calm and in control. She also wanted to ensure that she was not pulled off-track by her students. Not surprisingly, given these values, she used her experience mainly to learn how to maintain control. She had discovered that small events can quickly escalate and that she needed to learn to see them quickly and prevent them quickly. This background led her to focus on *potential* problems when she interpreted a situation. She saw that William was giggling and fooling around, and she knew that episodes like this tended to get out of hand. At the same time, she also realized that William was outgoing and liked to share his ideas in class. These ideas and observations led her to several conclusions: she wanted to prevent William from getting other students off-task, but at the same time she didn't want to criticize William or stop the whole class to discipline him. She wanted to bring William back into the group. And when she reviewed the episode, she was proud of herself for finding this clever approach to solving the disruption problem.

Two themes stand out in Defoe's line of thinking. One is the strong theme of avoiding distractions. In fact, all four of the episodes she nominated for discussion related to preventing potential mishaps from occurring. And in all four cases, her reason for bringing up the episode was that she was pleased that she had found a non-confrontational way to avert a disaster. And in each case, the things she saw were virtually invisible to me, even on replaying the videotape. The second thing that stands out here is Defoe's apparent lack of awareness of Andy, who was still confused about the notion of believability in advertising. In the interview, she never mentioned the impact of the episode on Andy, nor did she ever get back to Andy later, as she had said she would. So while Defoe's response to the episode as a whole could be construed as increasing William's opportunity to engage with the content at hand, it also reduced Andy's opportunity to engage with it.

Teachers' Responses to Distractions

When we asked teachers about these distractions, they expressed one of two general responses. Some teachers expressed resignation, perhaps with a touch of mild annoyance or frustration that such things happen. Other teachers expressed strong emotions: anxiety, disorientation, momentary loss of persona, and fear that they might lose their students' attention or their own train of thought. Of these two general responses, resignation is the most surprising. Teachers who were resigned to distractions appeared to accept them as part of classroom life, and often didn't volunteer these interruptions as episodes worth discussing in their interviews. We actually observed many more interruptions than teachers brought up. And although teachers did sometimes indicate frustration or annoyance about these distractions, none of them conveyed a belief that they could or should work actively to prevent them. None asked interlopers to leave or telephone callers not to call, and none indicated in their interviews any intention of pursuing a course of action that might prevent future distractions. Their resignation seems particularly surprising in light of the widespread concern we saw in Chapter 2 for maintaining momentum. The single most frequently mentioned intention was to avoid distractions. Given that pattern of intentions, why do teachers seem to shrug off so many momentum-threatening interruptions?

Perhaps cause and effect run in the other direction. That is, momentum is a prominent area of concern *precisely because* classroom tranquility is so often threatened by things that teachers think are outside their control. In their unstable environments, where people come and go from their classrooms and where their own implementation plans are so often foiled, teachers focus on the distractions they *can* control, which tend to be the things students say and do.

When teachers weren't resigned to distractions, they were distressed by them and often disoriented by them. Mr. Jaspers (grade 5 drama, 6 years' experience) offered a nice metaphor to describe the disorientation and loss of persona that can arise from a distraction:

> I kind of run through potential scenarios of things that will happen: "Well, we'll go this way, we'll go that way, this will happen. If they're not understanding after we do this, to further explain, it's going to jump to this"—that kind of thing. [This particular episode] is almost a moment where something would happen on stage, and you would fall out of character for a moment, and you start dropping, lose the play, what's happening, where are the lines, and you're not the character, you're just yourself, and you sort of have to regroup and find your way back into what was

happening. [This moment is] similar to that because teaching is bit of a performance. You do have your teacher role that you go into.

Mr. Awles (grade 3–4 science, 9 years' experience) also indicated a response of disorientation and confusion:

> It surprised me . . . because I kept going in my head, "Okay, now if I have them do this, everything will just flow." Well, it didn't. You know, because you're always looking at these activities and thinking they are just going to flow. Well, when they don't flow, then it's like you have to back up, and then you are really thinking, "Okay, now how am I going to do this one to get this one to go right?" because basically you're trying to get to where you want to get, but to get there it's like, "Okay this isn't that difficult. It wasn't that difficult for me. Why is it so difficult for them?" So you have to stop and rethink, and now you are having to rethink faster.

Distractions also generate anxiety, as Ms. Abundo demonstrated. She is a relatively inexperienced teacher, observed during her second year. As she was passing out a worksheet to her third-grade science class, she realized she would be short one copy, and, in her words, she "panicked." She couldn't leave the room to make another copy, and she didn't want to lose the flow of the lesson while figuring out what else to do. "It's like we're doing one thing after another after another. So those few minutes or so I could lose everybody. I could lose one or two kids, or I could lose the whole class in concentration." In a flash, Abundo's momentum was threatened by a copying miscalculation. She had to decide what to do about the handout shortage, try to maintain her composure, and try not to lose her students' attention. Abundo brought up this episode as a high-anxiety moment for her, even though it happened so quickly that it was barely noticeable on the videotape. The videotape showed a teacher distributing a handout and, at the end of the distribution, calmly asking two students to share one copy.

Experience does not diminish these fears, as a brief episode involving Ms. Macciolino demonstrates. When a student in her fifth-grade social studies class asked her what a "quality" was, this 35-year veteran appeared to respond calmly. But when we asked Macciolino about it, she said:

> I was feeling a little bit like I want to get on with it. I don't want to spend so much time answering his one question, because I've lost the other 24 kids. But I do want to answer his question. I mean his question was valid for him. It needed an answer. And I think we did get it, the answer, but it still was not something he was super clear about.
>
> [What was the problem then?] Because if I lost 24 kids at that point in the lesson, I was going to have a downhill, I was going to have an uphill battle all the rest of the way. Keeping the rest of them focused. It would have been much harder to pull them in at that point.

One reason these episodes are stressful is that they require decisions that teachers have not anticipated. Often teachers can't make decisions as quickly as they believe they should. Ms. Toklisch (grade 6 math, 10 years' experience) described her situation this way: "I always go into it thinking what I think is going to happen, and it never turns out that way. I tried to just let them talk [about a math problem] while I thought about what they were saying and how I was going to handle it, and while they were all talking I just—while they had something that they wanted to say I just wanted to let them say it. And then the whole time I'm thinking, 'Okay, do I push this, or do I just let them talk and go back and sort of refocus everybody?'"

These feelings of disorientation, anxiety, and indecision help explain why teachers are so intent on avoiding distractions in their classrooms. Whenever a distraction occurs, it is not only students who are distracted, but teachers as well. Teachers must make a complicated decision quickly, before they lose the momentum of their lesson altogether. And at the same time, they must regain their own composure.

It is difficult to know what to make of all these interruptions, implementation failures, and student disruptions. On the one hand, they can inhibit intellectual engagement simply by preventing concentrated attention to content. But when teachers expressed anxiety about them, it was because these events distracted the teachers themselves as much as they distracted students. When forced to turn their attention to another matter, teachers can lose their own train of thought, lose their own momentum, and consequently lose their ability to sustain attention to content. On the other hand, many of these episodes *appeared* to be relatively minor events, and the teachers themselves *appeared* to handle them quickly and calmly, so that there was no appearance that much was lost, even when teachers later indicated worry or distress over the episodes. Yet the fact that so many teachers indicated resignation when discussing such episodes suggests that they have learned to accept them as an inevitable part of classroom life. One wonders whether this resignation also motivates them to reduce their curriculum from big ideas to small ones so that there is less to lose when distractions occur.

I have described here three broad types of threats to classroom tranquility: interruptions, planning and implementation failures, and student distractions. One might think that teachers could do more to reduce all three kinds of threats, but they mainly sought to control only the student disruptions. These were prevented through a plethora of classroom rules and routines.

Classroom Rules and Routines

Faced with continual distractions, teachers rely on a set of rules and routines to stabilize their classroom environments. Routines help stabilize the learning environment in many different ways. First, they enhance *intellectual tranquility* by reducing the threat of distractions, thereby increasing the chances that students will be able to concentrate on the issue at hand. Second, they enhance *emotional tranquility* by encouraging and reinforcing students, thereby increasing students' willingness to participate. Third, they enhance *social tran-*

quility by creating norms of fair play, politeness, and mutual respect, thereby promoting a civil community in the classroom.

Despite the advantages of rules and routines, Americans have always been ambivalent about the role they play in controlling students. In an early and still-significant sociological study of education, Willard Waller (1932/1961) argued that schools were inherently despotic, that they were characterized by domination and subordination, and that teachers suppressed spontaneity because they were threatened by it. Waller also thought that teachers had to be so repressive because the curriculum was inherently boring and unrelated to life, so that teachers had to be despotic to get students to attend to it. Education necessarily entailed such content and students had to be induced to learn it.

Other researchers have portrayed classroom life with similar ambivalence. Philip Jackson (1968) showed that classrooms were characterized by crowds, praise, and power, and that each of these features had an impact on classroom life. The fact of crowds meant that students were always having their work disrupted and that they usually had to wait to be called upon or to get help. Praise was connected to power in the sense that teachers used praise constantly as a way to communicate to students about what constituted appropriate behavior. And of course, teachers had the power to control what happened to students.

At around the same time that Jackson's study was published, another researcher, Jacob Kounin (1970), took a more positive stance toward student control, arguing that control was an essential part of teaching. He began by investigating a type of teacher behavior that he called a "desist," an action that was designed to stop students from engaging in disruptive behavior. However, as his study proceeded, he came to see that teachers also engaged in a number of strategies aimed at *preventing* disruptive behaviors. Kounin found that effective teachers were able to attend to multiple events throughout their classrooms. For instance, when they formed students into reading groups and sat with one group, they were still scanning the activities of the other groups. By tracking multiple events simultaneously, they were able to insert their "desists" in a timely manner, before the distractions got out of hand. Moreover, by thinking about multiple things at once, they could respond to questions from students in one group even while they were working with students in another group, and even when the assignments differed across the groups.

Kounin's study provoked a tremendous interest in the differences between effective and ineffective teachers, and numerous researchers have since sought to learn more about the practices of effective teachers. Their work does not address problems of social hierarchy, but instead looks at the role that control and management play in increasing instructional effectiveness. Teachers whose students gain the most during the school year are those who are *most efficient* (Brophy and Good, 1986). They move from one activity to another quickly, with little wasted time. They keep students on task, keep tasks moving along, keep transitions brief, and keep textbook pages turning. Routines are important vehicles for achieving this efficiency by socializing students into coordinated roles (Brophy, 1999). Routines prevent student misbehavior, encourage student cooperation (Doyle, 1986), and help teachers maintain the momentum of their lessons.

Routines are the most enduring practices that teachers devise. When teachers construct their daily agenda, that agenda applies only to that day. When they develop responses to unexpected student comments, those responses apply only to fleeting events. But when they develop routines—standardized systems for determining how students will be called on, how materials will be distributed, how assignments will be collected and returned—these systems tend to endure, providing a framework within which *all* instruction is both facilitated and contained.

To give a sense of the role classroom routines play in teaching, I first provide a case study of one teacher's classroom routines and the line of reasoning that led to them. I then broaden my scope to describe the full range of routines developed by the teachers participating in this study, along with some of the effects these routines had on students' opportunities to engage intellectually with important content.

Ms. Aires' Routines

Ms. Aires (grade 4 language arts, 3 years' experience) was a Hispanic woman who taught mainly Hispanic students. The lesson we observed began immediately after the students returned from lunch. Aires had more noticeable routines than nearly any other teacher we observed, and her students, far from seeming oppressed, appeared to be eager to participate and to please her. The first thing we observed was a collection of routines used to bring students into the room after lunch. When it was time to fetch her students, Aires went outside, closing the door behind her as she left. She returned with her students lined up behind her, opened the door, leaned inside, and *turned off the lights.* Then she stood at the door as her students filed into the unlit room, *patting each one on the back and speaking his or her name.* One by one, the children went directly to their seats and *put their heads on their desks.* When they were all in place, Aires closed the door and *turned on the lights.* The students *then lifted their heads* and turned their attention to her.

The lesson itself consisted of three parts, with students rotating about the room to work on the three separate activities. Ms. Aires stayed at one location and worked with a different group during each rotation. When it was time for them to move to the next activity, she *rang a little dinner bell,* and students promptly jumped up and moved to their next activity. At one point, when she wanted everyone's attention, she *stood up and put her hands on her head.* As students noticed her, they also put their hands on their head, or they saw other students put their hands on their heads and followed suit. Soon all the students had their hands on their heads, were quiet, and were facing Aires.

Then she spoke to them.

It would be a mistake to interpret these many routines as evidence that Aires was overly authoritarian or that students were overly controlled. In fact her students appeared to be very fond of her and eager to participate in these routines. When she asked a question, hands went up eagerly, and when she stood and put her hands on her head, students seemed to want to do the same, and nudged each other to ensure that everyone cooperated. At one point in the lesson, a student interrupted to remind Aires of a routine that had been neglected. One had the sense, observing the lesson, that students wanted to participate in all these rituals.

Quiet and order were important to Ms. Aires, and the first thing she wanted to talk about in the interview was the noise students made when they rotated from one activity to the next. She wished her students would start quietly and walk slowly. She thought noise distracted students from their work and that distractions were a particular problem in this lesson because students had to work independently in their rotations, while she worked with just one group. So it was important that they be able to do that and not be distracted by noise. Moreover, from her experience, she had developed certain principles of practice specific to this issue. "I find that when they start out quietly, they kind of keep it that way. Like, when we go to the library, and I'm using a low voice and the librarian is speaking softly, that's how the kids will be. But if we start out loud, that's how the kids are going to behave. And I sort of relate that to the noise from chairs or from anything moving. And also if they're running, I kind of think that that's how they're going to keep on doing things, you know."

In addition to quiet, Ms. Aires liked order, and she had established rules and routines for almost every aspect of student behavior. At one point, when the students were working on their separate activities, a student left his group and tried to approach Aires, who was sitting with another group. She put her hand up as a policeman would, stopping traffic, and the student stopped in the middle of the classroom, midway between his group and hers. Quietly but sternly, she said, "You know what to do with that." The student tried to object, but she repeated her admonition two more times, and he finally retreated. In the interview, she explained this episode as follows. The student was approaching with a pencil, which she assumed he wanted permission to sharpen. She also thought, in retrospect, that the student's movement was really a ploy to get into the camera's view and be on the videotape. (The camera was pointed toward the group with whom Aires was working.) But, she said, students knew that they didn't need permission to sharpen pencils. Furthermore, there was also a rule that once students were in groups, they couldn't interrupt other groups. We asked Aires if she would have responded to such a student differently earlier in her career, and she said yes, that she would most likely have repeated the rule for the student, rather than just saying, "You know what to do": "I've learned that if I keep on giving them the answers, it's tiring for me. Not just in questions, but anything that they come up to me for. But also I think that they can learn more sometimes from their peers, asking their peers. Because I think that sometimes their peers can explain it to them even better than I can, in words that they can understand better, in some situation. And so I really want them to reach out to others, and help each other out, and learn to work cooperatively in their groups, too."

Ms. Aires' routines were designed to create a calm, quiet, and orderly classroom environment, but they also helped her by reducing the number of things she had to keep track of. For instance, one routine involved using a timer when students were working independently at their desks. This allowed her to peruse student work without having to simultaneously watch the clock. Another routine involved having a student change the language and format of the date on the board, which was written in Spanish in the morning and English in the afternoon, reflecting the language in which instruction was given. In the morning, for instance, the date would be "1 de marzo, 2002," in the afternoon, "March 1, 2002." Aires found that she frequently forgot to make this change, so she established a routine in which changing the date from Spanish to English became the responsibility of one of the students. When she discussed this routine, she said it satisfied several intentions: "Honestly, the reason why I thought about it was for them to help me, because I forget, and I thought it'd be nice, and it could be a little extra help for them, because then they get to do it in English and in Spanish, and it is done differently, and they tend to get it confused a lot. You know, a capital letter in English, and it's lowercase in Spanish. That the month goes first in English. So it's good practice for them, and I think they like it. They like having that job, too. But the reason why I first thought about it was for them to help me, because that's one of those little things that I do forget." In the interview we asked not only about these particular episodes, but about Aires' use of routines in general.

> I love them, actually. It's a nice way of communicating something to them. They know my signals, I think. Like, for example, to be quiet, obviously, putting my finger on my mouth. Also to lower their voice, I go like this [she makes a lowering motion with her hand], moving my hand, my fingers up and down. That means, instead of being just totally quiet, just lower your voice. Um, the bell, yeah; and putting my hands on my head.
>
> And it's a quicker response, too, I think. And it lets them help each other again. Like, they tell each other. One person notices, and they tell the rest of the people in their group. And it's very quick, actually. It can be very effective, and I really like that. Because sometimes I just want to tell them a little message in the middle of whatever they're doing, and let them continue. And I really like finger signals.

We asked her why these were so important, and Aires said:

> Like if they are talking loudly in an activity and I need their attention, and if I tell them to be quiet, my voice has to be higher than theirs so they can listen to me. And again, I find that when I raise my voice, they raise their voice, and it keeps going like a cycle. And this breaks that cycle, and it gives a silent type of signal to be quiet instead of speaking up higher. [So then you don't have to raise your voice?] Yeah, when I raise my voice, I do find that I'm not as calm myself, and I find that if I'm calm, I'm a better teacher, basically, than if I have a loud voice and I'm more like tense or stressed or wanting them to do things quickly. I have reminders to remember, "You've got to keep your voice down, speak softly and slowly." It's much better.

Ms. Aires' line of thinking. Although Ms. Aires' routines helped her maintain the quiet and orderly classroom that she desired, they had to be vigilantly maintained at all times. Aires has thought a great deal about these routines, and her line of thinking is instructive. She believes it is important for students to learn to work independently and for teachers to speak softly to students. She mentioned that the teachers she admires are people who speak softly, and she indicated that she has a personal need for a quiet classroom so that she can speak softly and still be heard by her children. She feels calmer when she can speak softly. Given this set of beliefs and values, she has accumulated certain principles about her student behavior that are relevant. She has noticed that they are easily distracted by noises, and that they get bored if the same routine is used too much. She has also noticed that noise levels tend to be maintained or to escalate. She has also acquired some ideas from outside sources, even one from her brother. All these ideas—her standing beliefs and values and her accumulated principles and strategies—contribute to her interpretation of her situation, which she views as one in which she must respond to strong pressure from her colleagues to keep her students quiet. She draws several conclusions regarding what she should do: she should establish norms of quiet, prevent students from disturbing one another, avoid raising her own voice, avoid repeating herself, get students' attention quickly and efficiently, change her signals regularly so that students won't lose interest, and reduce the number of things that she needs to keep track of. Notice that Aires has listed numerous intentions for her routines, including accommodating students' need for variety, accommodating her own personal need for a quiet voice to get students' attention, and making sure that things like date formats are changed when they should be.

Aires appeared to have generated a set of routines that were "friendly" to students. Recall that her portfolio of routines included patting each child on the back and speaking each child's name as the children entered the classroom. This routine probably enhanced emotional tranquility and presumably increased students' willingness to participate. Indeed, her students all seemed eager to participate and expressed excitement and pleasure when she told them what their forthcoming activities would be. The fear, then, that routines will necessarily create an atmosphere of domination and suppression does not seem justified. According to Aires, as well as many other teachers, routines increase the likelihood that students will be able to engage with important ideas by decreasing the chances that they will be distracted from those ideas.

But Ms. Aires' practices also demonstrate that classroom routines do not remove all the threats of distraction. Recall, for instance, the student from one group who tried to approach Aires when she was working with another group, presumably to ask permission to sharpen his pencil when he didn't need permission to do so. Such episodes are one reason Aires felt she had to be constantly vigilant in reminding students of the rules and procedures. Moreover, we observed one distraction that was actually *caused by the routines themselves.* This distraction occurred when Aires neglected to follow her own routine of changing the date on the board from Spanish to English every afternoon. The lesson we observed occurred immediately after lunch, just when the date should have been changed. However, no one changed the date from Spanish to English, perhaps because of the excitement of having a visitor and a camera in the classroom. Well after Aires had begun her lesson, a student noticed that the date was still written in Spanish and insisted that it be changed. But by the time the student pointed out the error, Aires didn't want to bother with the change because she was well into her lesson and was reluctant to lose her momentum. But the student wouldn't let it go. The date had to be changed because the class was now speaking in English. Finally Aires conceded. She asked the responsible student to change the date and then went back to the lesson. But the date was written high up on the board, and the student couldn't reach it. He approached the board, picked up some chalk, and then realized the date was too high for him to reach. He returned to his seat, picked up his chair, brought it to the front of the room, and climbed onto it.

Then he dropped the chalk, climbed down from the chair, picked up the chalk, climbed back up on the chair, erased the date, and rewrote it in English. Throughout all of this, Aires was trying to maintain her momentum and to keep other students attending to her rather than to the student who was trying to change the date. She proceeded with her lesson as if all this commotion was not going on.

Other Routines We Observed

The routines we observed were remarkably various. Teachers had developed routines for when and how students would enter the room and what they could do while waiting to be called to order, routines for calling students to order, for calling on individual students, for handing out materials and collecting materials, for grouping students—for virtually every conceivable aspect of classroom life. To illustrate this variety, consider one small task teachers must do: calling the group to order. Students are called to order numerous times in a day—not just at the beginning of the day, but after every learning activity that moves them into solitary or small-group work. As they work, they can become quite engrossed in the task at hand, and their conversation and activities can raise the noise level in the room so that it is difficult for the teacher to regain their attention when it is time to move on.

Most teachers have developed routines that don't require them to raise their voice each time. Some, such as Ms. Aires, make a point of changing their routines regularly so that students will continue to find them interesting. Aires' method of standing and placing her hands on her head has a ripple effect, for when students see her doing this they respond by putting their hands on their heads. This in turn enables other students to notice and respond either to the teacher or to other students who are emulating the teacher. Another teacher might ring a small bell or play a musical instrument or call out, "May I have your attention please?" Ms. Defoe counted backward from five to zero as her students gradually come to attention. When she reached zero, she would say, "Thank you for stopping at zero." Mr. Sadowski (grade 2 math, half a year's experience) used a clapping routine. When it was time to bring students back together, he clapped out a rhythm:

clapclap clap   clap clap

About half a dozen students responded by clapping the same rhythm in return:

clapclap clap   clap clap

Then Sadowski clapped out a second pattern:

clapclap   clap

This time, about 20 students responded:

clapclap   clap

Then Sadowski said, "I didn't hear everybody," and repeated his first pattern:

clapclap clap   clap clap

This time, all students responded in kind, and he began the group lesson.

We saw similar variety in many other aspects of classroom life. Many teachers had developed a routine for calling on children, and many of these routines were justified with language similar to reformers' language of universal access to knowledge. But for teachers who were calling on students, the intention was usually universal participation. Some teachers wanted to ensure that all students had an equal chance to get called on, and some wanted to ensure that all students *knew* there was a chance they would be called on, so that they would be more attentive. These teachers often had jars of popsicle sticks with students' names on them and randomly drew names from the jars during the Q&A portions of the class. Others wanted to ensure widespread participation and so chose students who hadn't spoken for a while. Still others wanted to reward good behavior, so chose the students who were sitting quietly in their seats with their hands raised politely. Still others preferred to call on their best students, in the belief that these students were more likely to provide the right answer and consequently to keep the Q&A portion of the lesson moving along.

Critics of teaching are chary of routines because they view them as a means of control. Several authors have suggested that teachers' efforts at classroom control can interfere with students' intellectual engagement and can motivate teachers to stick to mundane, trivialized forms of knowledge (Doyle, 1986; McNeil, 1985; Sedlak et al., 1986). Some teachers also conceded this point. Here is how Ms. Mathews (grade 4 science, 26 years' experience) expressed the problem: "You know, when you find yourself having to raise your voice, and your heart starts pounding, and you start realizing that things are not going the way you had planned, it's a scary feeling. And I know we've all been through it. And if it happens to you once, and you're just starting off, you want to avoid that at all costs. So probably the tendency is to stick with more of the traditional approach, and give them lots of paper, lots of writing, and sit in your seat, do your thing."

But for most teachers, routines were not intended so much to control as to foster a sense of community in the classroom and to encourage student cooperation. Table 4 shows the distribution of teachers' intentions for classroom routines across their six areas of concern. The most widely mentioned intentions for routines were to increase student willingness to participate and to foster a sense of community in the classroom. These intentions are quite different from the authoritarian motives that critics often attribute to teachers' routines. Teachers clearly view routines as important contributors to emotional and social tranquility. Routines give them a way of making sure that they treat students equally, that they acknowledge each student or have at least one personal interaction with each student, that they give students special attention, and that they help students learn to cooperate with one another. All of these can increase the likelihood that students will focus on the issue at hand and perhaps even engage with important ideas.

Table 4 Percent of routines motivated by each area of concern

Area of concern	All routines
Defining learning outcomes	5
Fostering student learning	26
Maintaining lesson momentum	34
Fostering student willingness to participate	39
Establishing classroom as a community	37
Attending to personal needs	24

Implications for Reform

This chapter describes two seemingly contradictory aspects of teachers' practice: the volume and variety of routines they use and the volume and variety of distractions they experience. Despite teachers' attempts to foster stability and tranquility in their classrooms, interruptions appear to be a defining feature of American classroom life, and these interruptions frequently reduce student opportunities to engage intellectually with important ideas.

Whether these features of classroom life really are defining features, and if so, why, are important questions. According to Stevenson and Stigler (1992), Asian classrooms are not susceptible to nearly as many disturbances as their American counterparts. These authors found that interruptions occurred in 47 percent of the American fifth-grade classrooms they observed, but in only 10 percent of the Asian classrooms they observed. Moreover, many of the problems teachers encountered were condoned, encouraged, or directly caused by school policies and organizational norms: P.A. announcements, children moving in and out of the classroom, other adults entering classroom, telephones ringing, and so forth. One lesson reformers could take from this chapter is that American school cultures themselves may threaten reform initiatives.

These episodes also suggest that routines themselves do not thwart intellectual engagement as much as teachers' fears of escalating disruptions do. Ms. Mathews explicitly stated that her fear motivated her to rely on more mundane pedagogies and content. Ms. Defoe took pride in her success at preventing escalations and missed the fact that, in the process, she also cut off a legitimate question from another student. I suspect the problem is that teachers are unable, in the thick of things, to think through a complicated substantive confusion while simultaneously thinking through the seriousness of momentary off-task behaviors.

The difficulties teachers had keeping students both on task and on script lends support to the hypothesis that the circumstances of teaching may be responsible for teachers' inability to respond to reform ideals. Teachers establish a wide variety of routines to increase the tranquility and stability of classroom life, but they cannot prevent all interruptions from outside, cannot prevent all student misbehaviors, and cannot prevent all potentially distracting off-script remarks.

4. Managing Conversations about Content

Conversation in classrooms often takes the form of mutual interrogation. That is, students may ask questions of teachers in order to clarify their understanding, and teachers may ask questions of students in order to learn more about what students do or don't understand and how they are thinking about the content. Regardless of the content being taught, and regardless of other learning activities, teachers and students will always interact with one another about the content. In fact teachers frequently plan question-and-answer sequences as integral parts of their lessons. Q&A sequences are independent learning activities, which may be scheduled to occur before or after other learning activities, but they are also often routines, in the sense that teachers devise standard ways of posing questions and students learn that there are standard ways of responding to these questions. As such, Q&A routines can prevent students from saying things that are so far afield from the issue at hand that they can derail the lesson. But despite teachers' efforts to control the conversation, students manage to say many things that don't quite fit into the day's agenda.

This chapter addresses three aspects of conversation between teachers and students. The first section provides examples of the variety of unexpected ideas students put forward. To the extent that these ideas are non sequiturs, they have the potential, just as misbehaviors do, to derail a lesson and to distract both the teacher and other students from the intended direction of the lesson. The second section describes the routines that teachers devise for interacting with students, and the third describes teachers' intentions for the practices we observed.

Unexpected Student Ideas

Even in the most carefully orchestrated classrooms, and even if no external interruptions, planning failures, or off-task behaviors occurred, teachers would still have difficulty enacting the scripts they envision. Without intending to misbehave, students can dream momentarily and lose the thread, or think they have the thread when in fact they are confused. Or one student's understanding is different from everyone else's, and the teacher has to decide quickly how to respond to these conceptual complications. These episodes arise not because students are off-task but because they are *on* task and are thinking about the content. They lead to *off-script comments* rather than *off-task behaviors.* That is, students are actively participating in the lesson the teacher has developed, but they say things that the teacher has not anticipated, ask questions that were not expected, or misunderstand the ideas in a way that the teacher has not envisioned. Once this happens, the lesson is no longer unfolding in the way the teacher imagined it would. In the interviews, teachers brought up student off-script comments and questions nearly three times per lesson, and these episodes represent only a portion of all that occurred.

There are myriad ways in which students may deviate from the teacher's envisioned lesson, and many of these deviations arise from enthusiasm rather than from disengagement. In their zeal, students volunteer ideas that they may believe are relevant or pertinent but that in fact take the class in a direction far from where the teacher intended to go. Their comments can create the most perplexing dilemmas teachers face. They threaten the lesson's integrity in two ways. First, simply by veering off course, they threaten the momentum of the lesson. But in addition, the simple fact that they have veered off course may suggest that the teacher did not accurately estimate her students' knowledge and capabilities when she planned the lesson in the first place. Such comments may imply that the entire lesson was misconceived.

Table 5 summarizes the number and types of off-script moves that were discussed in our interviews. These numbers do not represent all the off-script moves that occurred. Because there are usually more than 20 students in the classroom, and because it is difficult to ensure that they all have the same understanding of the content, it is highly likely that at least one student will deviate from the teacher's envisioned lesson.

The first type of off-script response from students occurs when students misunderstand either the content or the teacher's question, and their response reflects their misunderstanding. This category was by far the most frequent. The examples in Table 5 illustrate the difficulty for teachers of using their own questioning as a vehicle for keeping students attentive, for they could never be sure of the answers they would receive once the question had been asked. One thing to notice in these examples is that teachers often had an answer they were expecting, or "looking for," as they often said in the interviews, and they were surprised and taken aback when student responses deviated from those expectations.

Often these conceptual difficulties indicate that one student's thinking is out of synch with other students'. These discrepancies leave teachers with the difficult decision of whether to respond to the one student, and risk losing the attention of all the others, or to abandon the one student, knowing that he or she needs attention. Most of the situations that we observed involved a student who didn't understand an idea that everyone else did, but the reverse can also happen. For example, in Ms. Toklisch's sixth-grade mathematics class, a student came up with a highly refined and complicated solution to a mathematics problem, and put it on the board for the rest

Table 5   Examples of unexpected student ideas and questions

Number of events	Type of event
68	*Conceptual confusions,* including:
	Mr. Kimberly (grade 6 science, 22 years' experience) is introducing a lesson on pollution and air quality. He starts by asking students to think of places where the air doesn't smell so good. A student proposes saltwater air.
	Ms. Dawes (grade 4–5 language arts, 13 years' experience) asks what you could use for clothing on an island. A student proposes snakes and parrots.
	Mr. Wafner (grade 4 social studies, 25 years' experience) has asked students to work in groups but is not satisfied that the groups are functioning well. Afterward he introduces a discussion of how to do group work, aimed at heightening students' awareness of the need to cooperate when in groups. He asks how to do the reading when you are with a group, and a student says, "Alone." Wafner wanted a response that involved taking turns.
12	*Clarifying questions,* including:
	Ms. Lachamy (grade 6 language arts, 1 year's experience) is explaining to students how they are to do a task. A student asks what they will be doing the next day.
	Mr. Awles (grade 3–4 science, 9 years' experience) is showing students how to draw a side view of the ocean. She wants them to place their left hand along the left side of the page and then trace it with their pencil, to create a jagged downward line. A student says she is left-handed and therefore can't do this.
	Ms. Eckhard (grade 4 language arts, 6 years' experience) has students form groups to work on a problem. Within each group, one student is to record the work. One group can't proceed because students are too confused about the task.
14	*Other unexpected responses to the lesson,* including:
	Ms. Chalmers (K–2 science, 22 years' experience): In a lesson on light and shadow, a student introduces the fact that her kitten is named Shadow.
	Ms. Ames (grade 4 math, 1 year's experience): After small-group work, one student tattles on others in his group.

Table 5 continued

Number of events	Type of event
	Ms. Defoe (grade 5 science, 3 years' experience): In a lesson on physical fitness, a student makes a goofy comment about fat; others laugh.
	Ms. Taffner (grade 6 science, 7 years' experience): In a science lab, a student complains that the yeast stinks; others laugh.
	Mr. Jaspers (grade 5 drama, 6 years' experience): In a drama class where students are learning to improvise a role, one student improvises by running out the emergency exit and leaving the building.
94	Total off-script comments

of the class. The teacher understood the student's reasoning, but she also knew that it was beyond the reach of most of the others. Her dilemma was that if she spent too much time attending to this student's thinking, the other students would become bored and find other ways to interest themselves. Yet she couldn't ignore the idea either.

In the homework assignment for her fourth-grade mathematics class, Ms. Ames (who had one year of experience) had asked students to collect some data that they would then analyze during class. Ames saw that one of the students hadn't done her homework and had no data to contribute. However, as the students began their work, this student suddenly had data. Ames realized that the student was making up her numbers and that the numbers would be inconsistent with everyone else's data. The faulty data were outside the distribution of data the other students had collected. If she didn't confront the student about the faulty data, the entire project would lose its value for the rest of the class.

Yet another kind of off-script comment occurs when students ask clarifying questions. These often arise when the teacher is explaining the plan for the day, and a student asks a question that sets back the discussion. One such seemingly normal episode occurred in Ms.

Macciolino's lesson. Macciolino, with 35 years of experience, was a rotating teacher whom we observed while she was teaching grade 6 social studies in someone else's classroom. She had introduced the day's lesson by saying that she would ask a question and then go around the group for answers, and that everyone must come up with an answer. The hard part would be that they couldn't use an answer that someone else had already offered. Therefore, they should think of more than one answer to begin with, and they should listen to other students' answers so they won't repeat them. The exchange went as follows:

Macciolino: You're learning about explorers. I want you to think about something an explorer does, another word for an explorer, or a quality that an explorer needs. And if you look up there [at the board] you will probably all repeat each other's answers, so it may not be much help to you. So: another word for explorer, something explorers do, or a quality that an explorer needs. Since this is a harder question, I'm going to give you a whole minute to think about it.

S: What's a quality?

Macciolino: A characteristic.

S: What's a characteristic?

Macciolino: Something like, "I'm enthusiastic." That's a characteristic. You're curious. That's a characteristic, being curious. [To the other teacher, laughing:] Help me out, Ms. Longfellow!

Another S: Like feelings.

Another S: Like, something they have.

Macciolino: A way that you are that makes you special. If you are describing people, what kinds of words do you use to describe them. [To the group:] All right. Time to think.

Though she appeared completely composed on the videotape, and appeared to respond to the student's question in a matter-of-fact way, she indicated later in the interview that the question provoked a fear that she might lose the rest of the group while responding to this one student.

> [How do you decide when it's more important to focus on one kid versus, as you put it, losing the rest of the class?] Because if I lost 24 kids at that point in the lesson, I was going to have a downhill—I was going to have an uphill battle all the rest of the way, keeping the rest of them focused. It would have been much harder to pull them in at that point. Sometimes I find that children, especially when you first begin something and they don't yet see the bigger picture, it's easy for them to get diverted, and that is all it takes sometimes. To be diverted is this child asking something that is obvious to them, so they're not going to pay attention to it. He has to have an answer, but they're not going to be a part of that process . . . . It's a play between keeping them with you, so to speak, and getting him on board. [Ms. Macciolino, grade 5 social studies, 35 years' experience]

The third kind of off-script comment consists of non sequiturs. Often students who are high-achieving, attentive, and interested may volunteer comments that are completely irrelevant to the topic at hand. Because young minds are relatively undisciplined, any such off-topic comments invite more off-topic comments as the rest of the class adapts to the shifting subject matter. Table 5 above gives some examples of these innocent digressions.

Routines for Interacting with Students

In Chapter 3 I pointed out that classroom routines provide a structure within which daily lessons must be fitted. Because they surround and structure teachers' lessons, they can have a strong influence on student opportunities to participate and to engage intellectually. This confining role of routines is particularly apparent in the case of question-and-answer routines, which, as they become habits, control not only what kinds of questions teachers ask but also how they respond when students answer their questions.

Q&A routines are among the most essential teaching tasks, and American teachers have perfected a particular approach that has been documented throughout the past century and has been the focus of many efforts to improve teaching. Two articles published after midcentury (Gall, 1970; Hoetker and Ahlbrand, 1969) reviewed studies done throughout the entire first half of the twentieth century and found that this predominant approach consisted of rapid-fire questions that required factual recall and rapid-fire responses. By the 1980s, this approach to Q&As had received the name *IRE*, an acronym that refers to the fact that the teacher *I*nitiates, the student *Re*sponds, and the teacher then *E*valuates (Cazden and Mehen, 1990; Mehan, 1979). The *I* refers to initiations rather than to inquiries, because teachers initiate numerous interactions that don't consist of questions. For instance, a teacher can initiate an interaction by giving students a directive, providing them with information, or asking them a question. But well over half of all initiations observed in other studies asked students for specific information. Since then, analysts have noticed many ways in which this form of classroom discussion differs from ordinary conversations: in the classroom, the teacher knows the answers to the questions she asks, and the teacher controls everyone else's participation in the discussion (Corrie, 1997; Edwards and Westgate, 1994).

Q&A routines are important determiners of whether or how students engage with content, and they can control what teachers say as well as what students say. Teachers devise Q&A routines in order to streamline operations, reduce confusion, and make life more predictable and manageable. Many routines are designed to control what students say by creating norms both for the types of questions that will be asked and for the types of responses that are expected.

But despite these routines, students can become confused, frustrated, fidgety, or distracted. Their unanticipated comments and questions can create problems for teachers because they present a threat to momentum. They can quickly disrupt the story line the teacher is trying to maintain, and they can force the teacher into a new line of thinking as well because, by definition, she hasn't anticipated them. I pointed out in Chapter 3 that virtually any unexpected event has the potential to create disorientation, confusion, and anxiety in teachers as they quickly try to recover and to respond to the unexpected comment so that they don't lose their momentum. At the same time, the fact that such episodes happen routinely suggests that an important part of learning to teach must necessarily involve finding ways to *respond routinely to unexpected events*.

Here I examine three categories of Q&A routines that we observed in our classrooms, and show how these influenced teachers' responses to off-script student ideas that arose during those routines. I also examine some apparently routinized responses to unexpected student moves that appeared to be independent of Q&A routines, and which consist mainly of dismissals. Taken together, there are four kinds of routines for asking and answering questions:

> I-R-Reinforcements. In this type of Q&A routine, the teacher initiates, the student responds, and then the teacher reinforces the student's answer by repeating it or by complimenting it.

> Guessing games: In this type of Q&A routine, the teacher poses questions and systematically rejects student responses until she receives the response she has been looking for.

> I-R-Probes. In this type of Q&A routine, the teacher inquires, a student responds, and then the teacher responds by probing further, asking another question either to this student or to another.

> Dismissals: Dismissals are routinized ways of dismissing student ideas that are off-script and that the teacher doesn't want to attend to at the moment. They may or may not appear within a Q&A routine.

I-R-Reinforcements

Most of the Q&A routines we saw deviated slightly from the general model of the IRE in that the third part of the sequence—Evaluation—was not very evaluative. Instead, teachers' responses were consistently positive, so much so that I could relabel the sequences as *IRRs*, referring to *I*nitiation, *R*esponse, and *R*einforcement. In an I-R-Reinforcement routine, almost all the teacher responses consisted not of evaluating student ideas, but of reinforcing them.

That such a sequence is widespread should come as no surprise; my earlier examination of teachers' intentions indicated that teachers were generally loath to criticize their students and believed they needed to compliment and encourage them at all times. The reinforcement version of the Q&A responds to that concern, and is well illustrated by a session we observed in Ms. Lafayette's classroom during a lesson on phonics. In the course of this one lesson, Lafayette (grade 5–6 language arts, 28 years' experience) gave her students 3 "perfects," 14 "goods," 10 "excellents," 3 "thank yous" and 38 "nice jobs." In the interview, we asked Lafayette if it might be possible to offer students too much positive encouragement, to the point where compliments lose their meaning. Lafayette didn't think that was possible: "Philosophically I don't know if that could ever be true, that you give too many compliments . . . I want kids to believe they're good at things, and I want to build that feeling within that child. That they're good at this. I guess, because I am a special educator I believe strongly that everybody that we're working with needs to feel good about what they're doing and needs to feel that there may still be things to learn, but that if they take a risk and give an answer, they've done a good job."

Ms. Lafayette's line of thinking. Ms. Lafayette's line of thinking about her Q&A routine starts with a long-standing belief that people need to feel good about themselves, and that they won't make an effort to do anything if they don't believe they can succeed. She also believes that her job as a teacher is to make students feel good about themselves. From her experience as a teacher she has learned that her comments do have an impact on students' feelings, and she also recalls that when she herself was a student, her professors' comments had a similar effect on her. Lafayette also justifies her substantial reinforcement by pointing out that a lot of her students are discouraged about life (an observation that may have some merit—the school serves a low-income, depressed rural population) and that they are generally quite good at spelling, so there is little risk of inappropriate reinforcement.

Apart from the reinforcements, Lafayette's Q&A routine looks very similar to those documented by other researchers. Lafayette's questions came rapid-fire, one after another, mostly asking for factual recall. (The topic, short vowel sounds, lends itself more to recitation than to deep thought.) Many of them asked students to recite particular sequences they had memorized: the name of the vowel, a word containing the vowel with its short sound, and then the short sound itself. When students were able to recite the required sequence, Lafayette complimented them. However, her reinforcements did have some limits, and when students made errors, which was rarely, Lafayette was able to break out of her routine and correct the error. In the excerpt from her I-R-Reinforcement routine below, notice what happened near the end, when one student, Jeff, offered a wrong answer.

> Lafayette: How about this one [pointing to the *A* card]: Bernie, do you remember it?
>
> Bernie: *A,* apple, aaa.
>
> Lafayette: Nice job. Good. How about this one [pointing to *E*]? Chris?
>
> Chris: I don't remember that one.
>
> Lafayette: You don't remember it? Bernie?
>
> Bernie: *E,* Ed, eh.
>
> Lafayette: *E,* Ed, eh. Okay, good. So we say "*A,* apple, aaa," and that's the short sound of the *a.* "*E,* Ed, eh." We just had [points to *I*]:
>
> [Unknown] S: *I,* itch, *I.*
>
> Lafayette: "*I,* itch, *I,*" nice job. What's this one, Jay?
>
> Jay: *O,* octopus, ah.
>
> Lafayette: Good! So you say the name of the letter first, "*O,* octopus, ah." Nice job. Does anybody know any key words for *Y* as a vowel?
>
> Jeff: Yes, yuh.

Lafayette: Okay, you're talking about *Y* as a consonant. Nice job.
[As she speaks she pulls the *Y*-consonant card off the board.
Previously she was pointing to a *Y* in the set of vowels.] And
if you flip over that *Y*-consonant card, Jeff, you'll see it says,
"*Y*, yell, yuh." Right? So the "yuh" is the sound of *Y* as a con-
sonant, like at the beginning of the word "yes," as you said.
But the *Y* as a vowel has some different sounds, that you get
into when you start to study syllables that have that *Y*. Okay?
[Student nods.]

Lafayette: Okay. So for our lesson for today [Kelsey raises her
hand.]—Kelsey?

Kelsey: What about the word "cry"?

Lafayette: Cry, *y*, cry, *I*, good. Anything else?

Unknown S: Baby.

Lafayette: Okay. *Y, Baby, ee.* Nice job. Okay, so there are two
sounds *Y* can make as a vowel? Good.

In this episode, Ms. Lafayette asked Jeff for the sounds made by the
vowel Y, but Jeff responded by offering the sound that *Y* makes when
it plays the role of a consonant, rather than the sound it makes as a
vowel. Lafayette corrected Jeff's error, pointing out the distinction
between *Y* as a vowel and *Y* as a consonant, but still managed to say
"nice job" as she did. The fact that she was able to give this evaluative
feedback to Jeff means that her sequence does consist of more than
simply reinforcement, even though it includes a lot of that.

I-R-Reinforcements are particularly well suited to recitation, and
the example from Ms. Lafayette's lesson shows how they can help
students review and recite what they have learned. But they are not
guaranteed to be fruitful. In the I-R-Reinforcements in these 45 lessons, I saw three kinds of errors that limited the potential of reinforcement as a teaching tool: teachers may limit their Q&A to low-
level content, content that they are sure students can respond to correctly; they may avoid or dismiss student ideas that are complicated
and therefore difficult to respond to; or they may inadvertently re-
state and reinforce student ideas that are wrong.

Low-level content. When teachers aim for continual positive encouragement, and when they rely heavily on reinforcements in their Q&A routines, they tend to limit their routines mainly to questions that students are likely to get right. For if teachers can ensure, through their questions, that students will produce only right answers, they can also ensure that their evaluations of student responses will always be positive. Ms. Defoe's fifth-grade science lesson offered an example of an IRR that focuses on low-level content. Her lesson focused on an important but difficult idea: what makes a claim believable. Defoe's students had been studying physical fitness, but the unit also addressed the nature of scientific evidence and how to evaluate claims about products that would promote physical fitness. When we visited her classroom, Defoe was preparing her students to write "believable" advertisements for physical fitness products. The ads were to include the scientific evidence that would make their claims believable. To prepare students for this assignment, Defoe went through a Q&A routine designed to help them think about their task. In this routine, she could have asked her students a series of questions about what kind of evidence would make an ad believable, or she could have given some examples of ads and asked her students if they were believable or not. Instead, Defoe focused on a much easier question: she asked her students for examples of things that would count as physical fitness products. Students offered a variety of ideas—gyms, barbells, skateboards, bicycles, and so forth. As each student offered an idea for a product, Defoe repeated the idea and agreed that this was indeed a good example of a physical fitness product. While Defoe's Q&A routine helped students to think about products they might use for their advertisements, it didn't help them think about what sort of evidence they could use to promote their products. Yet the nature of evidence and how evidence makes claims "believable" is the more important—and more difficult—concept for students to understand. Instead of providing a Q&A sequence about what would make a claim believable, Defoe restricted her Q&A to examples of fitness equipment, a much easier topic for students to think about. Hence the reinforcement routine would work.

Teacher responds positively to wrong answers. I-R-Reinforcements can also restrict engagement when teachers become so habituated to positive responses that they inadvertently give students positive responses to wrong answers. Positive responses to wrong answers were relatively rare, and they appeared only in the context of I-R-Reinforcement routines. We saw three examples of these errors.

In the first example, Ms. Scott (grade 1 science, 3 years' experience) was closing out a unit on dinosaurs. She asked her students to generate a list of all the things they had learned about dinosaurs. Students participated eagerly, volunteering that dinosaurs were big, that some were meat-eaters, that the meat-eaters had sharp teeth, and so forth. As they offered their ideas about what they had learned, Scott responded with verbal approval to each idea, and also wrote the student's idea on the board. At one point in the lesson, though, a student suggested that dinosaurs don't have ears. Scott was visibly surprised by this proposal, and said, "I wonder how they can hear!" But after expressing her surprise, she turned and wrote the student's observation on the board with all the others. In her interview, Scott again expressed surprise over this student's comment, and speculated that the student might have got this idea from pictures of dinosaurs, which don't depict visible ears. But her own puzzlement over the remark didn't stop her from including it on the board with other students' observations about dinosaurs.

In the second example, Ms. Mines (grade 6 language arts, 26 years' experience) was teaching her students time-order words—that is, words that are used to help readers follow a sequence of events. They include words such as "first," "second," "third," "then," and so forth. Like Ms. Scott, Mines chose an IRR routine for her lesson, and she asked her students to generate examples of time-order words. As they nominated words, Mines wrote them on the board in the format that students would use in their writing. That is, she listed them like this:

First,

Second,

Then,

Mines capitalized each word and placed a comma after it to show students that these terms would be located at the beginning of their sentences. But she became muddled when a student nominated the word "when." Of course "when" can be used to indicate order provided that it is accompanied by a phrase or clause, such as "When that dries, you can . . ." But Mines's format on the board didn't allow for such a construction. Mines wrote the word on the board but didn't capitalize it or put a comma after it, so that her list looked like this:

First,

Second,

Then,

when

An odd compromise at best, and one that misleads students at worst. In her interview, Mines acknowledged that her presentation was misleading and insisted that she would clarify the confusion for students later. But she didn't clarify it in the lesson we observed.

In the third example, the teacher's response was not necessarily misleading, but it did send students mixed messages. This, too, was an I-R-Reinforcement routine in which students were generating multiple responses to a question. In this case, Ms. Eckhard (grade 4 language arts, 6 years' experience) realized at one point that students were generating ideas that others had already put forward, so she asked that students volunteer only ideas that were not already up on the board. Despite her admonition, three students nominated ideas that were already on the board, and she let them add their ideas to the growing list.

Guessing Games

Though the IRR was the most widespread form of Q&A sequence, we also saw a variant of Q&A that looked like a guessing game. Teachers who used this routine were not reluctant at all to tell students that they were wrong, but they also gave students little or no substantive basis for guessing what the right answer to their questions might be. Instead, they often said something like, "No, try again." In this form of Q&A, there was no visible rationale for what made an answer right or wrong, so that the likelihood that students would actually think about an important idea was severely diminished. Ms. Jibson (grade 4 math, 30 years' experience) demonstrated this form of Q&A in her lesson on fraction equivalences. She had designed an activity that involved fractions of which each was a half of the preceding number: 1, $\frac{1}{2}$, $\frac{1}{4}$, $\frac{1}{8}$, and so on. Eventually she wanted students to see that two halves form a whole, that two quarters form a half, and so forth. But she didn't tell students that this was the idea they would be thinking about. Instead, she described only the *tasks* that they needed to perform. She first gave students a long strip of paper and asked them to write "1 whole" on it. Then she gave them a second strip, the same length as the first, and asked them to cut it into two equal lengths, labeling each part "$\frac{1}{2}$." Then she handed out the third strip and asked students to cut four equal parts and to label each part "$\frac{1}{4}$." The guessing game began when she handed out the next strip of paper:

> Jibson: All right. Raise your hand if you think you know what we're going to do next with the orange strip. [Hands up.] All right. James.
>
> James: One-sixth.
>
> Jibson: No, but that's a really good thought. And we'll cut a sixth another day. Anybody got a different idea? Carla.
>
> Carla: One-fifth.
>
> Jibson: One-fifth. That's a very good idea too, because we've got halves, we've got fourths, so a fifth seems like it would be next. But that's not right, and a sixth isn't right. [Hands waving frantically.] What do you think?
>
> S: One-seventh?
>
> Jibson: One-seventh? Nooo. You're getting really good, I'm glad you're willing to try. All right, Brad.
>
> Brad: One-eighth.
>
> Jibson: One-eighth.

Ms. Jibson's line of thinking. That a teacher can say "no" successively to one student after another seems surprising in light of teachers' widespread concern about validating and reinforcing students. And in fact Jibson also subscribed to the value of positive reinforcement. But other areas of concern overshadowed this one in her deliberations. As a result, her line of thinking contains some major inconsistencies. On one hand, she believes she should "validate" student ideas and compliment them on their thinking, and that students should be relaxed and not nervous. She also believes that students need to be thinking about the content, should be asking questions, and should be eager to work. And, through a professional development program, she has acquired the idea that she should encourage students to make conjectures about mathematical relations. All these ideas suggest that students should be encouraged to think about the content and to participate in discussions. On the other hand, she also believes that her job is to ensure that students are working with "accurate, error-free information." And she has deduced from her experience that she should move quickly past wrong answers and not allow these to slow or derail the conversation. So Ms. Jibson is somewhat confused about her role. She wants students to feel free to speculate and to share their ideas, and she wants to validate all of their thinking, but she also wants to ensure that they are working with error-free information and to ensure that she quickly glosses over any wrong answers that are produced. It was less clear in the interview why Jibson thought mistakes should be swept under the rug. At one point she indicated that wrong answers slowed the discussion, but at other times she implied that wrong answers were a personal embarrassment and needed to be covered up.

It is hard imagine a classroom discussion in which students are free to offer conjectures, yet none make mistakes and the conversation is always error-free. Jibson reconciled these ideas in two ways. One strategy she used was to tease mistaken students. In her view, this strategy enabled her to correct the student, and thereby ensure that students had correct information, but it also made light of the error, so that it would not embarrass students or discourage them from future participation. The second way Jibson resolved the contradiction was with guessing games. She justified this particular guessing game by noting that her students should have been able to figure out this progression, because she had visited their classroom last year and taught this lesson as a visiting teacher, so at least some of her students had already worked with fraction strips. Moreover, she thought she could hear some students whispering "one-eighth," thus reinforcing her hypothesis that they should be able to guess the length of the last strips in the series.

Sadly, the result of all of these considerations was a form of Q&A in which Jibson quickly indicated when students were wrong and quickly asked for another guess, but never offered any ideas that might help students understand the mathematical relationships among the strips of paper they were cutting up.

Just as I-R-Reinforcement carries certain learning risks with it, so does the guessing game. For instance, teachers often failed to provide students with important content, and they sometimes responded negatively to ideas that were not actually wrong.

Failure to provide important content. Inherent in the guessing-game strategy is a tendency not to tell students what the central idea is or even to provide them with any substantive clues. The guessing game really is like a form of 20 questions, in which the teacher holds a secret and students must try to guess what it is without any hints.

Notice that Ms. Jibson was not afraid to give students negative evaluations when they guessed wrong. But neither did she offer any guidance on the central mathematical idea that controlled the entire set of strips. Students had rightly deduced that each successive strip was cut into smaller sections than its predecessor was, but they hadn't noticed that each successive segmentation was exactly half of its predecessor. The mathematical idea was not discussed. Jibson may have envisioned a Q&A sequence in which, after cutting up the first three strips, students would see that each strip was cut into twice as many sections as its predecessor. But they didn't see that. All they saw was that the strips were getting successively shorter. Because she hadn't anticipated their response, she hadn't prepared any clues or hints to offer students to help them see the mathematical pattern she was working on.

The arbitrariness of the "guessing game" version of the Q&A routines reduces student access to the content being taught because the content itself is not actually discussed. If Ms. Jibson had introduced the cutting exercise by saying that each successive strip of paper would be cut into twice as many pieces as its predecessors, or even that there was a common mathematical relationship between the length of each strip and that of its predecessor, students would have had an opportunity to think about the relationships among fractions when they tried to predict what sizes of strips would come next.

Negative responses to plausible answers. Just as teachers can get carried away with positive encouragement, so can they get carried away in guessing games. In guessing games, teachers are looking for specific responses from students. But they can confuse the students' actual words with the ideas that underlie them, and inadvertently reject sentences that are literally acceptable simply because they don't provide the exact phrase the teacher expected. In fact teachers often referred to these episodes by saying that the students' responses was not what they "were after," or not what they "were looking for," suggesting that they had a particular script in mind and that the students were not complying with it. In fact Ms. Jibson made this error at one point in her lesson, and later realized she had unfairly chastised a student. She said: "And as I walked around, um, I realized that number one, one thing that I did was that I said to the child, 'You did it wrong,' which was of course totally wrong, because I hadn't ever specified. So I thought, 'Why did I say that?' and then I did go on and say to them, 'Oh, but this was my mistake, let's look and let's think about it.'"

Mr. Sadowski's guessing game illustrates the problem of negative responses to plausible answers. Sadowski was teaching his second-graders how to organize data into charts and graphs. The project for this day's lesson was to graph their favorite seasons. He asked the students to write their favorite season on a yellow sticky note, then asked them to place their stickies in columns on the board. All the students who chose fall put their stickies in a column above the word "Fall," those who chose spring put their stickies in a column above the word "Spring," and so forth, so that when they were finished they had built a rough bar chart showing how many students had selected each season as their favorite. Then Sadowski asked students what to name their graph. He wanted them to call it "Our Favorite Season," because that was the label he himself had decided was best. He failed to give students any substantive idea to think about, and instead wanted them to produce the particular response that he was "looking for." Students offered different ideas, and Sadowski rejected them, continually reminding them to think about what he had asked them at the beginning of the lesson (he had asked them their favorite season). After students finally arrived at the right answer, a student suggested that we should call the graph "Our Weather Graph." Sadowski repeated that it must be called "Our Favorite Season."

I-R-Probes

The third variety of Q&A sequence ends with another question rather than with an evaluation, a restatement, or a reinforcement. The I-R-Probe consists of teacher *Initiation*, student *Response*, and an additional *Probe* by the teacher. The additional probing question may ask for clarification or elaboration, may ask for a rationale, or may ask other students to respond to the original student's ideas. This Q&A sequence can become just as habitualized as the other Q&A sequences, and we saw certain types of follow-up probes used repeatedly—questions that asked the student to elaborate, for instance, and questions that asked other students whether they agreed with the initial student's comment.

Although the I-R-Probe was the least frequently employed Q&A sequence in the lessons we observed, it deserves attention because reformers often cite it as the best strategy for engaging students intellectually. Ms. Mission (grade 6 math, 9 years' experience) used the I-R-Probe while teaching students about scatterplots. Students had plotted a line showing a relationship between the distance they traveled to school and the time it took for them to get to school. The relationship was not exact, of course, as some students lived closer but took more time to arrive, and others who lived farther away arrived relatively more quickly. Mission was using an I-R-Probe routine to ask students why some of the dots on their graph were above or below the line. As students offered hypotheses, Mission never provided any evaluation of a student's response to her questions, but instead followed each response with another question. Sometimes she asked clarifying questions ("So you're saying . . .?"), sometimes she asked other students whether they agreed with a particular student's hypothesis, and sometimes she asked them to connect their thought more directly to the graph ("Where would you see that on the graph?").

This Q&A approach raises the question: What does Ms. Mission do when students generate ideas that are flat-out wrong? Such an episode did occur in this lesson, and it occurred just as the bell rang, so Mission was under great pressure to resolve the problem quickly and let her students leave. By that time, the discussion had moved to how to find the median of a distribution. The particular distribution under discussion consisted of six families of different sizes. Mission had represented these families by stacking small cubes on her desk at the front of the room. For instance, a family of five was represented with a stack of five cubes, and a family of three was represented by a stack of three cubes. Mission then led the students through a discussion of these "families," asking about the range of the distribution, its mode, and then its median. Her Q&A routine was again an I-R-Probe routine. The stacks were arranged from shortest to tallest. Just before the bell rang, Jason correctly located the median of the distribution by placing a pencil between the third and fourth stacks. Mission, using her habitual routine, asked if other students agreed with Jason's placement. Another student, Jordan, said he disagreed. He approached the front of the room and moved the pencil so that it was in the wrong place. Just after he made his "correction," the bell rang. So Mission had both a confused student and a compelling time constraint as well. As students began packing bags, she called out and asked them to wait a moment.

Mission: Stay seated, guys. How many pieces of data do we have?
Chorus: Six.

Jordan: Oh, there are six?

Mission: Six families.

Jordan: Can it [the median] be on a family?

Mission: [to class as a whole] If there are six families, can it be
on a family?

Chorus: No.

Mission: Why not?

Ss: [miscellaneous comments] Nothing's in the middle.

Mission: Okay, there are six pieces. How many have to be on either side?

Chorus: Three.

Mission: Three? Okay. Jordan, do you want to put it so there are
three on each side?

S: We could cut a family in half.

Mission: We're looking for a median though.

Jordan: It would be right here.

Mission: Okay, we'll pick this up right after break.

Even with the pressure of time, and even when Jordan directly
asked Mission for guidance—"Can a median be on a family?"—she
offered no direct instruction to Jordan. She turned his question over
to the class for an answer instead of answering it herself.

In the interview, we asked Ms. Mission about this episode. From
other interviews, we knew that these unexpected student moves created anxiety for teachers; we knew that teachers faced a trade-off between responding to individual deviations and keeping the group on
track; and we also knew that teachers constantly felt that time was
passing too quickly. Finally, we knew that these pressures frequently
led teachers to gloss over student errors, and to tell themselves they
would address the problem later, as Ms. Mines did when her student
introduced a time-order word that didn't fit her pattern.

Ms. Mission's line of thinking. Mission's line of thinking begins
with standing beliefs and values that mostly have to do with how students learn, rather than with issues such as her own personal needs,
lesson momentum, or the classroom as a community. With respect

to how students learn, Mission said she believes that students learn from their mistakes, and that they need to feel comfortable making mistakes in public without fear of ridicule or rejection. This belief is similar to the beliefs other teachers have expressed about the benefits of students' being willing to take risks and to expose themselves in front of their peers. Mission combines this idea with a belief that it is important for teachers to model the process of continually revising one's thinking. From her experience teaching this grade level and this content, she also knows that students are sensitive to being "helped." They view "help" as a euphemism for failure, and she knows there are certain aspects of the mathematical concept of central tendency that students get confused about. She also indicated that she acquired this particular approach to pedagogy through a college math methods course in which the math teacher both advocated and modeled this approach to teaching.

Finally, she has learned over time that if one student makes a mistake or is confused there are often others who are confused as well. This realization alone may account for her apparent calm in the face of Jordan's mistake. Most other teachers perceive mistakes as individual events, and perceive the individuals as deviations from the rest of the group. Mission suspected that this student's confusion was not an isolated event at all, and instead reflected the understanding of the class as a whole. In the episode we observed, Mission saw that Jordan was confused about the location of the median and about how many families were in the set. She concluded that Jordan needed to struggle with this problem, rather than being told the solution, if he was to grasp the concept.

Probing further is frequently advocated as a Q&A routine that can foster greater intellectual engagement. Yet it was used only rarely by the teachers participating in this study. It is a good example of a reform idea that has been advocated but not adopted. Why? One important problem it creates for teachers is that, because it encourages students to intellectually engage with the content, it also increases the likelihood that students will say things that are difficult for teachers to anticipate or to respond to. When teachers use I-R-Reinforcement or guessing games, they can rely on routinized ways of responding to students, regardless of what students say. Even if students offer bad ideas, teachers can encourage them, reinforce their effort, and continue the Q&A series. But in the I-R-Probe routine, teachers can't rely on habitual reinforcements like "good job," nor can they rely on guessing-game devices, simply telling the student he is wrong and asking someone else to try. Instead, their habitual response is to ask another question. They can ask the student to clarify or elaborate, or can ask other students whether they agree, but if these questions don't shake students loose from their erroneous thinking, teachers have no other devices on which to draw. Probing further doesn't always work, and when it doesn't, it can create serious disorientation, anxiety, and indecision for teachers who can't find the ideal probe that will push student thinking in the right direction.

We saw a particularly painful example of this problem in Ms. Toklisch's sixth-grade class, where students were learning how to find the diameter, area, and perimeter of circles. Toklisch had asked her students whether they would get more pizza from two 9-inch pizzas or from one 16-inch pizza. On the board was a picture of the comparison (see Figure 1).

This was the "area" part of her agenda; she planned to address the problem of perimeter later. But the area problem didn't get resolved. Some students summed the two 9-inch diameters to a total of 18 inches and concluded that, because the two smaller pizzas had a larger total *diameter*, they must also have a larger total *area*. This outcome was perplexing for Toklisch because students had already estimated the area of the various sizes of pizza and had produced the following table:

Size	Price	Estimated area (in square inches)
9 inches	$6.00	about 63
12 inches	$9.00	about 115
16 inches	$12.00	about 180

So the students had already determined that the larger pizza had a larger area than two smaller pizzas would have. Yet they continued to

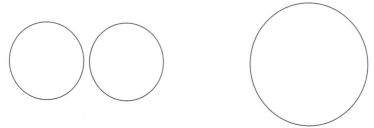

Figure 1. *Ms. Toklisch's problem: two 9-inch pizzas compared with one 16-inch pizza.*

think that two smaller pizzas would provide more to eat because the sum of their diameters was greater. Moreover, when Toklisch repeatedly asked students whether the diameter or the area told them how much they could eat, students agreed that it was area that mattered. So Toklisch faced a group of students who insisted that the area, not the diameter, told them how much they could eat, who had already determined that the larger pizza had more area, but who also now insisted that two smaller pizzas offered more to eat because their diameters summed to a larger number. She asked a series of clarifying questions (What is the area of the larger pizza? What is the area of the smaller pizza? Do we use diameter or area to find out how much we can eat?), but students didn't budge. Suddenly Toklisch realized that too much time had passed and that she had other content to cover. So she shifted to another learning activity with no resolution on this one. In the interview, Toklisch indicated that she was unhappy with her behavior during this episode.

Ms. Toklisch's line of thinking. The line of thinking that guided Ms. Toklisch through this episode starts with a standing belief that students should learn to judge the mathematical worth of an idea, rather than accepting the teacher's word for what is true or not true. She also had participated in a professional development course that was intense and life-changing, moving her to this belief (I call it a "standing" belief because she has held it for some six years). She also knows, from experience, that students are frequently confused by the relationship between diameter and area. They are accustomed to buying pizzas on the basis of their diameters, so the idea that the "amount you get to eat" is a function of area, not diameter, is difficult for them to grasp. Believing that students need to work this through for themselves, she concluded that she should persist in her I-R-Probe until they sorted it all out. Yet when she suddenly noticed the clock, she dropped the discussion altogether and introduced her next topic. When Toklisch viewed her tape, she criticized herself, saying that she should have stayed with the topic longer. However, she also said that this group of students had been particularly difficult to teach, tended to be reticent and sluggish, and that she was very far behind in the textbook.

Dismissals

Teachers need ways of handling off-script comments that don't discourage students but at the same time don't allow the entire lesson to become derailed in pursuit of an irrelevant idea. One way to do this, which appeared to be habitual, was to dismiss a student's comment, usually by appeasing the student with a comment such as "We'll talk about this later." Recall that Ms. Defoe used this strategy to dismiss Andy, when he asked a question that was very difficult to answer at the time that William began acting out. We also saw Mr. Sadowski dismiss a student during his Q&A about labeling his graph. After he had finally generated the correct title, "Our Favorite Season," a student asked: "Should we put an s at the end, so it says 'our favorite seasons'?" Sadowski responded by saying, "Let's answer that question when we get to the end, okay?"

The problem with dismissals is self-evident. Though they allow the teacher to move ahead with the lesson as planned, and do not appear to be punitive, they give students a clear message that some ideas won't be talked about, even if they seem relevant and important to students. Dismissals clearly discourage students from investing intellectual energy in their learning.

Teachers' Intentions for Their Interrogation Practices

Two kinds of interrogation practices are central to teaching: Q&A routines and responses to unexpected student ideas. Sometimes un-

Table 6 Percent of conversation practices influenced by each area of concern

Area of concern	Teaching practices	
	Q&A routines	Responses to student comments
Defining learning outcomes	15	20
Fostering student learning	52	35
Maintaining lesson momentum	25	54
Fostering student willingness to participate	36	34
Establishing the classroom as a community	20	24
Attending to personal needs	5	15

expected student ideas appeared in the context of a Q&A routine, and sometimes they arose at odd moments in the lesson. An examination of teachers' intentions for their interrogation practices provides further insight into why they do the things they do. Table 6 summarizes teachers' intentions for their Q&A routines and for their responses to unexpected student ideas.

The table helps us see once again the contradictory ideas that govern teaching practices. When teachers develop their Q&A routines, they think about how to foster student learning and how to increase student willingness to participate. On the other side, when it comes to unexpected student ideas, teachers are more often motivated by a felt need to maintain momentum; hence their dismissals and other strategies for skipping quickly past these unexpected offerings. The combination of these sets of intentions demonstrates the tensions teachers must routinely resolve in their conversations with students.

Implications for Reform

Active and engaged students are highly likely to generate ideas that teachers don't anticipate. By definition, students are novices in these content areas, so they are likely to misinterpret central ideas and to offer odd or unusual comments as they try to make sense of new ideas. The ideas that they offer can distract the teacher from her own train of thought, confuse other students, introduce an issue the teacher would prefer not to address, and in general disrupt the flow of the lesson. Moreover, any one of these distractions has the potential to provoke other distractions. A student who makes a joke encourages others to make jokes. A student who volunteers that her cat's name is Shadow encourages others to share their pets' names. A student who is lost and needs special attention gives other students an opportunity to chat with each other or to tease one another while the teacher responds. Unless these distractions are handled quickly and calmly, they can escalate to the point where all students are out of step and the teacher will need to retrace her steps in order to bring them all back together, moving in unison once again along the desired path.

Teachers' Q&A routines do control, to some extent, the likelihood that such distracting ideas will be offered. But they sometimes do this by discouraging intellectual engagement. When teachers rely on habitual reinforcements, they also frequently rely on questions that are easier to answer, thereby reducing the chances that anyone will say something that can't be reinforced. When teachers rely on guessing games, they provide students with no intellectual supports to help them find the answer, so that students cannot think seriously about the question at hand.

The third approach to Q&A routines, which relies on probes, creates its own problems. Teachers who relied on probes tended to increase students' intellectual engagement, but these teachers also had a much harder time directing student thought toward the conclusions they wanted students to reach. Their experience offers a bitter pill for reformers, for it tells us that as engagement increases, so does the risk of losing access to the central idea.

Remarkably, teachers brought up far more episodes involving *off-script students* than they did episodes involving *off-task behavior*. Most of the episodes that teachers worried about related to students who were actively participating in the lesson, not to students who had found other ways to amuse themselves. The dilemma for reformers is, if teachers succeed in engaging students intellectually, then students, in their enthusiasm, are likely to share their partial thoughts and their misconceptions with the group, creating for teachers the problem of how to respond to these comments while also keeping the larger group on track and maintaining momentum. Given how frightened teachers are of distractions, it is easy to imagine that many teachers would actually prefer *not* to have students too enthusiastic about the content, because they would rather *not* have students volunteering all their thoughts. This is an ironic outcome, particularly in light of teachers' own rhetoric about wanting students to be willing to taking risks and to participate.

But it is also apparent that teachers differ both in their tolerance for off-script ideas and in their ability to respond quickly and appropriately to them. This mix of tolerance and responsiveness leads each teacher to develop teaching practices that keep intellectual engagement within manageable boundaries. If reformers can find ways to alter these boundaries, either by increasing teachers' tolerance for ambiguity or by increasing their ability to respond to unexpected ideas, they may increase teachers' willingness and ability to engage students intellectually.

Reformers might also think about the kinds of teacher knowledge that are relevant to their manageable boundaries. Some reformers believe the main impediment to intellectual engagement is that teachers themselves are not sufficiently versed in the subject matter to be able to respond to the variety of ideas students generate. The episodes examined here, though, suggest that even when teachers appeared to have a good grasp of the content, they were still frequently nonplused by students' unexpected ideas. The problem for them appeared to be less that they didn't understand the connections between students' ideas and the ideas they wanted to pursue, and more that they didn't know how to *guide students* toward the ideas they wanted to pursue. While there were indeed teachers whose understanding of particular concepts was not particularly deep, there were also many whose understanding of both subject matter and students' understanding of the subject matter appeared to be quite elaborated, and yet they were stymied about how to respond adequately to students' enthusiastic but off-script ideas. One lesson for reformers might be to provide professional development that addresses ways of responding when students produce unexpected ideas. This is a nuts-and-bolts problem that teachers routinely face but that tends to get relatively little attention in reform literature.

Less easily addressed is the problem of managing time while also increasing students' intellectual engagement. Often, teachers' dismissals were motivated by a need to move forward with the planned agenda and by a recognition that not all ideas can be pursued. Even when students stick closely to the teachers' agenda, teachers can't permit too much engagement, because the more engaged students are with a idea, the more they will want to pursue it. Yet eventually they must move on. Ms. Toklisch told us that the first year she adopted her problem-oriented approach to teaching, she got through only half the textbook. She realized then that she needed to contain student discussions if she was going to cover all the content she needed to cover. If there is a lesson here for reformers, it may be to think harder about the trade-offs between content coverage and active intellectual engagement.

5. Constructing the Day's Agenda

Whereas classroom routines are established over time and tend to control students and teachers across many days and months, each day's lesson is unique because it has a distinct agenda that aims to foster student learning of specific content. The day's agenda normally includes at least three kinds of teaching practices: establishing a learning outcome for the lesson, portraying the content relevant to that outcome, and developing one or more learning activities that give students an opportunity to interact with and assimilate the content.

These three parts of the lesson work together to determine what students actually learn. To understand how they mesh, consider Ms. Lachamy's language arts lesson. Lachamy, with one year's experience, taught mainly Hispanic sixth-graders. On the day we observed her class, she was focusing on paragraph structure. When we asked Lachamy why she taught paragraph structure, she said that the content itself was part of both her district and her state writing standards: "In terms of writing and organization, we have a district standard for sixth-grade writing, and then there's the state standard. And the state standard and our district standard are very closely aligned. They list very explicitly that [students] will be able to write a multiparagraph expository essay, showing good organization, using transition words, etc. It also talks about that they will be able to use—there's a bunch of grammatical requirements in it. They'll be able to spell, use commonly misspelled words correctly, use correct capitalization and punctuation. All of those elements are in both state standards for the sixth grade in terms of writing, and the district [standards]." At the same time, Lachamy indicated that she had selected paragraph structure as her personal focus for the year because she thought that organization was the most important part of this standard, and that spelling and grammar were less important, even though they were also in the standards. "So I did, out of what the district said in terms of writing, I didn't take the whole thing. I said, Okay, I'm going to focus on organization because I think being able to express yourself in an organized manner is important, and I think it's important to their success and their future school and their English and in social studies and in writing any kind of report, and in college, and you get a job, and you're asked to write up a memo, or type up a report, you need to be able to express yourself in written form." Notice that, even though the state and district described what students should be able to do, Ms. Lachamy still had values of her own that interacted with the state and district ideas about what students should learn. Her idea about the importance of organization led her to emphasize organization more than other parts of the state standard. In addition, she had ideas about what paragraph structure consisted of that added to what was in the standard. Elsewhere in the interview, she said: "Well, part of it has to do with, in terms of sixth-grade writing, our students at the school are generally very, very low in their writing skills, and if they're low in first grade and second grade and so on, by the time they get to sixth grade, it can be pretty poor, and you have a lot of work to do at sixth grade if they don't come to you with very good writing skills. . . . So my objective this year was that the students would be able to write a multiparagraph essay, well organized, *that contains topic sentences, supporting details, and transition words,* etc." (The italics mark Lachamy's additions to the district standards.) So Lachamy's formulation of her learning outcome both reduced the scope of the standard, by focusing more on paragraph structure than on grammar and spelling, and increased the specificity of the standard, by adding ideas about what constituted a well-organized paragraph. These ideas were not mentioned in the standards, but Lachamy believed that paragraphs consisted of specific parts: there should be a topic sentence, followed by at least three supporting sentences, and then a closing sentence.

With this learning outcome in mind, Lachamy *portrayed the content* to students by giving them a formula for an organized paragraph. She told her students that their paragraphs (about what they liked about a book they were reading) should look like this: "I found this book interesting. One reason it was interesting was because . . . Another thing I found interesting was . . . Finally, I thought the book was interesting because . . . Etc." This definition-by-example, then, constituted Ms. Lachamy's portrayal of a well-organized paragraph.

Next, with the learning outcome defined and a portrayal completed, Lachamy was ready for her students to engage in the third component of her lesson, the *learning activity*. Her learning activity for this day was to have students write paragraphs that had these constituent parts. But knowing from past experience that organized paragraphs were especially difficult for her students, Lachamy had developed an activity that would break the paragraph into its constituent parts to make each part more visible to the students. The idea was that students would write each sentence on a different strip of paper and then glue the strips sequentially onto a page. Moreover, each type of sentence would be written on a different color of paper—topic sentences on pink slips and supporting details on green. She gave students very explicit instructions about how to make their paragraphs: (1) list five interesting things about the book they had read; (2) generate five topic sentences (one for each interesting thing); (3) write each topic sentence on a pink slip of paper and glue that to the top of a blank page (the result being five sheets of paper, each with a pink strip across the top containing one sentence); (4) list three reasons, details, or facts to accompany each topic sentence; and (5) write those on green slips of paper and then glue those onto the sheets (so that each sheet would contain a pink strip at the top with a topic sentence and three green strips with supporting details underneath the pink one). Lachamy spent quite a bit of time laying this procedure out for students, and had a pile of precut green and pink strips of paper ready for them. To the left of her overhead projector, which listed these tasks, she had a poster sheet that listed transition words, and she referred to the poster a couple of times to remind them to use transition words when they wrote their various supporting sentences.

So Ms. Lachamy's agenda looked like this: (a) the *learning outcome* was paragraph structure; (b) the *portrayal* was a definition of a organized paragraph as one that had a topic sentences followed by three supporting details and a conclusion; and finally, (c) the *learning activity* consisted of five steps: writing interesting things about the book, writing a topic sentence for each interesting thing on pink strips of paper, gluing the strips, and so forth.

Ms. Lachamy's line of thinking. Though I have separated these three parts of the day's agenda analytically, it is also possible to examine a line of thinking that stands behind the entire agenda. In this case, Ms. Lachamy's line of thinking starts with a strong belief in the importance of organization in writing, which led her to emphasize organization more than spelling and grammar, even though the state and district curriculum standards gave equal weight to both. In addition, she has a particular view about what organized paragraphs look like that involves topic sentences and supporting details, specifics that are not mentioned in the standards. In addition to these ideas about the content, Ms. Lachamy has accumulated certain principles of practice regarding how students learn. For instance, even though she got the idea for "accordion paragraphs" from her principal, who in turn had got it at a workshop, the idea appealed to Lachamy because she already believes that students need to distinguish their topic sentences from their supporting details in order to see whether their paragraphs are organized. Her experience, then, has disposed her to be attracted to a strategy that makes the parts of the paragraph very visible to students.

Like most teachers' lines of thinking, Lachamy's yields multiple intentions for her agenda. Helping students learn to organize their writing is one, but there are several others, including making sure she doesn't lose them, making sure they are on task and engaged, helping them structure their thoughts, and representing the concept of an organized paragraph in a way that is "hard to miss." This array of intentions should not be surprising, for teachers frequently have multiple intentions for particular practices. Still, one might expect that the intentions that drive teachers' daily agendas would address student learning outcomes more than other areas of concern. To see whether teachers' intentions for their agendas were more likely to address student learning outcomes than other areas of concern, I tallied all the intentions teachers mentioned for each of these three types of practices—establishing learning outcomes, portraying content, and developing learning activities. Table 7 summarizes the proportion of all intentions for these practices that addressed each area of concern. It shows that, when teachers were defining learning outcomes, the majority of their intentions did address content. Yet even for this task, teachers also thought about other areas of concern. Their decisions about what to teach were based not only on what content should be covered, but also on what would interest their students, on their own personal needs, and even on community norms in the classroom.

Table 7   Percent of lesson construction practices influenced by each area of concern

	Teaching practices		
Area of concern	Defining learning outcomes	Portraying content	Designing learning activities
Defining learning outcomes	60	34	29
Fostering student learning	63	48	47
Maintaining lesson momentum	8	23	31
Fostering student willingness to participate	10	20	31
Establishing the classroom as a community	3	9	13
Attending to personal needs	7	9	13

Moreover, when developing the other parts of their agendas—portrayal of the content and learning activities—concerns about lesson momentum and student willingness to participate became more salient. So even though most of teachers' intentions for their agenda reflected concerns about content coverage, these were by no means the only concerns driving the final agenda.

The remainder of this chapter examines the origins of each of these three parts of the daily agenda and the resulting lessons themselves in light of reformers' ideals.

Establishing Learning Outcomes

Several years ago, Andrew Porter and his colleagues (Porter, 1989; Porter et al., 1989) did an extensive study of teachers' decisions about what content to teach. They found that, absent any outside influences, teachers depended on their own values and convictions as they established their learning outcomes. At the same time, teachers also appeared to respond readily to policy guidance, particularly when they agreed with it. At the time of that study, few states or districts had very coherent policies regarding curriculum content, but now many do, and perhaps the most notable reform success story told in this book relates to the effects of these policies. Teachers referred more to district or state policies when they gave a rationale for their learning outcomes than to any other type of practice we asked about. Table 8 shows where teachers got their ideas about learning outcomes, and sorts them according to source. The predominant source of ideas about learning outcomes was institutional policies, which includes textbooks, curriculum guides, student assessments, and accountability systems. A few teachers got ideas for learning outcomes from professional development courses, and a few got ideas from their own teaching experiences or from experiences at home or in other contexts. These numbers suggest that policymakers who want to increase the quantity and quality of school content should focus more on defining that content, for teachers apparently do pay attention to such guidelines.

However, the fact that teachers were influenced by curricular guide-

Table 8   Sources of ideas for learning outcomes

Number of references	Source of ideas
45	*Institutional policies and practices*
12	Textbook or manual
14	Curriculum guides
3	School-specific policies
10	Tests or accountability systems
6	Miscellaneous other policies
5	*Professional development*
3	Curriculum materials
2	Ideas about content
5	*Informal learning*
2	Lessons from experience
3	Everyday thinking (conversations with friends, experiences at home, etc.)

lines doesn't mean that those guidelines were transferred directly from the reformer's desk to the students' desks. A great deal of translation occurred en route. Ms. Lachamy's agenda demonstrates this point. Even though she attributed her learning outcome to state and district guidelines, and even though she appeared to be very familiar with those guidelines, she also conceded that she had defined a learning outcome that suited her own values and her perception of her students' needs. She reduced the amount of attention she gave to grammar, increased the attention she gave to organization and paragraph structure, and added specific criteria for paragraph structure that were not part of the state framework.

The specifics of Lachamy's line of thinking are unique to her, but the structure is not. Most teachers who referred to state or district guidelines or texts used their own prior ideas to interpret those guidelines. In fact, in our interviews we routinely checked teachers' reliance on these outside sources with a "devil's advocate" question: When teachers said they taught some content because it was on the test, in the book, or in the state standards, we followed up by asking: "Do you always teach everything in the [test, text, or standards]?" Almost to a person, teachers answered no and then clarified that *in this case* they followed the guideline because *in this case* they happened to agree with it.

But defining the lesson content or learning outcome is only one part of the day's agenda. Even if policymakers were able to completely influence teachers' decisions about *what to teach,* they could have little influence over the important question of *how to teach.* At issue, then, is how teachers portray new ideas to their students and what kind of learning activities they use to acquaint students with that content. These practices require the teacher to translate content into something students can grasp, recognize, think about, and ultimately understand. But translations can be tricky, as the next two sections reveal.

Portraying Content

By "portraying content," I mean the way in which teachers introduce new content to students who do not yet know what they are to learn. Often this means "showing" it to students. Teachers can do this by providing rules of thumb or lists of prescriptions, or by giving students pictures, diagrams, or enactments of some sort. Some approaches to portraying content look like literal portraits—a picture of the solar system, for instance, or a diagram of an atom; others are verbal descriptions, such as Ms. Lachamy's description of an organized paragraph; and still others are even more subtle, as when teachers pose a problem to students and hope to introduce a new idea through the problem. For instance, when Ms. Toklisch introduced the concept "area of a circle" to her sixth-graders, she posed a problem having to do with how much more pizza was available in a larger versus a smaller pizza. Students already knew what the diameter of a circle was, and they knew that pizzas were usually thought of in terms of their diameters. The problem she presented was her way of alerting students to a new issue, namely the area of a circle. It was her way of portraying that content.

Toklisch's example suggests that portrayals and learning activities are not always entirely separate. Some portrayals are themselves learning activities, and most learning activities also provide important messages to students about the content. Portrayals that are also learning activities are sometimes called "gateway activities," because they are designed to introduce students to new ideas. In other cases learning activities are separate from formal portrayals of content but still convey certain messages about the nature of the content. For instance, Ms. Lachamy's learning activity of having students write topic sentences on pink strips of paper and supporting details on green strips of paper suggests that each sentence can serve only one purpose in the paragraph and that each sentence can be partitioned from the others. So the activity itself also contributes, often unintentionally, to the portrayal of content.

Overall, I saw three main ways in which teachers portrayed content to students:

> *Direct presentations:* Teachers presented new content directly, often with the aid of text written on the board or on an overhead projector. Some teachers provided complicated demonstrations that involved physical props—globes, piles of sand, kettles of boiling water—designed to show students something.

> *Gateway activities:* Many teachers embedded new content in a learning activity that was designed either to introduce a new idea or to illustrate one.

> *Hiding content in procedures:* Teachers who used this approach rarely mentioned content explicitly. Instead, they told students what to *do,* by saying things like, "Open your books to page 124" or "Draw a large circle on your page," without saying what students would find on page 124, what the circle represented, or what the central idea was that they would be thinking about.

The third approach is clearly the weakest, but the first two present their own problems.

Direct Presentations

We saw a variety of presentations and demonstrations in the 45 lessons we observed. Teachers used overhead projectors, blackboards, pictures, charts, and bulletin boards; and they sometimes organized complicated demonstrations that required them to gather together a lot of materials.

Ms. Abundo (grade 3 science, 2 years' experience) demonstrated evaporation by boiling a kettle of water in her classroom. The demonstration required her to get the pot of water and a burner set up before the lesson. She also had brought in some ice to show students how heat would also melt ice, turning it back into water again, when she placed it on the lid of the pot.

Ms. Chalmers wanted to show her early elementary students that the darkness they saw at night resulted from the fact that they were on the shaded side of the Earth. She set up a film projector to serve as her "sun" and stood before it holding up a globe. She had envisioned this entire scenario, including how she would arrange all her students so that they would be able to see a "side view" of the Earth—one side of it in the sunlight and the other in the shadow. As she turned the Earth, she asked the children questions about what people in different parts of the world would be doing at a given time (e.g., as darkness approached, they would be getting ready for bed; as the light approached, they would be waking up). Though this demonstration required moving the entire class to a different room, and was complicated to arrange, Chalmers wanted her students to be able to see that the darkness they saw at night was the result of a shadow that was formed when our side of the Earth turned away from the sun. She provided this demonstration as part of a unit on light and shadow.

Such demonstrations are intended to introduce new ideas to students. They render abstract ideas more concrete and render complicated ideas more simply. Yet there is a very great risk of error in such presentations, and errors quickly lead to confusions. And the more complicated the demonstration is, the greater the likelihood that something will go wrong. For instance, when Ms. Chalmers finished showing her students how the Earth's rotations put different sides of it into light and shadow, and how these rotating phases of light and shadow create day and night, she spontaneously decided to show them how the Earth's orbit contributes to the seasons. She hadn't originally planned to do this, but now she felt it would be a good idea, since she already had all the equipment set up for it and had the students arranged to be able to see it. However, once she added the demonstration of orbit and season, students became confused and lost the idea of rotation and of a shadow rotating around the Earth as the Earth itself rotated. The new content was added because it was *logistically* an opportune moment to do so, but it was not *conceptually* a good addition, and Chalmers later regretted having done it.

Ms. Abundo encountered a different sort of problem with her props. After she showed her students water evaporating and melting, she moved to a poster-size picture that she had created to show them the entire water cycle. The picture showed a cloud on the upper left side, with rain coming down from it, and the sun shining on the upper right. Below both was a landscape that included a stream. Abundo had taken the idea for this picture from her teachers' manual. In fact the textbook publisher had provided a poster for this purpose, but Abundo felt the publisher's poster was too dark for students to see, so she had made one of her own. Then she made labels that students could affix to the picture—one for condensation, one for evaporation, and one for precipitation. Last she made some curved arrows that students could affix to the picture to show the direction of water movement and to make the water cycle explicit. Abundo first asked students to affix the labels. One student put the word "precipitation" over the raining cloud, another put the word "evaporation" over the stream, and a third put the word "condensation" between the sun and the cloud. Then she asked her students to put the curved arrows onto the picture. However, it turned out that she put her glue on the wrong side of the arrows, so when students attached them to the picture, they pointed backward. Figure 2 shows Abundo's development of the water cycle. When students completed the third step, the picture showed water going up from the stream to the clouds, where precipitation was supposed to occur, then from the cloud to the sun, where condensation was supposed to occur, and then from the sun back down to the stream, where evaporation was supposed to occur.

Original poster

Poster with labels

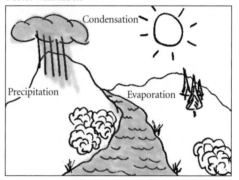

Poster with labels and arrows

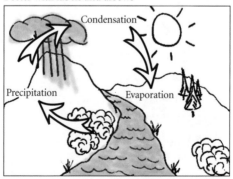

Figure 2. *Ms. Abundo's portrayal of the water cycle.*

Demonstrations that relied on complicated props were relatively rare in these lessons, and I suspect the reason was that the use of props greatly complicates the logistics for teachers and threatens to disrupt momentum. Those teachers who did make an effort to engage in complicated demonstrations often inadvertently confused rather than enhanced student understanding.

Gateway Activities

Teachers who used gateway activities created learning activities that either posed problems for students to solve or required students to manipulate materials in a way that would reveal something important about the content. These activities were usually designed to illustrate an idea. For example, Ms. Mathews (grade 4 science, 26 years' experience) used a complicated procedure to demonstrate the layers of the Earth: she asked her students to enact each layer. She began by asking for a volunteer to play the role of the inner core. Then she asked a handful of others to be the outer core, and so forth. As she arranged students, she listed the main features of each layer and told each group of students what they needed to do in order to enact their part of the Earth. Once all the parts were assigned, students simultaneously played their various roles, rocking, swaying, or reciting phrases that represented their features. Then she reviewed again the layers that each group of students represented.

Ms. Fosnot (grade 1–2 math, 7 years' experience) used a gateway activity to show her students the importance of having a standard unit of measurement. She began her lesson by reading her students a story about a king who wanted to have a bed made for the queen for her birthday. To estimate its size, the king asked the queen to lie down on the floor and then paced off the distance around her. He concluded that the bed should be three feet wide and six feet long. However, the carpenter's apprentice who eventually made the bed was much smaller than the king, so when he used his own feet to measure off the bed, the bed was not large enough to fit the queen. After Ms. Fosnot read this story, she had her students measure beds for the queen. Students worked in groups of four or five. Each group had a large sheet of brown wrapping paper which they would use to measure and then cut out a bed for the queen. Each group could decide whose feet would be used to measure the bed.

Because Fosnot had planned such a complicated gateway activity, her mind was on the forthcoming activity itself when she read the story to her students. Consequently, she forgot to show students the pictures of the king and the carpenter's apprentice, and the pictures emphasized the differences in size between the king and the apprentice who actually made the bed. So when students made their beds for the queen, they still didn't grasp the point that different sizes of feet would yield different sizes of beds. Even after the exercise, when the teacher posed as a queen and tried to lie on the various beds, students appeared to have missed the reason why their beds differed in size.

Ms. Katlaski (grade 6 math, 7 years' experience) also had an orchestration problem when she tried to convert her content into a learning activity. She wanted her sixth-graders to understand multiplication with fractions. This is a very difficult concept for students to understand. Multiplying with whole numbers yields larger products, but multiplying with fractions yields smaller products. To help her students "see" how multiplying with fractions worked, Katlaski used an activity recommended by her textbook, in which students would fold a sheet of paper in different ways. The particular mathematical problem that Katlaski posed was this: $\frac{1}{2} \times \frac{2}{3}$. To show students what this product would look like, she wanted them to fold their paper first lengthwise, into two halves, and then widthwise, into three thirds. She also intended to have them color the different portions, so that they would be able to see where $\frac{2}{3}$ overlapped with $\frac{1}{2}$. Their sheets would look like Figure 3. The top row was to be filled in with one color to represent the $\frac{1}{2}$ (represented here by diagonal lines descending from left to right), and the two columns representing the $\frac{2}{3}$ were to be filled in with a different color (represented here by diagonals descending in the opposite direction). The crosshatched area, the intersection of the two, represents $\frac{2}{3} \times \frac{1}{2}$.

But Katlaski hit two snags when moving her students through this

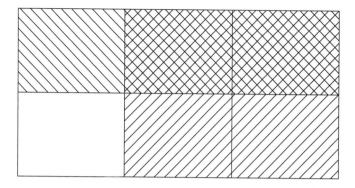

Figure 3. *Ms. Katlaski's portrayal of* ½ + ⅔.

process. The first problem came when Katlaski forgot to tell students to color one of the halves before they moved on to refold the sheet into three thirds. The second occurred when students had difficulty folding their sheets into thirds. It was physically too complicated an act for them to carry out. This problem, coupled with the fact that she had forgotten to tell them to color one of their halves, led to great consternation and confusion in the lesson and the portrayal she had hoped to present to the students was lost.

Even when teachers keep track of all these details, however, complicated portrayals can confuse students, particularly when different activities rely on different materials or metaphors to portray the same idea. Ms. Mission (grade 6 math) explained such a dilemma in the context of her lesson on central tendencies. She was using learning activities that her textbook had recommended, but she had discovered through the years that two of them conflicted. In one activity a distribution of families of different sizes was represented with different stacks of cubes. A stack of five cubes represented a family of five, a stack of three cubes represented a family of three, and so forth. The very next learning activity asked students to draw a line graph showing how many families had three members, four members, five members, and so on. Mission had discovered that students regularly confused the line graph and the stacks of cubes, and plotted the *number of cubes in each stack* rather than plotting the *number of stacks of each size.* So again, her physical materials complicated her portrayal of this content.

Complicated demonstrations and learning activities can be confusing. An important substantive idea is harder to keep track of when activities involve multiple props, and it is easy for teachers, as well as students, to forget where they are and where they are going. Instead of enriching the content in the lesson, these activities can distort it.

Hiding Content in Procedures

The third main way in which teachers portrayed content was to not mention it at all. This may seem a surprising approach, but in fact this technique was relatively common. When we observed Mr. Awles (grade 3–4 science, 9 years' experience), he was presenting a lesson on the ocean, a topic Awles claimed he loved to teach. The learning outcome he sought was for students to learn that different kinds of life existed at different depths in the ocean, and to recognize that each depth constituted a specialized environment. His introductory lesson consisted of three main learning activities:

> Students wrote in their journals three facts and two opinions about the ocean.
>
> Awles engaged in a Q&A routine, asking students to offer their facts and opinions about the ocean.
>
> Students drew cross-sectional pictures of the ocean that would be used in future lessons to locate different kinds of life forms.

Each of these learning activities was introduced with almost no mention of the content of the lesson. For instance, Awles introduced the first activity like this: "This is one of my favorite subjects in studying science. How many of you have been to the ocean? (Students raise hands. Awles counts hands.) How many of you *swam* in the ocean? (More hands.) Okay. In your science journal, I want you to write down three facts that you know about the ocean and two opinions you have about the ocean." He introduced the second learning activity like this: "Now if I call on you, I want you to give me a fact or an opinion. Valerie?" As students offered their facts and opinions, Awles acknowledged every idea but discussed none. In fact, on two occasions when students said they had a comment about someone else's fact or opinion, Awles said, "We aren't discussing right now. We're just listing." Finally, he introduced the third and main learning activity like this:

> I know you guys have more to say, but right now we're going to move on to the next piece, so put your journals away and get out your blue crayons and your white paper. [He waits for students to get ready.] The reason we have two pieces of paper is because I found out two different pieces of information. And I thought, "Well, I could give you one, but who's to say that the other one isn't true, too?" So we're going to work on one first, and then we'll work on the second one. And this one has to do with Cassandra's question, how deep is the ocean, and with Lena's fact about the colors, and with Andrew's fact about the colors.

This third learning activity was intended to introduce the idea that the amount of light available varied with the depth of the water. Awles had decided to introduce the unit by having students draw a cross-sectional picture of the ocean, complete with depths, which they could use later to locate various life forms at their appropriate depths. The picture of the ocean that he wanted his students to draw looked like Figure 4. But Awles never told his students that this was his plan. Nor did he say what purpose these drawings would have. In fact, even though he put a drawing on an overhead projector to serve as an example, he covered up all but the left side, so that students could not see what the whole picture would look like as he told them to draw the line on the left side. Here are his instructions for how to draw this picture. The numbers show the amount of time that had passed in the lesson when each instruction was given.

> 13:52 Hold up your left hand. Now put that down on your paper, put it next to the edge. That is going to be your shoreline. Wait. I'll show you. The edge of your paper is going to be your shore-

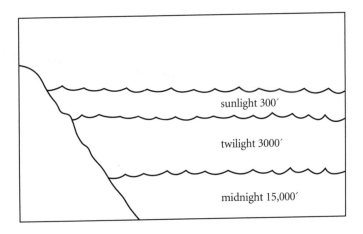

Figure 4. *Mr. Awles's cross-sectional portrayal of the ocean.*

line, and you are going to make a shoreline going down angle. Just make an angled shoreline going down to the bottom of your paper.

17:27 Now take your very very lightest color of blue and draw a wavy line across the top like this. Your lightest, lightest color of blue.

19:12 Now what you are going to do is, I'm going to use just one shade of blue, because that's all I have, but you have three or four colors. So you are going to use different colors. Your first line is going to go straight across. First we have to draw the top of the water. All you are going to do is make a zigzaggy line across the top of the page. You've got your shoreline at the top, so don't go higher than that. Use the lightest blue you have.

20:06 Now, this has to do with what Melina talked about when she said her fact. Now, you're going to go down—if you hold up your fingers, and you spread them about an inch—you are estimating an inch. No more than an inch. If you are looking at your little finger, it would be about the first knuckle of your little finger. Go down that far and make another zigzag line. Same color of blue is fine.

21:56 Now, in between here, as you can see, I have the word "sunlight." Would you write that on the edge of that, please? Put the word "sunlight" in there. And then I have in there, "300'." Three hundred feet. So the sunlight only goes down 300 feet. So put 300 and put a slash mark next to it. That means feet.

23:21 Now take your next blue. The medium color blue.

24:15 If we used our little finger and our one-knuckle length to measure the first one, and it was 300 feet, and the next layer goes to twilight, and that goes to 3,000 feet, do you think it's two knuckles, or do you think it's three knuckles? [Students call out "three."]. So make the next line three knuckles down and use a medium color blue for that.

25:15 Oh, I know what I forgot, and I see Akea doing it. Take your first shade of blue and color in all of your sunlight area. Color in all of your sunlight area with your first shade of blue. Then take your second color and color in the second section. So when you get all done, it's all one color and then you'll be able to see, and that way, Antonio, it won't bother you. Color in your first strip, all the way across. Color that in. And then color in your twilight zone. You've got to color in the whole piece, even in the middle. Even over the words.

28:50 For those that are done, after we have done the sunlight, and you can see that we only go to 300 feet, and then we go to the twilight, and that was only 3,000 feet, then we go to midnight zone, and that is 15,000 feet. So now, make your line on the bottom of the paper for the floor of the ocean. Write down "midnight, 15,000 feet," and color that zone in. Make sure the whole thing is your midnight zone. You can see I have only three zones there: sunlight, twilight, and midnight.

32:42 Okay. For your shoreline, Cassandra asked what color you could use for the shoreline. What color can you use for that? [Students call out "Brown, tan."] Brown or tan. So take out that crayon and do your shoreline. [Students ask: "What about the sky?"] Not yet. We're not doing the sky yet.

34:26 When you are done, get out a tan or cream color and color your sand.

Awles's guidance was entirely procedural. The substantive meaning of these drawings was not made explicit until minute 21:56, when he asked students to label the top section of the ocean the "sunlight" zone. The entire lesson was devoted to these pictures, and almost nothing was said about the ocean itself. The time in between Awles's procedural directions was filled with student questions that were also about procedures:

Can we use crayons?

Can I use a ruler?

What color should it be?

Does this look okay?

Can we just take our hand and go like this?

Mr. Awles's line of thinking. This technique of hiding content in procedures was not unusual. Many teachers moved students through their lessons by telling students what to *do* next, rather than by directly addressing the content itself. To some extent, these practices also reflect habits. Over time, teachers have probably discovered that students need specific, concrete guidance. Mr. Awles had also concluded that students lacked confidence, for they routinely asked clarifying questions such as those listed above. His line of thinking for this method of portraying the ocean includes two main ideas. One relates to the students, the other to the ocean itself. He lives in California, near the ocean, and each summer he visits friends who live on the ocean. He brings back artifacts to share with his students. But recently he joined a local university study group. Through that group,

Awles acquired the idea that students need more than just a collection of specific details (in his case, specimens); they need an overview of the ocean, a framework on which to attach those details. So he had been working on a new approach to teaching the ocean, one in which he purposefully postponed pulling out his specimens until students had an overview.

The second main idea running through his thinking relates to students and how they think and learn. From his experience teaching, he has noticed that students need very concrete instruction and that they are also very insecure. He has concluded from these observations that he should give his instructions in tiny increments, with a lot of reinforcement as students successfully completed each step. Hence he does not provide an overview of the content or a purpose of the activity. Moreover, Awles has concluded from his experience that class discussions tend to be nonproductive; they veer off track and prevent him from accomplishing his learning outcomes. So he tries to discourage students from actually discussing the content. These observations led him to the lesson we observed, in which he tried to restrain himself from enthusiastically sharing his specimens, tried to restrain his students from discussing the content, and instead focused the entire lesson on the tasks of drawing a picture, line by line. He produced a lesson that was almost content-free.

These three methods of portraying content—direct presentations, gateway learning activities, and hiding content in procedures—are not mutually exclusive. Ms. Mathews, who portrayed the Earth's layers by having students represent each layer, used a gateway learning activity that also translated the content into a set of procedures and repeatedly outlined tasks that students would do as they portrayed the content they were studying.

None of these approaches to portraying content is automatically superior to the others. The third method, in which content is converted into procedures, does seem weakest, in that it removes content and ideas from view. But the first two methods are not free of problems. Presentations seem to invite more unanticipated student comments, as when Ms. Chalmers' student volunteered that she had a kitten named Shadow; and many teacher mistakes occurred when teachers tried to keep track of a complicated set of materials, either for a demonstration of their own or for a gateway learning activity. Moreover, these problems cannot be attributed to teachers' poor planning, for many of the portrayals that teachers attempted, and even the materials they relied upon, came from their teachers' manuals, and often teachers talked at length about how they had planned and envisioned the lesson. The classroom problems we observed were not necessarily the result of poor planning, lack of substantive knowledge, or other popular diagnoses. They seemed to result from overly complicated activities and an overreliance on props. If anything, the message we see in these portrayals is that simpler presentations or gateway activities are likely to work better.

Learning Activities

I have already described some learning activities that were used to portray content. But learning activities also play an important role in getting students to interact with content. Virtually all lessons, at every level of education, involve some sort of learning activity—something students are supposed to *do* that will enable them to internalize the content. This doing may take many forms, including reading and writing, group discussions or debates, watching a play or putting on a play, conducting an experiment, or solving a problem. If the content provides an important idea, the learning activity should *intellectually engage* students with that idea.

Perhaps if this study had included high school classrooms, we might have seen learning activities that consisted mainly of watching and listening to the teacher present the content. Certainly college-level learning activities consist mainly of listening and note-taking. But in elementary classrooms, teachers plan a wider range of activities for their students, and most teachers developed lessons involving more than one activity. There might be a homework review, then a presentation of some new content, and then a learning activity during which students work with the new content in some way. Each lesson consists of a sequence of events that move students through the day's agenda. A very common sequence of activities is this:

Homework review, typically via a Q&A session

Presentation: introduce new content, typically with a visual aid

A learning activity involving the new content

Closure: gather papers, materials, give assignment for the next day, etc.

Learning activities are combined in a wide range of ways to create lessons. Ms. Lachamy's lesson demonstrates the simplest form of a daily agenda, for it included one learning outcome (write an organized paragraph), one portrayal (an example of a paragraph that has the requisite parts), and one learning activity (writing sentences on green and pink strips and gluing them together to form paragraphs). One of the most complicated lessons we observed was in Ms. Bowes's fifth-grade math lesson, where we saw twelve discrete learning activities, all engaging students with the same concept: geometric symmetry. Here is an outline of her lesson:

1. Bowes gave students equilateral triangles and then engaged in a Q&A routine about how to prove these triangles are equilateral.

2. She asked if students could fold their triangles to create two equal parts, and if they could do this in more than one direction.

3. Bowes presented the concept of symmetry and defined it. (Notice that this definition followed two learning activities that involved the concept of symmetry.)

4. She gave students letters of the alphabet and asked them to see how many lines of symmetry they could find for their letters. Students worked in pairs.

5. She asked students to report their findings to the rest of the class. As each pair reported, she asked them what letter they had, asked them to show it, asked how many ways they tried to fold it, and what they concluded.

6. She asked students to open their math journals and write a definition of symmetry. She already had one on the overhead projector for students to copy.

7. She gave groups of students some new shapes to test. These shapes included squares, pentagons, and hexagons. Again, they tried to see how many lines of symmetry they could find. Then they reported what they found in their shapes.

8. She asked if anyone had noticed a pattern. The pattern is that the number of lines of symmetry equals the number of sides the figure has: a triangle has three, a square has four, and a pentagon has five.

9. Students again opened their journals, this time to write the observation that, for regular polygons, the number of lines of symmetry equals the number of sides.

10. She gave students still more shapes to study. However, these were irregular polygons, so the new rule didn't work. Students ascertained this fact and explained it to the teacher.

11. Bowes then presented a set of oddly shaped drawings on the overhead projector, each with multiple lines dissecting it, and asked volunteers to come up and ascertain which lines were lines of symmetry. She then asked other students to give thumbs up or thumbs down if they agreed or disagreed.

12. She then placed on the overhead projector several half-shapes and asked for volunteers to draw the other half of the shape in such a way that the total would be bisected with a line of symmetry. As students worked on these, she commented on their strategies (One counted squares, another traced the other half, etc.).

13. Finally, she asked students to open their math books, and she gave them an assignment (problems 1–18). She discussed the problems with the students, talked about how they could do

them. Most were similar to those the students had just worked on, so the discussion was on how to trace a drawing, how to draw the other half when only half is shown, and so on.

Saying that the *content* of Bowes' lesson was geometric symmetry doesn't do justice to the lesson itself, which was a content-rich lesson that included a complicated mix of portrayals of symmetry and intellectually engaging learning activities.

Ms. Bowes' line of thinking. We interviewed Ms. Bowes at length about how she constructed this lesson. One thing that stands out about her line of thinking is the attention she pays to how students learn. She begins with a premise that students learn more if they can "see and do," rather than just reading, and that multiple activities offer multiple ways of remembering. She adds to this belief a number of observations from her own experience, including that students learn more from hands-on activities, learn more by writing things down, and learn more when they work in groups. In her interpretation of the situation, she noted that the content, symmetry, followed logically from the unit on geometry that was already under way. Though she didn't mention the textbook as an influence in her decision to teach this content, apparently it was: at the end of the lesson, she gave students an assignment from the textbook. However, she did mention that the examples in the book were not sufficient and that she had developed a number of additional learning activities to strengthen the concept. Like most teachers' lines of thinking, Bowes's has led to numerous intentions, including helping students understand symmetry, providing as many and as varied examples as possible, giving them some examples that foreshadow the homework, modeling how to do the homework, avoiding being repetitious, and avoiding transferring her own anxieties about lesson momentum onto the students.

Notice that the particular learning activities that Bowes developed also followed from her acquired principles of practice. She had determined, for instance, that students learned more when they wrote notes about what they were studying, so on two occasions during the lesson she had students write their findings in their math journals.

And she had determined that small-group activities increased student willingness to participate and that the process of sharing findings and listening to other students' findings strengthened the classroom community, so she included some activities of this sort in her lesson as well. She mentioned more than once the need for students to manipulate physical materials, and she included numerous activities that gave them a chance to do this. These standing beliefs and accumulated principles and strategies, then, accounted not only for her use of multiple learning activities but also for the specific activities she developed.

One interesting point to notice in Bowes's discussion is that, even though she acknowledged that state and local curricular requirements were increasing, and that state assessments were putting added pressure on her, so that she was continually anxious about how much needed to be done, there was no evidence that this pressure directly influenced her lesson design. That is, she mentioned these things in passing, but never indicated that, for instance, the content of symmetry was in a mandated curriculum or on the state assessment, or that she needed to hurry through it because there were so many other things yet to cover. And even though she indicated that these external pressures made her intensely aware of time, she nonetheless taught an 84-minute lesson, one of the longest we observed. Perhaps these pressures influenced other lessons in more direct ways, but this particular lesson appeared to derive more from her own understanding of the subject matter and her own theories of learning than from any institutional policies.

Teachers developed a variety of learning activities, and they used them in a variety of ways. I have sorted these learning activities into three main types:

Teacher-led projects or discussion: These activities typically involve a Q&A sequence in which the teacher leads the entire class through either a project or a discussion. Mr. Sadowski's students worked on a teacher-led project when they wrote their favorite seasons on sticky notes and created a graph of their favorite seasons, and Ms. Toklisch's students worked on a teacher-led project when they compared the areas of two small pizzas with that of one large pizza.

Prescribed individual seat work: In these activities, students work individually, and usually silently, on a task the teacher has prescribed in advance for them. Ms. Lachamy's students engaged in prescribed seat work when they wrote their sentences on green and pink slips of paper, Ms. Bowes's students engaged in prescribed seat work when they wrote their definition of symmetry in their math journals, and Mr. Awles's students engaged in prescribed seat work when they wrote facts and opinions in their journals.

Decentralized exploratory projects: In these activities, students work either individually or in pairs or small groups to explore a phenomenon, perhaps by doing an experiment or by measuring or collecting data. Usually, after they work on their projects, there is a whole-group Q&A session during which students report back to the whole class what they learned from their explorations. Ms. Bowes relied heavily on decentralized exploratory projects in her lesson on lines of symmetry. So did Ms. Fosnot when she had students measuring a bed for a queen.

Teacher-Led Projects or Discussion

Teacher-led discussions or projects, reviewed in Chapter 4, provide useful examples of how the day's agenda is shaped and constrained by Q&A routines. The specific content that teachers focus on in their Q&A routines derives from the day's agenda, but the kinds of questions teachers pose and they way they respond to student answers are habitualized routines. Indeed, Chapter 4 provides examples of situations in which teachers actually reinforced student answers that were wrong, because their Q&A routine was so strongly ingrained. Moreover, these routines do not prevent students from offering ideas that are far afield from the intended agenda, and these unexpected comments can be disconcerting for teachers.

Prescribed Individual Seat work

Seat work involves giving students specific assignments and asking them to work on these at their desks. Examples include doing problems 1–8 on page 82 of the math book, writing something in a journal, or copying something from the board. In all cases, the specific work is predefined by the teacher, and students work individually and usually silently.

One important aspect of seat work that is rarely discussed by teachers is the amount of time required to prepare students for this work and to make sure they understand the task. For example, when Ms. Lachamy asked her students to write topic sentences and supporting detail sentences on pink and green slips of paper, she spent about 10 minutes explaining the task. The preparation took up 23 percent of the total lesson time, and students didn't finish their tasks in the allotted time. Long preparation times are not unusual for either seat work or decentralized explorations.

Decentralized Exploratory Projects

Decentralized exploratory projects are usually more open-ended than prescribed seat work or teacher-led projects and discussions. In explorations, students are examining, experimenting, or generally exploring some phenomenon. Ms. Bowes's students were engaged in decentralized explorations when they tried to find the lines of symmetry in the letters of the alphabet, and Ms. Fosnot's worked on decentralized explorations when they measured out beds for the queen. We saw numerous examples of decentralized explorations in these lessons. Students measured circles, plotted graphs, conducted various experiments, mixed chemicals, and studied the steps involved in eating Oreo cookies. As they worked on their projects, the teacher often circulated and offered suggestions or asked questions about their findings. Though there was tremendous variety in these activities, there were also some common elements. In most cases, for instance, students worked together, either in pairs or in small groups, and the classrooms were noisy with movement and conversation. And in most cases the decentralized activity was followed by a whole-group Q&A routine in which each group reported its findings to the rest of the class.

In addition, in most cases, when teachers watched our videotapes of their lessons, they were surprised and disappointed at how many students were off-task. They had been unaware of these digressions during class because they were working with individual groups, but when they watched the tapes, they routinely saw students who were wandering abut the room aimlessly, sitting at their desks staring off into space, or playing with unrelated materials.

Each type of learning activity presents its own advantages and its own threats to learning and to momentum. Teacher-led discussions have the advantage of keeping the teacher entirely in touch with what students are thinking, since all student comments are public; but they are also risky because students can say things that the teacher is not prepared for. Prescribed seat work has the advantage of keeping student activity relatively circumscribed, but it can be very time-consuming, since teachers can spend as much as a third of the lesson explaining to students what they will be doing in the remaining time. Finally, decentralized explorations give students an opportunity to examine ideas in a way that builds on their own prior thinking, but they also run the risk that students will move off task once they are working independently.

The examples presented here lead to some general observations about learning activities. One is that learning activities are profoundly important. What students learn and how well they understand what they learn depend heavily on the learning activities that teachers devise. Yet learning activities can fail in any number of ways. If they don't interest students, students may not be willing to participate. Or students may be willing participants because the activity is fun, but the activity may not require *intellectual* engagement. Notice, too, that none of these three types of learning activity is automatically superior to any other, and none is guaranteed to engage students intellectually with important content. This observation runs counter to the assumptions of many reformers that a particular pedagogy is imperative to foster student learning. In fact the value of each approach depends heavily on how it is used. For instance, individual seat work in Ms. Bowes's class consisted of writing notes about symmetry after exploring the concept with some physical materials, but in Mr. Awles's class it involved writing facts and opinions about the ocean without any substantive introduction to the ocean or any stated purpose for the activity. Similarly, exploratory activities in Ms. Bowes's class were driven by specific questions about lines of symmetry, but in Ms. Fosnot's class students made beds for a queen without grasping the concept that standard units of measurement were important to their task. Each type of learning activity has the potential to address important content, to engage students intellectually, and to ensure universal access to knowledge. Each also has the potential to sap content, to distract students, and to exclude some students.

One final observation about both portrayals and learning activities is that teachers' choices for these activities are influenced by all six areas of concern, and especially by their theories about how students learn. The lines of thinking that were examined in this chapter illustrate teachers' tendencies to take most or all areas of concern into account as they establish their learning outcomes, their portrayals of content, and their learning activities. Most teachers also made some reference to their state standards. Yet the particular ideas they carried with them through their lesson agendas were remarkably varied. These differences seemed to follow largely from their theories of learning. Ms. Bowes believed that students needed a variety of experiences with the content and that they needed to "see and do" rather than simply reading. She developed a series of activities that enabled students to find symmetry in many different types of shapes. Mr. Awles believed that students needed to receive instructions one small step at a time, or they would become confused and frustrated. He spent almost an hour leading them as they drew a relatively simple sketch of the ocean. Ms. Lachamy wanted a device that made paragraph structure so obvious that it would be "hard to miss." She asked students to write their paragraphs on green and pink slips of paper. These differences in views about how to foster student learning determined the kind of learning activities that teachers developed, and in turn determined students' opportunities to engage intellectually with the academic content.

Implications for Reform

The main components in each day's agenda include a learning outcome, a portrayal of the content associated with that outcome, and one or more learning activities that will provoke students to interact with the content. Reformers have tended to focus mostly on decisions about what the content and learning outcomes should be, and to pay less attention to how content is portrayed or to the kind of learning activities that are used. And they have been very successful in influencing teachers' decisions about content and learning outcomes. Most teachers in this study mentioned state or district policies when they explained the rationale for the learning outcomes they sought. Many also mentioned textbook or associated materials when they accounted for their learning activities and their portraits of content. Apparently teachers relied on these materials not only for ideas about learning outcomes but also for ideas about how to present content and how to engage students intellectually with it.

So the first lesson reformers can take from these practices is that guidance about content standards, though necessary, is not sufficient. Messages from states and districts regarding content have been influential in the sense that teachers are aware of these standards and do attend to them, although they make numerous adjustments to suit their own beliefs and values.

Yet despite the widespread influence of content standards on teachers' daily agendas, many of these lessons appeared to be drained of important content. Certainly one reason these lessons lost their intellectual steam is that they were designed to accommodate multiple areas of concern, not just content coverage. Each learning activity must foster learning, but it must also enable teachers to maintain momentum, ensure student willingness to participate, accommodate teachers' personal needs, and so forth. In his study of learning activities, Walter Doyle (1986) concluded that some types of learning activities are simply more suitable to the circumstances of teaching, but that these more suitable activities make meaning vulnerable.

Another reason these lessons lost intellectual steam was that logistical complications distracted both teachers and students from the content. We saw numerous lessons in which teachers attempted learning activities that involved multiple groups of students working with multiple materials that should have introduced them to an important idea, but the logistics of the activity itself distracted everyone from the idea.

So the second lesson reformers can take from these practices is that complicated materials and activities frequently distract both teachers and students from the content they should be thinking about. This is an important lesson, for many reformers believe that more complicated lessons are more likely to be intellectually engaging, and that simpler activities, such as seat work, necessarily entail less important content or less intellectual engagement. The activities we observed do not support this hypothesis. Either kind of learning activity can be infused with content, and either can be devoid of content. Either can be intellectually engaging, and either can be tedious. So although learning activities are important determinants of students' intellectual engagement, there is no necessary connection between these broad categories of activity and any of the reform ideals.

6. Sources of Problems in Teaching

The previous chapters have reviewed a series of tasks that are essential to each classroom lesson: creating a tranquil environment through a series of classroom routines, managing conversations with students through Q&A routines and responding to their unexpected ideas, and constructing an agenda for each lesson that includes a learning outcome, portrayals of content, conversations about content, and learning activities. Teachers may devise any number of strategies for accomplishing these tasks, and, as we have seen, there are also many ways in which their strategies can go awry.

It is now time to return to the question posed in Chapter 1 about why teachers have not risen to reformers' challenges. Five hypotheses have been put forward to account for the mysterious gap between reformers' ideals and teachers' everyday practices: teachers' lack knowledge and guidance, their beliefs and values differ from those of reformers, their dispositions interfere with their practice, or the conditions of teaching themselves militate against reform. To these, I have added a fifth: that reform ideals are unrealistic. This chapter begins the process of testing these hypotheses by examining the full range of problems that teachers encountered. The first part of the chapter reviews all episodes that could be construed as problems, and the second examines these episodes more closely in order to ascertain the underlying sources of the problems.

Defining Problems

Depending on whose perspective one uses, and on how critical an eye one uses, it would be possible to argue that the 45 lessons we observed contained either dozens of problems or only a handful. Teachers themselves pointed to many instances in which they were dissatisfied, and they used a variety of criteria in their self-criticisms. Observers also saw things they questioned, often applying differing standards for their judgments. Sometimes the two assessments agreed; sometimes they didn't. In addition, there were disruptions of the sort mentioned in Chapter 3 that created problems, and these were unrelated to the teacher's practices. I use three perspectives in this examination: teachers' own assessments of their practices, a hypothetical reformer's assessment of the same practices, and an assessment by a hypothetical parent that focuses not on the teachers' practices but instead on the myriad confusions, mistakes, interruptions, and prop failures that occurred and that appeared to be unrelated to teaching practices per se.

I also use slightly different units for analysis in these three examinations. When examining problems identified by teachers, I stick to the 499 episodes that constitute the core of the study, that is, episodes that were discussed in the interviews, and in particular the 181 episodes that were brought up by teachers themselves. However, when I examine problems from the reformers' and parents' points of view, I include events that were not discussed in the interviews. I refer to these as "events" rather than as "episodes" as a way to distinguish them from the episodes that were discussed in the interviews.

Teachers' Self-Criticisms

Teachers' self-criticisms were typically based on one of the six areas of concern reviewed in Chapter 2. Teachers perceived their practices as inhibiting or working against one or more of those concerns. In our interviews regarding the 45 lessons, teachers criticized 46 episodes in their own lessons. Table 9 summarizes their self-criticisms by area of concern.

The table shows that teachers were more frequently dissatisfied with their ability to foster student learning than with any other area of concern. This result is consistent with earlier findings shown in Table 2 suggesting that teachers' *intentions* were more often focused on this area of concern than on other areas. However, all the areas of concern are interrelated, and when teachers talked about the importance of any one of them, it was often because they viewed that one as influencing others.

Many of these practices would not have been criticized by reformers—or even noticed, in many cases. Yet they represent genuine concerns and legitimate things for teachers to worry about. For instance, Ms. Taffner (grade 6 math, 7 years' experience) criticized herself for beginning to ask summary questions about the content before her students had finished their individual projects. She realized, on watching the tape, that students weren't ready to think about her questions. Ms. Eckhard (grade 4 language arts, 6 years' experience) criticized herself for forgetting to turn off the classical music she had been playing before her class began. On viewing the tape, she felt that this background music was very distracting. Ms. Taswell (grade 6 math, 14 years' experience) criticized herself for destroying the mo-

Table 9   Teachers' self-criticisms of practice, by area of concern

Number of criticisms	Area of concern
1	Defining learning outcomes
17	Fostering student learning
11	Maintaining lesson momentum
6	Fostering student willingness to participate
7	Establishing the classroom as a community
4	Attending to personal needs
46	Self-criticisms out of 181 episodes nominated by teachers for discussion

mentum of a lesson in which she was demonstrating a math problem that referred to amounts of broccoli. She couldn't think how to spell "broccoli," but instead of letting it go and continuing with the mathematics, she revised and revised her spelling and finally looked it up. In the interview she argued that she shouldn't be such a perfectionist because she loses her momentum over things like this.

Other teachers criticized themselves for moving too quickly from one segment to another, interrupting students, failing to respond to students, and neglecting small details. All these things could have reduced students' access to knowledge or their opportunities to engage intellectually with content. But the things that teachers noticed and criticized about their own practices were often things that we, as observers, either didn't notice or couldn't see. Teachers were much more aware of small events than we were.

Reformers' Criticisms

In light of the three main ideals promoted by reformers, I looked for episodes in which important ideas were suppressed, students' intellectual engagement was suppressed, or universal access to knowledge was suppressed.

Important Ideas Are Suppressed

There were several ways in which important content was suppressed in the lessons we observed, and some have already been examined elsewhere; in Chapters 4 and 5 I have described numerous ways in which Q&A routines, portraits, and learning activities hid content behind obscure guessing games or complicated lesson procedures. A few others warrant some discussion here. The episodes that are most likely to concern reformers are those in which teachers made substantive mistakes in their lessons—that is, episodes in which teachers were not merely suppressing content, but were actually misrepresenting it. We observed both major and minor misrepresentations. Minor errors occurred when teachers misspoke themselves, got confused, or said something that could be misleading, but there is no evidence that the statement was intentional, that it reflected the teacher's own misunderstanding of the content, or even that it confused or misled students. For instance, when Ms. Todd (grade 5 math, 20 years' experience) was teaching her students the metric system, she held a long Q&A session in which she posed numerous metric conversion problems, such as how many centimeters there are in 3 meters and how many grams in 2 kilograms. The problems got more and more complicated as the lesson proceeded, and they switched back and forth among meters, liters, and grams. Ms. Todd misspoke herself several times, saying meters when she meant liters, or grams when she meant meters. But students didn't appear to be confused by these slippages.

Other errors were more misleading but still relatively minor. For instance, when Mr. Awles was showing his students how to draw the three major layers of the ocean, he suggested that they use their fingers to measure depths. He first told them to measure down one knuckle from the top line and to draw their second horizontal line there. The resulting interval, measured from the top of a child's finger to his or her first knuckle, represented the "sunlight zone" of the ocean, which was 300 feet. To get them to mark the "twilight zone," which went down another 3,000 feet, he said, "If we used one knuckle to measure 300 feet, would we use one knuckle or three knuckles to measure 3,000 feet?" Students called out "three," and Awles agreed. So one knuckle represented 300 feet and three knuckles, or three times 300, came to 3000 feet. In the interview it was clear that Awles hadn't thought at all about the substantive correctness of this calculation. Instead, he was thinking about the fact that students didn't have rulers and that he needed to quickly develop an ad hoc method of measurement. His main intention was to ensure that the students left a greater distance between the second and third lines than they had left between the first and second lines. Nor is it clear that this was confusing for students. They all understood that 3,000 was a lot more than 300, and, if pushed, they probably would also have said that it was 10 times as much. Small errors such as these occurred throughout these 45 lessons, and teachers often noticed them when they reviewed the videotapes. What is less clear is the extent to which these errors really misled students.

The second type of erroneous teaching involved incomplete, confusing, or downright wrong portrayals of content. I found only one erroneous portrayal in the 45 lessons. It occurred in Ms. Buford's fifth-grade class, which began with a "problem of the day." Though the class we observed was a math class, the problem was not a math problem. It was this:

> Today is neither Sunday nor Friday.
> Tomorrow will be neither Tuesday nor Thursday.
> Yesterday was neither Monday nor Wednesday.
> What day is today?

After students worked on this problem by themselves for a time, Buford initiated a discussion about the process they had used to solve the problem. She asked them not to say what their solution was, but instead to talk only about their strategies. Those who spoke described their approach in many ways, but the essence of all the approaches was that they had simply eliminated all the days that were mentioned in any of the sentences. Through this process of elimination they inferred that today must be the day that was not already mentioned. Their approach missed entirely the fact that many of the "nots" listed in the problem did not refer to "today." After hearing three or four versions of how students eliminated their days, Buford agreed that the process of elimination was a good one and moved on to the main portion of the math lesson.

There is one additional way in which content was suppressed. In a very small number of cases, the entire lesson appeared to be seriously disorganized and confusing. One of these was Ms. Masters' lesson on physical and chemical change. Masters had interrupted her original curriculum unit so that her sixth-graders could participate in a national geological data collection project. On the day we observed her class, Masters was returning to her original unit. She opened her lesson by reviewing the earlier lessons on physical and chemical change.

She had several visual aids on the wall. A series of 8½- by 11-inch sheets of paper lined the wall above the blackboard, each illustrating one of the experiments students either had already done, or would do, for this unit. Taped onto the board itself were larger posters summarizing findings from experiments they had already done. She also relied on a set of overhead transparencies that summarized earlier lessons. During her review she moved back and forth among these displays, pulling down the projector screen to show a transparency, then raising it to refer to one of the posters on the wall behind it. But sometimes she forgot to pull the projection screen back down when she showed the next transparency, so that the image was projected onto the array of posters and charts, making each layer of information compete with the others.

Masters wanted students to remember the distinction between physical changes and chemical changes. Physical change occurs when two substances are mixed together but can later be separated again, as when sand settles to the bottom of a container of water. Chemical changes, on the other hand, are irreversible. At one point she pulled a beaker of Kool-Aid from the top of a file cabinet to remind students what chemical change looked like. She wanted them to notice that this mixture still consisted, even after several weeks, of just one substance; that it hadn't separated back into two parts. But when she asked students how many different things they could see in this mixture, students said they could see two different things. Mold had grown in the beaker since its last use and was floating visibly on the surface of the Kool-Aid.

After Masters finished her review, students worked in small groups on an experiment that involved mixing things together. When they finished, Masters called everyone together to discuss what they had learned from their experiments. She tried to organize the conversation so that students first discussed hypotheses, then observations and then conclusions, but many students didn't understand the distinction, and those who did couldn't confine their remarks to only one aspect of their reasoning. Their comments addressed every aspect of the project, despite Masters' efforts to impose her version of order on the conversation. Masters also tried, again unsuccessfully, to get students to phrase their hypotheses and observations in scientific language, but students referred to their mixtures with terms like "sludgy" and "lumpy." Masters became frustrated and angry, partly at how little students had remembered about physical and chemical changes from before their digression, and partly at their inability to reason and to talk scientifically about their experiments. Eventually she gave up trying to guide the students in any way. The lesson closed with students offering ideas and comments willy-nilly, without any critique, guidance, or direction from their frustrated and angry teacher.

Intellectual Engagement Is Suppressed

Whereas most of the episodes in which content was suppressed occurred during teachers' portrayals of content or during learning activities, most of the episodes in which intellectual engagement was suppressed occurred during Q&A routines, when either teachers' questions or their responses to students may have discouraged students from thinking about the content. Many were extremely brief exchanges, and easy to miss when first viewing a videotape. Episodes in which teachers responded to unexpected student comments or questions were briefer still, often amounting to a single discrete exchange. Yet these tiny interactions do have an influence on students. Some of them misinform students; others discourage them from engaging intellectually with the content. When a teacher says, for instance, "We'll talk about that later," she is telling students not to think about the ideas, but instead to sit passively and let the teacher take care of these issues. Similarly, when teachers reject plausible ideas from students, with no indication as to why their idea is not acceptable, they discourage students from further thought.

Chapter 4 provides examples of these interactions. One form of interaction not described there bears examination now. It involves the teacher's suppression of intellectual engagement by failing to respond to student questions. A lesson by Mr. Kimberly (grade 6 science, 21 years' experience) provides an example. Though many teachers seemed to have difficulty responding to student questions and ideas, Mr. Kimberly seemed especially unable to do so. His lesson was on the atmosphere, and more specifically on the troposphere. Though students had some difficulty at the beginning of the lesson understanding Kimberly's terminology, once they grasped the issue, they were excited and had many questions and observations to make. But Kimberly discouraged nearly all of these in one way or another.

Kimberly opened the lesson by portraying air as an example of a resource, which he defined as something nature provides that we can use. He reminded them that they had studied water earlier, and that water was a resource too. He then asked: "Does air fit our definition of a resource?" Most students appeared to be nodding or saying yes, except Michael, so Mr. Kimberly asked Michael what his reasoning was for disagreeing. Michael said that different places around the world had different resources, and since the entire world had air, it couldn't be a resource. Michael's argument suggests that he understood resources as being attached to specific locations. He could have picked up this idea from the unit on water, or perhaps from a unit on minerals as resources. Kimberly could have addressed Michael's conception of a resource by comparing air to other kinds of resources that are location-specific, but he chose not to. Instead, Kimberly repeated his criteria for a resource, this time in Q&A form:

Kimberly: Is air something we get from nature?
Ss: Yes.
Kimberly: Is it something we can use?
Ss: Yes.
Kimberly: Is it a resource?

Immediately after this exchange, another student said he also didn't think air was a resource, because we didn't ask nature to invent it, and nature didn't give it back to us, but instead it was already there for us to use. Again Kimberly repeated his criteria, pointing out that air was from nature and we used it, and therefore that it was a resource. In each case, his students were intellectually engaged with the concept of a natural resource and had their own thoughts about what made something a resource, and in each case Kimberly chose not to address their ideas, to explain the difference between his definition and theirs, to show them which kinds of resources fitted these definitions, or to do anything to help them see the relationship between his definition and their own prior ideas.

Kimberly then moved on to the next part of his portrayal, which was a physical demonstration. He told students that the atmosphere went up 62 miles, but then said this was really a very thin layer. To illustrate, he draped an overhead transparency sheet over a globe and said this thin cover was the equivalent of 62 miles. A student said he was confused: How can something that thin also be 62 miles thick? Kimberly said: "It's a comparison. It's a comparison. It's a comparison. This is 25,000 miles around [hand encircles the globe] and this is 62 miles high [the transparency]. It's a comparison." At this point, numerous students began speaking simultaneously, saying things like "He's taking everything and making it smaller" and "Now I'm really confused." The commotion in the room suggests that students were actively attending, but also still confused on this point, but Kimberly apparently felt he had finished his portrayal and moved on to his learning activity, with no further discussion of the relationship between the transparency draped over the globe and the 62-mile-high atmosphere.

The learning activity involved filling out a worksheet. Kimberly's approach was to lead the students through it, helping them figure out what to write in response to each question. The first question asked students to define a resource. Students seemed unclear on what to write, so Kimberly said, "Something from nature that we can use. Write it down." At this point, a student asked if the air could ever get a hole in it. Then another responded excitedly, saying, "It *does* have a hole in it!" Numerous excited voices then filled the room. Kimberly tried to quell this enthusiasm by using his hands to ask them to lower their voices and saying, "We'll get to that. We really will. (Still numerous voices) There is not, there is not a hole in it. [Still numerous voices.] MAY I HAVE YOUR ATTENTION PLEASE! Time out. Kate. Dylan. Eyes right here. [Quietly:] I asked you to write down the definition of a resource, not have a big conversation about it. Remember the definition: Something you get from nature that you can use. Write that down for me, please."

After students wrote the definition of a resource, Kimberly moved on to the second question, which asked for a definition of atmosphere. Again he gave them the definition they were to write. The room continued to be noisy as students wrote the definitions he had given them. Kimberly then circulated through the room to see what students were writing. One student hadn't written anything. He stopped at her desk and said, "Resource. Atmosphere. What is it?" The student shrugged sullenly, and Kimberly walked off to another desk without offering the student any further help. She continued to sit still, staring blankly at her paper.

Later Kimberly introduced the term "troposphere" to students, saying that it was the part of the atmosphere that was closest to us, the part "that we really use." It extended above the earth for 10–20 miles. He then asked students what they thought we got from the troposphere, and pointed to a student. The student said, "I don't know, but some of us are really confused." Instead of asking the student what was confusing, or asking how many others were confused, Kimberly didn't respond to this comment at all; he simply called on another student.

Then Kimberly went into the components of the troposphere. He handed out a circle graph with three different-sized sections marked off and asked students which one they thought represented oxygen (a guessing-game question, since he had given them no basis for answering this question). After several students offered guesses, he said oxygen was the middle-sized wedge. The largest was nitrogen, and the smallest represented inert gases, which he described. Then he said there was a very tiny slice on the chart that looked like no more than a heavy line, which had other types of gases, such as hydrogen and carbon dioxide. As students considered this news, two interesting exchanges occurred. In one exchange, a student asked about nitrogen, thinking it might be a dangerous gas. Kimberly said, "You've been breathing it for 12 years! Has it hurt you yet?" Then another student asked if nitrogen made you sleepy, if it was a sleeping gas. Kimberly said, "In that case, you'd be sleeping all the time, because you're breathing nitrogen right now." Then a third student asked if nitrogen was that stuff that makes you laugh, that the dentist gives you. Kimberly said, "There may be nitrogen in there, but it's combined with other things." The entire sequence suggests that students were confusing nitrogen with nitrous oxide, but Kimberly didn't seem to pick up on that confusion, and he didn't address their underlying concern until after several exchanges. Finally he told them that the gas used by dentists was nitrous oxide, but he said nothing more about the relationship between nitrous oxide and nitrogen.

The second exchange that followed from Kimberly's circle graph had to do with the very thin slice that contained "other gases." When he was explaining that slice, a student asked if it wouldn't contain nitrogen and oxygen as well. I had the impression that the student was having difficulty translating the slices of the pie, which separated all the gases, from the actual air, in which they are all mixed together. But Kimberly didn't respond to the student's question at all. Instead, he said that the gases in that slice accounted for less than one percent of the atmosphere and therefore the slice was too small to see on the graph.

Throughout his lesson, Kimberly encountered students who appeared to be very interested in the atmosphere, who appeared to be trying to connect this new content to things they had already heard about, and who asked several questions in an apparent effort to clarify their thinking. But in nearly every case, Kimberly either didn't respond at all to their questions, or responded in a way that didn't acknowledge their confusion and didn't help them understand the relationship between this new content and other ideas they already had.

Mr. Kimberly's interview was replete with expressions of anger and annoyance toward his students. He complained about the fact that they pierced themselves and had tattoos, that they didn't dress properly in cold weather, that they were more interested in each other than in learning. He also complained about the district and state accountability systems, which forced him to teach very specific content according to very specific schedules. Kimberly perceived his students as undisciplined, their parents as uncaring, and the district as too demanding. He felt he was trapped between a community that didn't really care about education and a district that expected too much. He resented all parties for putting him in an untenable situation. When we asked about his interactions with students during the lesson, Kimberly interpreted the noise level as evidence that students were *not* interested in this content. And when we asked about the students who asked him about nitrogen, he averred that they really knew the answers but were purposely trying to goad him. With respect to another confused student, he said that it was hard to spend time with one confused student when the rest of the class was not confused. He also said that if a student really wanted to learn, he should be willing to stay in during recess to ask his questions, for then Kimberly would have time to respond.

Universal Access Is Threatened

One of the ways in which reformers pursue the ideal of universal access to knowledge is to recommend that classroom instruction not be organized in a way that favors some students over others. In fact most practices that threaten universal access occur *outside* classrooms, as when students are placed in "tracks" that receive different amounts of content and different opportunities for intellectual engagement, or when schools serving different communities impose different standards on the teachers they hire. Within classrooms, there are two ways in which universal access may be threatened: teachers can group students and then offer different curricula to each group, or they can call upon some students and ignore others. When reformers see students grouped according to ability, they worry that students in the lower groups will be taught less. They also worry that teachers may call mostly on boys, on whites, or on the smarter students, leaving others less engaged.

In their interviews, teachers discussed 27 classroom participation routines—that is, practices involving either grouping or calling on students. When teachers divided their students into groups, they used a wide range of strategies, but in only three cases did they divide them according to ability. Some used games that led to random arrangements, some used odd principles such as grouping students by birth order, and some let students sit with their friends. Many teachers rearranged their groupings regularly, believing that it was good for students to learn to work with different people. Most of these strategies were not designed to facilitate different instruction or different curricular goals for each group, but were simply ways of dividing the entire class into smaller units, each of which participated equally in the entire lesson. Ms. Aires divided her students into three groups so that they could rotate among three separate learning activities, but the lesson was designed so that each group eventually participated in each activity. She called her learning activities "rotations." Aires said she did this in part because it provided a way for her to work with one small group at a time and to assess their progress. We also noticed, though, that one of the learning activities involved listening to a book-tape while reading the book itself, and the room contained about eight headsets for this activity; so some sort of grouping was necessary anyway for students to use this technology. Similarly, when Ms. Fosnot had students measure paper beds for a queen, she formed the students into groups, with each group working together to measure out their bed; but all groups did the same activity. This tendency to form the class into smaller groups in order to engage in particular learning activities was very widespread, but we saw no evidence that the groups were treated differently or that they received different instruction.

Two of the three examples of ability grouping occurred in a district that required ability grouping for a particular school subject in which the curriculum was designed to allow students to move at their own pace. The third example appeared to reflect a decision by the teacher. This was Ms. Taswell, who argued that her grouping practice put less pressure on her low achievers and was less intimidating for them. However, at one point in the interview she also conceded that she had less interest in teaching her low-achieving students.

In observing how teachers called on students, we routinely watched for biases and found no evidence of teachers favoring boys, girls, whites, blacks, or Hispanics. Many teachers had devised methods for calling on students that would ensure universal participation. Several put students' names on popsicle sticks and drew a stick from a jar to determine which student they would call on after each question. Others called on students whose hands were raised but often announced that they were seeking a student who hadn't talked yet.

More of a concern to reformers might be the handful of teachers who called on students whom they expected to give a correct answer. This approach could ultimately exclude some students from active participation in the lesson and encourage them to disengage. Only two teachers said they used a selective approach to calling on students, and they accounted for this practice by saying they wanted to ensure that they got the right response so that they could proceed apace with their intended script. Both also believed that non-responding students could learn from these exchanges, even if they were not directly called upon themselves.

The interviews suggest that most teachers were greatly concerned about universal participation in their lessons. Sometimes their efforts in this area were herculean. Recall Ms. Buford, who wanted so much to keep Juan in her classroom, rather than expelling him for his tantrums, that she altered the atmosphere of the entire classroom to create a more subdued and less energized tone. Ms. Chalmers had a severely handicapped student in her classroom who could not communicate but who did make loud crying noises, almost continually, throughout the lesson. She and her other students had to raise their voices to be heard above his sounds. Neither Chalmers nor Buford indicated a belief that their special children should be removed from their classrooms. Both were committed to including everyone and maximizing their opportunities to learn.

The Parent's Criticisms

Neither the set of episodes that teachers criticized nor the set of events that reformers might criticize covers the numerous missteps or errors during the lessons that had nothing to do with teaching practices. But although the various kinds of disruptions described in Chapter 3 are not attributable to teaching practices, they are relevant to teachers because they inhibit momentum and student willingness to participate, raise teachers' anxiety levels, and can distract both teachers and students from the topic at hand. Teachers often feared that they would need to recycle back through a lot of material in order to recover from the interruptions. Interruptions are also relevant to reformers because they have the potential to reduce both attention to content and intellectual engagement. If students have vague, half-formed ideas in their heads at the time of the disruption, they may lose their understanding altogether during the interlude and thus lose contact with important content.

I tallied 19 interruptions by outsiders (people entering, telephones ringing, public-address systems) and 12 implementation problems (missing material, lesson sequences, etc.). These are conservative estimates, since I never systematically reviewed the entire set of lessons with such a tally in mind. The prevalence of these various distractions offers one clue to why teachers pay so much attention to lesson momentum. It is not easy to attain. Yet as teachers strive to accommodate regular disruptions, they may introduce practices that further reduce intellectual engagement. Ms. Taswell, for instance, knew that her first period would be interrupted several times: some students would arrive late, the tardy bell would ring, and a public address announcement would follow that. Taswell didn't like being interrupted, so she didn't start her first lesson until all these interruptions were finished. Instead, she found a way to *entertain* students in this interval. Taswell and nearly all her colleagues had settled on morning routines that postponed instruction for about 15 minutes, with the intellectual value of these interim activities varying from one classroom to the next.

Sources of Problems

I started this book by listing hypotheses that are frequently used to explain why teachers haven't responded to the reform ideals of the past century. Now, with a collection of specific problems that teachers encountered in these lessons, it is time to return to those hypotheses and see how well they account for these problems. The hypotheses were:

Teachers need more knowledge or guidance in order to alter their practices.

Teachers hold beliefs and values that differ from reformers' and that justify their current practices.

Teachers have dispositions that interfere with their ability to implement reforms.

The circumstances of teaching prevent teachers from altering their practices.

The reform ideals themselves are unreasonable or actually impede practice.

Most policy discussions assume that teachers are largely responsible for their own practices, and that the way to improve teach*ing* is to improve teach*ers.* Hence they focus more on the first three hypotheses. Yet many of the problems described in this book appear to spring from the situation itself, not from teachers' knowledge, values, or dispositions. The possibility that the reform ideals are unrealistic also needs to be considered. Discussions with the teachers suggest that they were already committing as much time and energy to their work as one could reasonably expect. They spent their evenings preparing materials for their lessons and spent their own money purchasing things they needed. They sought advice from members of their family and from others about how to solve problems they faced. These findings suggest that the job itself may be more demanding than many of us want to concede, and they give us reason to suspect that perhaps reformers want too much.

Because teachers direct activities within their classrooms, we tend to perceive them as *in charge,* and therefore to assume that whatever they do must reflect their own personal strengths or weaknesses, rather than the situation itself. This conclusion could be an example of what psychologists call *attribution error* (Nisbett and Ross, 1991). This is how attribution errors work:

Imagine that you are observing Ms. Mission's mathematics lesson on median and range. Students are looking at a distribution of family sizes that looks like this:

2, 3, 3, 4, 5, 6

and are trying to locate the *median* of this distribution. A student asks whether the median could be a "half"—that is, he wonders if the median can be $3\frac{1}{2}$ rather than either 3 or 4. In response, Ms. Mission reminds students that newspapers often refer to average families as having 2.4 children. As a reader of newspapers, you, the observer, know that newspapers are using means, not medians, for such statements. So as an observer of this classroom, you infer that Ms. Mission lacks sufficient content knowledge, for she has publicly confused median and mean. You have good reason to assume this is true, for you *saw her* make this error. But in this case, Ms. Mission nominated this episode to discuss in her interview precisely because she realized that she could have misled students by introducing something about means into a conversation about medians. She grabbed her example spontaneously, and then immediately realized that it was a bad example because it conflated means and medians. So if we attribute this teaching practice to Mission's lack of content knowledge, we are guilty of a common kind of *attribution error*. Had Mission had time to think about the student's question, she might have been able to generate a better example; but classroom lessons don't allow that time.

In the sections below, I examine evidence supporting each of these hypotheses.

Teachers Lack Knowledge or Guidance

Perhaps the most widely held hypothesis for the failure of reform is that teachers lack the full complement of content knowledge and teaching skills that they need to engage in excellent teaching. Lack of content knowledge is most often suspected, but it is also the most difficult to discern. Less than a handful of teachers in this study specifically stated that they were unsure of their content knowledge, and they weren't necessarily the same people whose performance suggested that they were unsure of the content.

Even in cases in which lack of content knowledge seems a potent source of teaching problems, it is often difficult to estimate the severity of the problem. For instance, it would be easy to conclude that Ms. Buford lacked content knowledge because we watched her directly teach her students, incorrectly, that the "process of elimination" was the correct approach for determining what day it is today. But the problem itself was not part of the regular curriculum. It was not part of the math curriculum, the language arts curriculum, or the science curriculum. Buford's "problem of the day" filled the space each morning from the time students arrived through the time her building principal gave announcements over the public-address system. Buford didn't begin the "real" curriculum until after the announcements. So her lack of content knowledge appeared in an activity that was not part of the official school curriculum and might not have appeared at all had there been no daily P.A. announcements.

There were also smaller episodes, whose significance was less clear, in which teachers demonstrated lack of content knowledge. For instance, when Ms. Mueller (grade 6 science, 3 years' experience) was teaching students about soil erosion, the term "slope" came up a lot. At one point she told students that this term was the same as the slope they had been studying in math (which was taught by another teacher); but as soon as she said this, she realized that she really didn't understand the term "slope" as it was used in mathematics and that she wasn't really sure whether her statement was true. So in this case, the teacher worried that her lack of content knowledge *in mathematics* might have caused her to mislead her students *in science.* Certainly it would be nice if she had a better understanding of slope as it is used in mathematics, but the extent to which this lack of knowledge created problems as she taught *science* is not clear.

Not surprisingly, the most difficult episodes to understand are those in which there appeared to be a lack of content knowledge, but the role of content knowledge was not discussed in the interview. For instance, in our interview with her about her lesson on believable ads for physical fitness products, Ms. Defoe indicated no concern about her lack of content knowledge, nor did she demonstrate a presence of content knowledge as she critiqued her lesson. Yet her lesson contained so many episodes in which she suppressed both important content and intellectual engagement that one wonders if she was intentionally avoiding the content because she was not knowledgeable about it. She used her question-and-answer session to ask students for examples of physical fitness products (a relatively easy topic) instead of asking for examples of evidence that would make an ad believable (a very difficult topic). In addition, in her portrayal of the content Defoe never defined believability as depending on evidence. Instead, she reminded students that ads for elixirs that make people stronger were inherently not believable because we know that people have to exercise to become stronger. Thus she offered an example of an unbelievable ad, but never offered any criteria for believability. And when Andy volunteered that he had seen an ad for an elixir that would make him stronger, and that the ad seemed believable to him, Defoe did not address his confusion. Instead, she dismissed Andy by saying, "Okay, well, we'll talk about that later, okay?" and turned her attention to William. This combination of behaviors suggests a pattern of avoiding difficult substantive issues. But in her interview, her rationales for the episodes were always related to her strong fear of distraction and her strong need to keep all her students on task. Hence her decision to dismiss Andy and focus instead on William. Still, when looking over the entire lesson, one sees a consistent avoidance of content.

Mr. Kimberly's lesson on the atmosphere could also be interpreted as reflecting a lack of content knowledge. Although his portrayal of the atmosphere did address the central concepts of the lesson, he failed numerous times to respond to student questions or comments. The sum of these interactions leads one to suspect that Kimberly didn't respond to students because he was uncertain about the content and consequently unsure what to say. But we also know from Kimberly's interview that he held very negative and resentful attitudes toward his students, so his attitudes, rather than his lack of content knowledge, could have accounted for his behavior.

Perhaps the most difficult lesson to interpret, in terms of teachers' knowledge of content, is Ms. Katlaski's lesson on fractions. Although Katlaski herself said repeatedly in the interview that she was unsure of her content knowledge, her lesson was rich in content, and she rarely suppressed important ideas. Yet her instruction was uneven and included both educative and misleading episodes. A particularly educative episode occurred during homework review. She began the review by simply reading to students the correct answers for each homework problem. Then she asked if students had questions about any of the problems. A student asked about question 4, and the conversation proceeded as follows:

> Katlaski: Number 4: Okay. "Enrico read one-fifth of a book on Saturday and one-eighth of the same book on Sunday. What portion of the book does he still have to read?" Ooooh. A little bit tricky on this one. Tell me what to put here, Ajay.
>
> Ajay: You put one-fifth minus one-eighth. And then, you have to make a—
>
> Katlaski: Okay, I have a question here. He read one-fifth of the book on Saturday. He read one-eighth of the same book on Sunday. Why are we subtracting?
>
> Ajay: Because for one thing it says, "What portion of the book has he not read??
>
> Katlaski: Sure. You're right about that. You're right. We have to subtract to find that. But isn't this how much he read on Saturday (pointing to $\frac{1}{5}$)? [Ajay nods.] And then if we take how much he read on Sunday away from it, that'd be like—What you're making me think of is saying, "Okay [she picks up a book to illustrate the portions read], I read this much of the book on Saturday [she separates out about a fifth of the book], and then on Sunday I read this much [she removes

some of the pages from Saturday's reading]. Is that what the
question is saying?

Ajay: No.

Katlaski: Okay. Let's read this question again and see what it's
saying. Okay. [Again, with the book in hand] How much did
he read on Saturday?

Ss: One-fifth.

Katlaski: This much. [She separates off about a fifth of the
pages.] Okay. How much did he read on Sunday?

Ss: One-eighth.

Katlaski: An eighth. [She separates off a few more pages.] Okay.
Now how much has he read so far? Someone show me the
equation that would tell me how much he has read so far.
Josh?

Josh: One-fifth plus one-eighth.

Katlaski: [Merging the two sections of the book] Okay. Can you
see how we've put it together? [Students nod.] Good. And
then you're in the middle of the next step. Because guess
what, guys? This is a multistep problem. You can't just do it
with one and be done. When we find the answer to this,
what's it going to tell us?

Katlaski's teaching style was relatively direct. She walked her students
through the problem step by step. She didn't skip over the central
idea, as Defoe did during her instruction on believable ads. And she
didn't avoid students' confusions, as Mr. Kimberly did. In this episode, she quickly perceived the nature of the students' confusion and
used a book to enact the story problem physically, holding up successively a fifth of the pages and an eighth of the pages.

But in other portions of the lesson, Katlaski had difficulty explaining concepts to her students. After the homework review, she introduced the day's topic, which was multiplying by fractions. In her introduction, she seemed to circle around the concept itself, apparently
unable to articulate it clearly, but repeatedly telling students that it
was a hard concept to get.

Katlaski: Most of you are not familiar with multiplying and dividing fractions. This is a—it's not that it's such a challenging math process, but the concept, getting it in your head, is a little bit harder. So even though normally I don't make you worry about the diagrams, and that kind of stuff, normally you have a good enough foundation for understanding that kind of stuff, we're going to be doing a little bit of that today. I'm going to have to ask you for your patience, because you're probably not going to want to spend a lot of time on this. But we're just going to spend a little bit on it to get it into your head, the idea of multiplying with fractions. . . .

　We're going to be spending our next chapter multiplying and dividing fractions. You're very familiar with multiplying and dividing. That's fine. It's a little bit different when you do it with fractions, and here's why. Let's take a look at this problem, it's a pretty good illustration of why it's a different ball game. Once you adjust your brain to how multiplying fractions works, you're not going to have any trouble. You just need to get yourself a good picture.

　I think one of the hardest parts to multiplying fractions is to estimate if you're correct or not, you know, to do your "about" answer, to doublecheck your work. Because until you get the general idea through to your brain, it throws you off a little bit.

Katlaski never did actually tell students what would happen when they multiplied two fractions. Instead, she went directly into a story problem from the text that was intended to illustrate the process. But as she walked her students through a diagrammatic representation of the story problem, she failed to point out to students what the mathematical process was that they were doing. The italicized text below signals the place where one might have expected her to give a pithy summary of what it means to multiply with fractions.

Katlaski: Okay, a little bit of a story problem here. "Marcus had a dozen cookies. He took six to school in his lunch. He gave a third of those cookies with his friend. What part of the dozen cookies did he share with his friend?" We're going to illustrate this problem. What do I draw first? Where do I start, Elizabeth?

Elizabeth: Twelve circles.

Katlaski: Twelve circles. Okay, and then, he took six of them to school. How am I going to represent that up here?

Students: Cross off six cookies.

Katlaski: Okay. So these are the at-home cookies [pointing to the crossed-off circles], maybe his sister ate them, and these are the school cookies [pointing to the six circles not crossed off]. And the, when he got to school, he shared a third of his cookies with a friend. Christie. How am I going to represent that?

Christie: Divide the six cookies three ways, like every second cookie has a line after it. [She is suggesting that the teacher draw vertical lines to separate the row of six cookies into three groups of two].

Katlaski: Okay, so how many cookies did he give to his friend?

Students: Two.

Katlaski: Two. All right. "What part of the dozen cookies did he share with his friend?" Here's where it gets a little hard. We can say two cookies really easily, but now we want to say it as a fraction. And not just a fraction of the cookies he took to school, a fraction of all the cookies he started with. So take into account aaaall the circles that you see. Sam?

Sam: *Two — twelfths* or one-sixth.

Katlaski: *Two — twelfths* or one-sixth. If you agree, give him a big thumbs-up. [Continuing] *Now, if we were to say . . . Well, let's just go on to a different one. See, here's the thing. When you're multiplying with fractions, it might throw your brain off a little bit to begin with because, when you're multiplying typically, do you end up with a smaller or a larger number?*

Ss: Larger.

Katlaski: Usually larger. When you're multiplying with fractions,

we're going to take a look and see, do we end up with a
smaller number or a larger number? That's the big thing
we're hitting here in the next few minutes. Because it throws
your brain off if you let it.

In this sequence, Ms. Katlaski worked out the problem together with
the students, but at the end she failed to articulate what this problem
had to do with multiplication with fractions. Students could have responded to all her questions, gone through all the steps, and not real-
ized that they had just multiplied two fractions, $\frac{1}{2}$ and $\frac{1}{3}$, to arrive at
the final result of $\frac{1}{6}$. Katlaski knew that students could easily be confused when multiplying fractions, yet couldn't seem to find a way to
explain to them what was happening during this process and why the
numbers worked out as they did. In her interview, she repeatedly said
that she didn't have a very good grasp of the content.

Katlaski also rejected a legitimate student idea during this portion
of the lesson. This occurred when she introduced the problem of
multiplying fractions with whole numbers. Her sample problem involved the number 9, and Katlaski wanted to show students that they
could convert 9 into a fraction by simply putting a 1 under it, like
this: 9/1. Instead of just demonstrating this strategy, she posed the
question to her students: "How can we make this 9 into a fraction?"
and a student responded that they could multiply it by 4/4. Katlaski
rejected this idea. In the interview, she conceded that she rejected the
student's idea partly because she was "looking for" 9/1, but also
partly because she wasn't sure the student's idea would work. By the
time of the interview, she had thought it through and was sure it
would work, but in the moment of the lesson, she couldn't think fast
enough to respond appropriately. Hence a lack of content knowledge
led to rejecting a plausible idea from a student.

Katlaski is an unusual case for two reasons. First, she devoted far
more interview time to criticizing her own content knowledge than
did any other teacher. And yet, despite her substantive difficulties,
her lesson was very densely filled with subject matter and was more
content-rich than many other lessons. She offers a particularly im-

portant contrast to Ms. Defoe, whose lesson on believable ads omitted any discussion of the concept of believability; and to Mr. Kimberly, whose portrayal of the troposphere suggested that he may have understood the content but that he was unwilling to share that content with students.

Altogether there are eight episodes that could reflect lack of knowledge of content:

> 1 portrayal that suppressed content (Defoe's lesson on believable ads)

> 2 Q&A routines in which a teacher dismissed students who needed help (Defoe of Andy; Kimberly of many students)

> 1 Q&A episode in which a teacher rejected a student idea that was plausible (Katlaski's student's proposal to convert 9 by multiplying it by 4/4)

> 1 Q&A routine in which a teacher accepted an idea that was not plausible (Ms. Scott, to the student who suggested that dinosaurs didn't have ears)

> 1 portrayal in which the teacher explicitly taught a wrong idea to students (Buford's problem of the day)

> 1 portrayal in which the teacher used a metaphor that she was unsure of (Ms. Mueller's reference to slope in geology versus a slope in math)

Teachers Hold Beliefs and Values That Differ from Reformers'

The second hypothesis used to account for the failure of reform is that teachers hold different beliefs and values from reformers' and strive toward different ends. Chapter 2, which describes teachers' intentions for their practices, provides ample evidence that their concerns are different from those of reformers. One difference is that teachers are concerned about a broader range of issues than reformers are. In addition to thinking about reformers' ideals, teachers think about the classroom as a community, their own personal needs, student willingness to participate, and lesson momentum. All of these are important aspects of instruction, though they receive less attention from reformers. In addition, even within a given area of concern, teachers' intentions are often slightly different from reformers'. Whereas reformers want intellectual engagement, teachers frequently settle for any kind of engagement. Consequently they may seek activities that are fun instead of intellectually engaging. And instead of thinking about universal access to knowledge, they think about universal *participation* in classroom activities and conversations, a difference that could lead them to focus more on activity than on learning itself.

Another difference lies in the relative importance attributed to different areas of concern. Whereas reformers place intellectual engagement high on their list, I found many cases in which teachers didn't want a high level of engagement because that led to more off-script comments, which made it harder to keep the lesson on its intended course. Teachers in this study appeared to seek an optimal level of student engagement that was not too low but also not too high—certainly not the value that reformers embrace.

This discrepancy again raises the possibility of attribution errors. Reformers who are persuaded that the key to reform is to increase teachers' knowledge are likely to interpret teachers' reluctance to engage students as evidence that they lack the *knowledge* needed to manage high engagement. They might argue that if teachers had a deeper knowledge of content or knew better ways of managing discussions, they would be less fearful of high intellectual engagement in their classrooms. Perhaps. Yet there were many episodes in this study in which teachers had substantial content knowledge but still didn't know how to respond to student ideas. One occurred in Ms. Toklisch's class when she introduced the problem of how to find the area of a circle. In response to the problem Toklisch presented, one of her students presented a complicated solution that was correct but was also beyond the grasp of most other students. Toklisch was astonished. She understood the student's idea completely, but also knew that none of the other students would understand it. In her interview, she indicated that this approach to estimating the area of a circle didn't normally come up until after several lessons on circles. So the problem Toklisch faced was not how to respond to an idea she wasn't sure of; it was how to respond to one student whose ideas were vastly different from those of all the others. And of course her response had to be immediate. More knowledge might have given her more hypotheses or proposals to consider, but it would not have made the decision itself any easier. When teachers seek to contain student engagement, the reason is not necessarily that they themselves are uncomfortable with the content. It is frequently because they can't respond to the disparities among the different ideas students offer and also keep all the students involved in a single conversation.

This difference between teachers and reformers in the perceived value of intellectual engagement is the most prominent example of a difference in values between reformers and teachers.

There were also many cases in which differences in beliefs were apparent. For instance, Ms. Lachamy held several beliefs about writing and learning to write that may have interfered with her ability to respond to reform ideals. She had specific criteria for paragraphs: they must contain one topic sentence, three supporting details, and a summary sentence. She also had a theory of learning that motivated her to have students write these different kinds of sentences on different colors of paper. Lachamy wanted her students literally to see the different parts of the paragraph by having one category of sentence appear on pink paper and another category of sentence appear on green paper. But the procedure of creating these multicolored paragraphs was so complicated that everyone's attention was diverted from the content to the procedure. So Lachamy's beliefs led to a lesson that was quite different from the kinds of lessons envisioned by reformers.

Teachers' theories about how to promote student learning and how to promote student willingness to participate also came up frequently in interviews. For example, Ms. Bowes explained her use of many different learning activities to study symmetry by saying that students need to see, feel, and touch, and that they need as many different examples as possible. In her case, her theory of student learning increased both the content saturation of the lesson and students' intellectual engagement. On the other side, Mr. Awles's ideas about how students learn hindered their opportunities to interact with content. Awles curtailed discussions of content because he believed they never went anywhere and were a waste of time. Awles also devised a nearly content-free learning activity, asking students to draw a cross-sectional view of the ocean, one line at a time, with no apparent purpose for the exercise. He believed that students were too insecure to work on large projects and that they needed step-by-step directions on what to do. When we pointed out that his students still had numerous questions about this task, and thus still exhibited insecurity, Awles concluded that he should have broken the work into even tinier pieces. His combination of beliefs led to a lesson about the ocean that replaced the content with a set of procedures for drawing and coloring.

Throughout our interviews, teachers offered a wide range of theories of student learning and student motivation. Many of these were well outside the range of plausible psychological theory. One teacher used a principle of compatible birth orders to group his students, for instance, a strategy that had no support in learning theory but that also didn't appear to have any harmful effects on students. Another teacher formed groups by giving students problems that couldn't be solved. On the day we visited, she told students to form groups that had the same number of people as there were fingers on a hand. Students became confused, not knowing whether the thumb counted as a finger. As they argued among themselves about what to do, she grinned at the dilemma she had created. In the interview, she said that ambiguous problems taught students how to work with one another to solve problems. She regrouped students every day, each time using a different problem to form the groups. There didn't appear to be any instructional harm in these episodes, but they did take time away from more substantive instructional activities.

Although it isn't possible to specify their exact number, it is possible to identify episodes that could be accounted for by the beliefs-and-values hypothesis. They fall into two broad categories:

> Numerous cases in which concern about lesson momentum and the prevention of distractions took precedence over intellectual engagement

> Several cases in which theories of student learning or student motivation led to learning activities that focused attention on procedures instead of on content

Teachers have Dispositions That Interfere with Their Ability to Implement Reforms

Dispositions differ from beliefs and values in important ways. Psychologists generally use the terms "beliefs" and "values" to refer to ideas that are acquired through experience, and use the term "dispositions" to refer to behavioral or emotional tendencies that appear to be more biologically based. People have dispositions toward introversion or extroversion, for instance, and toward flexibility or rigidity. Dispositions are harder to infer from observation, because all of us are sometimes flexible and sometimes rigid, depending on the situation. The only way to be sure a person has a disposition toward, say, flexibility is to see him tilting in that direction in numerous situations. But we have only one situation, one lesson, for each teacher; so it is more difficult to tell whether the observed behavior represents a continuing disposition or whether it is simply a response to a particular situation. It is somewhat easier to infer that one's beliefs or knowledge influences the behavior we observe, because we can argue that the person wouldn't have done something if he didn't know how or believe it was important. And in the case of this study, teachers often outlined their knowledge, beliefs, or values to justify their actions.

Even with this caveat, there were some lessons and episodes that appeared to result from dispositions more than from the situation itself. Three dispositions were particularly salient: a disposition toward disorganization, a disposition toward rigidity, and a disposition toward hostility.

Disposition toward Disorganization

Many instances of disorganization and disorientation were associated with specific classroom circumstances—for instance, with the use of complicated props, with off-script students, and with teachers' work schedules. These circumstances reflect school policies and organizational norms. But some teachers seemed to have a pronounced disposition toward disorganization. For instance, Ms. Masters' lesson on chemical and physical changes was disorganized from the beginning, when she projected overhead transparencies onto wall posters, to the end, when she failed to guide students through their interpretation of their experiments. In fact when we called Ms. Masters the evening before our visit, to confirm the time, she still hadn't decided what she would be teaching the next day. Ms. Todd also demonstrated a variety of problems that seemed to fit a general pattern of poor planning. In her lesson on metric conversions, students were to learn the relationships between meters, centimeters, and millimeters, between grams and kilograms, between liters and kiloliters, and so forth. In her interview Todd said that this was very difficult material for students to learn, and she acknowledged that she was nearly always dissatisfied with her success when teaching it. She also indicated repeatedly that she was dissatisfied with this particular lesson, and discouraged that the students seemed not to grasp the central idea. Yet several of her problems resulted from her own lack of planning. First, she had skipped some earlier chapters in the textbook that would have helped students with this content, in particular a unit on dividing with decimals, and didn't realize until she began this lesson that students needed that background in order to understand relationships among the metric units. Then, as she moved through the lesson itself, she introduced the metric units out of sequence. She had intended to begin with the largest units (kilos) and work through to the smallest (millis) so that students would see these units in relationship to one another. But in the moment, she introduced the terms out of sequence, and then, when she saw her students' notebooks, she realized they had entered the units into their notebooks out of order and that this sequence could later confuse them. Finally, in her discussions with students, she regularly switched from one unit to another. She might say, for instance, 10 milliliters, but write 10 mc on the board. Or she might be discussing meters and suddenly switch to liters. It is not clear how serious this third problem was, since students did the same thing in their own sentences and no one seemed confused by these switches.

Ms. Todd herself brought up all these problems. When she explained the sequencing problem, she put it this way: "I had not thought about doing this particular—having them write it out that way. Therefore, when I just started being spontaneous, it didn't come out right. And that often happens. I'm very spontaneous in the classroom. I have things planned out, but then we go in a different direction, and it may or may not work." Later in the interview, she returned to the issue of planning versus spontaneity and said, "I think some people are natural teachers and some are not, and I think I am a natural teacher. *I don't think a lot about what I do.* I just do it, and realize afterward that 'This was a pretty good way to do that.' And I'm pretty spontaneous in the classroom."

Todd was a conscientious teacher and seemed to want her students to learn this content. And her students didn't seem as lost or confused as she feared. Still, her preference to do things spontaneously and her belief that she was a "natural teacher" suggest that her teaching might suffer from her lack of organization and self-discipline.

Disposition toward Rigidity

Another disposition that created problems for teachers was a tendency to cling too closely to their envisioned script, disallowing any deviations from it. This rigidity sometimes caused teachers to reject student ideas that were plausible because the student didn't use the exact phrase the teacher had expected. In fact teachers often said, both in their interviews and to their students, that a student's response wasn't what they were "looking for." Some of these episodes are described in Chapter 4 as examples of ways in which teachers suppressed intellectual engagement or important content.

From the teacher's point of view, there are advantages to sticking closely to the script. Certainly this practice helps teachers maintain their momentum and avoid distractions; it no doubt also protects teachers from the uncertainties that are created when students offer unexpected ideas, and it gives them a way to respond to these that doesn't require them actually to think through, in the moment, the plausibility of each sentence students utter.

Frequently associated with the disposition toward rigidity are a disposition toward anxiety in the face of distractions and a fear of their potential to disrupt lesson momentum. These anxieties and fears were so widespread that I am inclined to attribute them to another hypothesis, the circumstances of teaching, rather than to the people who happened to become teachers. Still, there were variations among these teachers. Some seemed to overcome their anxiety and remained calm in the face of unexpected events. For instance, instead of being nervous or worried when a student generated a wrong idea just as the bell rang, Ms. Mission reasoned that if one student was confused, probably others were as well, so it made sense to stick with the issue until it was resolved. And instead of worrying that her students would become bored and restless if they spent too long on one idea, Ms. Bowes taught one of the longest lessons we observed, with every single learning activity focused squarely on the concept of symmetry.

Disposition toward Hostility

Occasionally it appeared that teachers had such hostility or negative attitudes toward their students that they failed to respond to students' questions and confusions. It is possible, for example, that a negative attitude led Ms. Taswell to group her students by ability, for when she accounted for this practice, she said that the lower-ability students were more tedious to teach than the upper-ability students, and she conceded that she probably didn't spend as much time with them as she spent with other groups.

Mr. Kimberly displayed the most extreme hostility. He was persistent in his cynicism, his disgruntlement, and his criticisms of his own students. In his interview he attributed his cynicism to the circumstances of his teaching—to district pressure to increase student achievement in the face of a community uninterested in educational pursuits. But other teachers faced similar circumstances and did not respond as he did.

In all, there were 3 teachers whose entire lessons could be accounted for by the dispositions hypothesis, and several other episodes that also appeared to reflect teachers' dispositions:

> *Disposition toward disorganization:* 3 teachers changed the sequence of their lessons only to discover that this new sequence didn't work; 2 teachers had entirely disorganized lessons.

> *Disposition toward rigidity:* 2 teachers accepted student ideas that were not quite right; 6 teachers rejected student ideas that were legitimate; 4 teachers dismissed legitimate student ideas or questions. Many of the teachers who suppressed student engagement may also fall into this category.

> *Hostility and negative attitudes toward students:* 1 teacher formed an ability grouping because she wasn't interested in teaching the low group; 1 teacher failed repeatedly to respond to legitimate student questions and confusions.

The Circumstances of Teaching

The fourth hypothesis often used to explain why teachers do not respond to reform ideals is that the circumstances of teaching are responsible for the teaching practices we observe. Certainly one important circumstance is the students themselves. Although we assume that teachers should be able to manage students, students create problems for teachers even in the best-run classrooms. Another circumstance is the props and materials teachers rely on. Another consists of the institutional rules and organizational norms that govern schools. Institutions establish the context in which teachers work, and they can make that context more or less tranquil and more or less supportive of instruction. Many of the distractions teachers experienced were condoned by institutional norms, and some were even side effects of well-intentioned reforms. Finally, the circumstances of teaching include broad social values and norms, which may not foster ideal teaching practices.

The Students Themselves

Students present a challenging combination of qualities for teachers to manage. Most of the time, they are enthusiastic participants in lessons. But they are also novices at thinking about the topic at hand, so their thinking is highly likely to move in unexpected directions as they struggle to grasp new ideas. Moreover, since there are many of them in any one classroom, the possibilities for conversations to veer off course are endless. Each such digression creates a dilemma for the teacher: if she attends to this student's idea, she may lose the attention of other students; if she tries to maintain the attention of all the rest, she may inadvertently dismiss this student's idea, thus discouraging him or her from further engagement.

Students can quickly become bored and distracted. Therefore, off-task behaviors—most of which are relatively minor—are also virtually guaranteed. Even the quietest rooms contain a lot of dropped pencils, chairs scraping the floor, meanderings about the room, and small whispers here and there. Noisier rooms simply magnify these rumblings. Against this backdrop of general turmoil, however, appear episodes of a larger magnitude, as when two Asian boys and a black boy in Ms. Rollins' lesson became enmeshed in a contest of racial slurs and epithets that persisted throughout the lesson and were an important aspect of every episode discussed in the subsequent interview.

So students can disrupt lessons in two very different ways: when they are enthusiastic, they disrupt lessons by offering partially formed ideas that have the potential to move the conversation in an unintended direction; and when they are bored, they disrupt by teasing their neighbors. Teachers cited 66 episodes involving student-initiated questions or ideas, far more than they cited for any other type of episode. They named very few *behavioral* distractions, even though we could see far more of these occurring in the classrooms. There is no reasonable way to tally disruptive student moves, for students are constantly moving, shuffling, and shifting, and which shuffles count as distractions depends heavily on the teacher's tolerance level.

The fact that teaching often consists in trying to maintain a single conversation with as many as 20 or 30 youngsters practically guarantees that it will slip off course many times during any given lesson, even in the best of circumstances. Teachers differed in how they interpreted and responded to these episodes. Some student comments or questions created tremendous stress for teachers, while others were deftly handled. When students made mistakes in Ms. Jibson's class, she felt embarrassment for the student and also felt compelled to scurry past the error, to cover up the embarrassment as quickly as possible. But when students made mistakes in Ms. Mission's class, Mission assumed that if one student was confused, others were as well; instead of skipping quickly past the error, she dwelled on the confusion until it was straightened out. Regardless of the degree of anxiety they create, student-initiated episodes substantially complicate the process of teaching and require teachers to develop adaptive strategies that may not be consistent with reform ideals.

Teaching Materials and Props

Every single lesson we observed depended heavily on props. Teachers had charts, graphs, and bulletin-board displays all over their walls and regularly referred students to them ("Remember last week when we learned the five ways of . . .?") They used overhead transparencies, homemade pictures and posters, and numerous physical models. Walls were covered with posters and charts, and the teachers had others materials gathered at the front of the room. They often moved quickly back and forth among these many displays. In addition, they had numerous materials for their students to use. Ms. Toklisch had a collection of more than 100 disks—pie tins, Frisbees, coffee-can lids, jar lids of all sorts—that students could use to measure circumferences and diameters of circles. Ms. Bowes had a large set of cut-out shapes, all laminated in plastic, that students could use to find lines of symmetry. Ms. Lachamy had cut up dozens of green and pink strips of paper for her students to use to write their topic sentences and supporting details, and Ms. Fosnot had brought in large sheets of brown packaging paper for her students to use to measure out beds for a queen. Props were everywhere.

Two points can be made about these props with respect to problems in teaching. First, even though institutions can provide such props, and even though some do provide them, most of the props we saw were homemade and appeared to be lesson-specific. To show students how thin the atmosphere was, Mr. Kimberly had cut darts into an overhead transparency so that it would curve over the globe as the atmosphere curves over the Earth. And to show them how much of the troposphere consisted of various kinds of gases, he used a spreadsheet program to create a pie chart and then printed copies for everyone. In their interviews teachers never mentioned that they shared materials with other teachers or that the school provided them. Nor did they indicate that they ever discussed the relative value of these materials with their colleagues. It looked as if each teacher created, each day, and all alone, all the materials that he or she planned to use.

Second, props often didn't help. That is, either the props themselves contained problems so that their message was unclear, or they added so much complexity to the lesson that they increased both teachers' and students' confusion. The use of lesson props was a prominent feature in teachers' self-criticisms of their practices. In some cases the props themselves were faulty, in some cases the teacher misused them, and in some cases the teacher wished in retrospect that she had used different props. In *every* case of self-criticism about portrayals, props played an important role in the portrayal and in the teacher's dissatisfactions with it.

Institutional Policies and Organizational Norms
Teachers work in bureaucratic institutions whose policies and organizational norms can be more or less supportive of their work. We found many teachers who seemed overwhelmed, as if they were

rushing from one thing to another and didn't have time to organize their materials or their thoughts. We heard numerous accounts of teachers misplacing or forgetting to bring important props for their lessons. One teacher made a handout and left it at home on the kitchen table. Another left her handout in another teacher's classroom. Another began her lesson feeling disorganized because she had just finished hall duty and had no time to compose herself or her thoughts. The sum of these episodes gives the impression that teachers do not have tranquil environments in which to work.

It is easy to think of teaching as a process of simply following the textbook and explaining each new concept as it appears, so that no time is really needed to plan a lesson. But each lesson is itself a complicated orchestration of portrayals, learning activities, and Q&A routines, all of which involve students, a schedule, the distribution and collection of materials, and so forth. Even if a particular portrayal or learning activity has been used before, it may not have been used for a year, and memories of how it worked last year may now be vague. Teachers also typically teach many lessons each day, and in addition have responsibilities for overseeing students in the hallways, in the lunchroom, or on the playground before school and during school breaks. When they have free time, they must read student papers or update gradebooks, meet with colleagues, meet with parents, and plan five or six lessons. So it should not be surprising that they are sometimes forgetful or that their lessons are not smoothly orchestrated or conceptually coherent.

Moreover, each lesson involves complex content that students can easily misunderstand. It needs to be thought about, and teachers, as well as students, need to immerse themselves in it. No teacher can anticipate every issue that may arise during a lesson, but they would certainly be better able to respond to these issues if they were fully immersed in the content themselves instead of having to rush into it from some unrelated places with unrelated problems.

I did not directly study the institutions in which these teachers taught, so the only evidence I have of institutional influence is its explicit presence inside the classroom. During these 45 lessons we observed P.A. announcements, telephone calls, unannounced visitors, and students who came and went in midlesson, all occurring with the tacit approval of the school administration. Several schools had devised policies that increased, rather than decreased, the number of interruptions teachers experienced. One school had an in-house suspension policy that allowed any teacher with a mischievous child to take that child to another teacher's classroom. Another had a variety of extracurricular classes, called "specials," and encouraged students to enroll individually for these. The result was that teachers routinely had to adjust their lessons as students came and went in midlesson. Another school had both P.A. announcements and tardy bells every morning. Schools that provided teachers with telephones apparently did not also provide them with answering machines, and teachers routinely answered calls they received midlesson. Each of these policies left a visible residue in the lessons we observed.

The Broader Social Context of Teaching

Willard Waller (1932/1961) first suggested that the activity of teaching itself creates the kinds of personalities we observed in teachers. He argued that the job requires teachers to maintain both dignity and social control and to speak seriously to children about childish things. In their efforts to control students, teachers lay down a number of rules, but children strive to empty these rules of their meaning, either by mechanizing them or by ridiculing them. Waller maintained that teachers learn to adapt to this milieu, so that both their personalities and their practices reflect it.

In the mid-1970s another sociologist (Lortie, 1975) listed several features of teachers' work that discourage a rigorous approach to the work. For instance, he noted that there is virtually no induction into teaching. Teachers become fully responsible for their own classrooms just a few months after they finish being students themselves. The transition is sudden and forces teachers to rely on spontaneous ideas, thus reinforcing in them the notion that teaching is idiosyncratic and depends heavily on "personal style." Lortie also pointed out that teaching is a careerless profession, in that the teacher's work is virtually the same after 30 years as it was in the first year. This, he argued, leads to a perception of the work as more like an avocation than a profession. It is something that people come to, leave, and return to at will, not something they invest in, think hard about, or strive to improve. Finally, Lortie pointed out that the act of teaching itself is fraught with ambiguities. It is very difficult to know at any given point whether students are really understanding the issue at hand. Teachers regularly experience situations in which students seemed to "get it" yesterday but to have lost it entirely today. And they encounter situations in which students appear to spontaneously and miraculously "get it." The uncertainties inherent in teaching and learning motivate teachers to seek more easily attainable goals, learning outcomes they know they can achieve. Hence they may aim simply to move through the textbook rather than to ensure that students are mastering difficult ideas.

These authors have made a compelling case for the role of the broader social context of teaching in fostering a relatively banal approach to practices. If they are correct, many of the beliefs, values, and dispositions outlined above may actually derive from the circumstance of teaching rather than from the inside teachers themselves.

I found at least 125 episodes that could be accounted for by the circumstances-of-teaching hypothesis. The following list summarizes these episodes by each condition.

The students themselves

92 episodes in which students presented conceptual problems or non sequiturs that had the potential to disrupt momentum

28 episodes in which student misbehavior (talking, teasing, fighting) threatened synchronized thought

5 episodes in which classroom discussions produced spontaneous confusions that caused teachers to misspeak as they tried to respond to events

Lesson materials and props

2 episodes in which teachers didn't have enough handouts and had to make adjustments

2 episodes in which the props contained errors themselves or were misleading in some way

3 episodes in which props were so complicated that they made
the lesson difficult to organize, and other problems followed
from that

2 episodes in which the learning activity required students to
make their own materials, and that procedure overshadowed
the substance of the lesson

Institutional policies and organizational norms

4 episodes in which teachers forgot to bring needed materials

5 episodes in which outsiders entered classes when lessons were
under way

5 episodes in which outsiders called the teacher on the telephone

Numerous students entering or leaving classrooms in midlesson

3 P.A. announcements

1 episode in which a severely handicapped child was placed in a
regular classroom and cried out loudly throughout the lesson

Broader social context of teaching

A wide range of practices that could reflect teachers' assumptions about their social role more than their assumptions
about how to teach or how students learn

Reform Ideals Are Unreachable

The final hypothesis put forward in Chapter 1 is that teachers' apparent failures to respond to reform ideals are due not to teachers'
knowledge, their beliefs or values, their dispositions, or even the circumstances of teaching, but to flaws within the ideals themselves. Reformers are idealists, after all, and they may hold a vision of teaching
that is simply unreachable.

There are three reasons to believe that the ideals themselves may
be unrealistic. One is that the kind of teaching that reformers seek
may entail more time and energy than teachers actually have. As it is,
even to produce the teaching practices we saw in these lessons, teachers routinely worked at home in the evenings, used their own money
to purchase supplies, and solicited help from friends and spouses to
prepare the lessons we observed. They often sought out professional

development courses on their own and paid the required tuition with their own money. Perhaps teachers simply have no more time or energy to devote to meeting reform ideals. Other studies of reform have suggested that this might be the case. For instance, David Tyack and Larry Cuban (1995) suggested that one major reform, the eight-year study, exhausted participating teachers, and that when the official initiative was over the teachers returned to their previous practices instead of retaining the new ones. Michael Huberman (1994), too, found that teachers were uninterested in reform, either because they disagreed with the reform's intent or because they had been involved in, disappointed by, and tired by an earlier reform initiative.

Another reason to look with skepticism at the ideals themselves is that there are times when they cannot all be attained simultaneously. We saw in Chapter 2, for instance, how Ms. Buford responded to an emotionally volatile student in her classroom. She was committed to the third reform ideal, universal access to knowledge, but to attain it she had to compromise the second ideal, intellectual engagement. She adopted a very low-key, monotonous tone in her instruction and discouraged students from participating actively in the lesson.

Yet another reason to suspect that the ideals are not realistic is that they conflict with other areas of concern that teachers think about but that reformers tend not to think about. For example, teachers tend to suppress intellectual engagement because they know that they must maintain lesson momentum and cover as much content as possible. Reformers have idealized visions of intellectually stimulating lessons, but they tend not to address the difficult trade-off between intellectual engagement and content coverage. Ms. Toklisch, whose Q&A sessions looked closer to the reform ideals than most of the Q&A sessions we observed, said that the first year she adopted this approach she managed to get through only one-third of her textbook. And in fact on the day we observed her class, we saw her suddenly change topics in a moment of panic when she realized that the class discussion was not leading to an orderly conclusion and that other topics also had to be covered during the lesson.

Finally, we may be skeptical of the reformers' ideals simply because the sum of all hindrances to ideal teaching, represented by all the hypotheses reviewed here, renders the ideal too difficult to reach. Even if the ideals themselves were feasible in principle, they could not be attained unless (a) teachers' knowledge was enhanced, (b) their beliefs, values, and dispositions were changed, and (c) the circumstances of teaching were substantially altered. But these aspects of teaching may themselves be linked to larger features of society in such a way that they are not very changeable. To the extent that teachers' beliefs and values reflect those of society more broadly, and to the extent that the circumstances of teaching have been created by society as well, then teaching practices also reflect society as a whole. If any of these conditions obtain, then the circumstances of teaching that hinder progress toward reform ideals are so intertwined with society as a whole that reformers cannot alter them.

Implications for Reform

The episodes examined in this chapter demonstrate the myriad ways in which things can go awry as teachers try to portray content and organize learning activities, manage question-and-answer sessions, respond to unexpected student ideas, and sustain a set of classroom rules and routines. The sheer difficulty of engaging all students intellectually and ensuring that they have access to important content raises the possibility that reformers may expect too much from teachers. In some cases, well-intentioned reformers actually make things worse: in their efforts to solve one problem, they create others. This was the case in Ms. Masters' lesson: she was seduced by the possibilities of having her students participate in a nationwide data collection effort, offered by a well-intentioned independent group that wanted to contribute to reform. But in order to participate she had to abandon her unit on physical change and chemical change, and that decision created other problems later on.

Teachers' tendencies to create overly complicated learning activities probably also derive from reform rhetoric. I suspect that some of the more complicated lessons we saw were designed for our benefit. That is, teachers knew they would have a visitor in their classrooms and may have taken on more complicated projects than they normally would have, because they believed this was the kind of classroom work that outsiders like to see. Reforms nearly always advocate relatively complex classroom activities, involving physical demonstrations, laboratory experiments, manipulatives in mathematics, and so forth. Yet the more complicated the lesson, and the more props on which it depends, the more chances there are for something to go wrong.

Each hypothesis for why reforms fail can account for some of the problems we saw. Sometimes teachers didn't know their content very well, and sometimes teachers' dispositions created problems for them. Often their own beliefs and values differed from reformers' ideals, and still more often the inherent circumstances of teaching created problems. These latter two possible sources of problems in teaching are not necessarily independent. For example, the value teachers place on maintaining lesson momentum at the expense of intellectual engagement may not really be an enduring personal value, but instead a preference developed in response to the task itself: maintaining a single coherent line of thinking with 20 or more novice thinkers who also tend to be rambunctious and quickly bored would be difficult for anyone. Many teachers might prefer to maintain lesson momentum, and the sense of accomplishment that momentum provides, than to engage students intellectually and confront all the ambiguities and difficult choices that intellectual engagement entails.

Reform ideals are not well suited to the realities of classroom life. Many reformers advocate relatively complex lessons, involving group activities and numerous materials and props, using pedagogies called "progressive," "discovery," or "constructivist." Even if these ideas are based on sound learning theories, they may actually increase the likelihood of distractions in the classroom, thus defeating their own purposes.

7. Sources of Improvements in Teaching

A lmost anyone observing a lesson can see the misstatements, failed props, content-deprived learning activities, and so forth. But only teachers themselves are aware of improvements in their practices: the myriad large and small problems they've solved, the innovations they've devised, and the new efficiencies they've created. Many of these improvements are developed privately, at the teacher's own initiative. Others are developed in response to outside pressures, especially those of policymakers and professional developers.

We may also find important differences between problems and improvements. The kinds of influences (teachers' knowledge, beliefs, dispositions, or the circumstances of teaching) that create problems for teachers may be different from those that stimulate improvements. For instance, many of the problems examined in Chapter 6 would not be eliminated by improving teachers' knowledge and capabilities, yet improvements in practice may result from improvements in knowledge and capabilities. On the other side, even though the circumstances of teaching produce problems for teachers, many of these circumstances can't be altered. For instance, a common problem teachers face is the conflict between responding to one student whose ideas differ from everyone else's, versus attending to everyone else. The circumstance itself cannot be changed, but teachers could be given more knowledge in the hope that this will help them.

The "knowledge hypothesis" is popular in part because knowledge remains one of the easiest things to provide to teachers. Those in positions of authority, such as policymakers, can provide prescriptive knowledge through curriculum frameworks that outline the content of instruction, through student assessments that convey desired learning outcomes, or through performance assessments that try to control the processes of instruction. Reformers elsewhere can offer professional development programs aimed at enhancing teachers' knowledge or capabilities. Sometimes these two approaches are combined, so that teachers receive professional development that focuses on a particular curriculum or a particular student assessment.

Virtually all teachers' references to improvements in practice were motivated by new ideas rather than by changes in beliefs or by changes in the circumstances of teaching. The question we turn to now is whether and how new ideas, specifically from external sources such as professional development programs and policymakers, help teachers improve their teaching practices. I take three approaches to answering this question. First I review 10 lines of thinking that have been described in previous chapters in an effort to locate and examine external influences within each line of thinking. The aim of this analysis is to see how external sources appear to influence teachers' thinking about their practice. Next I examine what teachers learn from referring to their own experience, without the aid of external influences. Seeing what and how teachers learn from experience helps us judge the relative value of adding knowledge from outside sources. Finally, I examine the full range of changes in practice that teachers themselves described, to see whether and when these changes were stimulated by outside sources such as policy guidelines or professional development programs, and the extent to which these outside sources actually improved teaching practices.

Evidence of Learning in Lines of Thinking

Table 10 lists the lines of thinking examined in this book. Each row summarizes one teacher's line of thinking. It shows the original beliefs and values, what new idea was acquired (if any), and how that new idea influenced the teacher's practice. The teachers are listed in ascending order according to how much they were influenced by a new idea. Thus, the first three rows show teachers' lines of thinking that were not influenced at all; in their interviews these teachers made no references to new ideas or to changes in practice over time. Next are the lines of thinking of two teachers who acquired new knowledge but did not consequently change their practices; instead, the knowledge served mainly to reinforce their prior ideas and practices. This is a relatively minor influence, and in fact we can't be sure that it is an influence at all. Thus, the lines of thinking of half the teachers in the table were formed with little or no apparent external influence.

Next come teachers whose lines of thinking changed and for whom new knowledge motivated a change in practice. The first two (Ms. Aires and Ms. Lachamy) made relatively minor changes in order to deal with specific problems. Each consulted another person about the problem, and the other person offered a suggestion that the teacher tried out. Ms. Aires sought a way to get her students' attention without raising her voice; her brother suggested that she use a dinner bell, and she did. Ms. Lachamy sought a way to help her students learn to organize paragraphs; her principal lent her a manual on the use of "accordion paragraphs," and she adopted its recommendations.

Next are two teachers whose newly acquired ideas contradicted prior ideas, and who consequently experienced conflicts. Mr. Awles's original line of thinking included a belief that students need to receive information in small, discrete steps and that it is counterproductive to engage them in discussions of content. In the past, he had taught the ocean by enthusiastically showing students all the artifacts he had brought back from his trips. But from a professional develop-

Table 10 Influence of acquired principles of practice on lines of thinking

Teacher	Teaching practice	Standing beliefs and values	Source of new ideas	Influence of new ideas
Ms. Defoe	Responding to Andy and William	Teachers need to be in control of events	None mentioned	N.A.
Ms. Bowes	13 learning activities on symmetry	Students need multiple concrete experiences	None mentioned	N.A.
Ms. Buford	Persona to accommodate Juan	Teacher is a behavior role model	Workshop mentioned but only as an aside	N.A.
Ms. Mission	Responding to Jason's wrong idea as the bell rang	Teacher needs to model thought process for students	Experience in an undergraduate college course reinforced Mission's ideas	Reinforced established beliefs and values
Ms. Lafayette	Extensive reinforcements during her phonics Q&A routine	Students have insatiable need for validation	Experience as a graduate student	Reinforced established beliefs and values
Ms. Aires	Complete set of classroom routines	Good teachers remain quiet and calm	Suggestions from principal, brother	Helped pursue established values
Ms. Lachamy	Learning goal, portrait and learning activity using pink and green strips	Students need to distinguish topic sentences from supporting details	Principal offered a handbook on "accordion paragraphs"	Helped pursue established values

Mr. Awles	Learning activity of drawing a picture of the ocean	Kids need things broken down into discrete steps	Professional development program introduced the idea of giving students a context for new science content	Created some conflict, didn't sit well with established ideas
Ms. Jibson	Guessing-game approach to a Q&A routine	Student errors are embarrassing and must be quickly glossed over	Professional development program introduced the idea that students need to make conjectures as they think about math	Conflicted with established beliefs, led to disjointed thinking
Ms. Toklisch	Q&A routine to solve the pizza problem	Students need to figure this out for themselves	Professional development program introduced a different theory of student learning which was life changing	Fundamentally altered beliefs, caused anguish and eventually major changes in practice

ment program he acquired the idea that he should begin each unit by introducing the central idea. So for his ocean unit, he should first provide students with an overview of the ocean and help them see where and how life survived in different parts of it, rather than simply showing them a potpourri of artifacts. The new idea motivated Awles to leave his artifacts in storage and to introduce his unit on the ocean by having students draw a cross-section. The combination of this new idea (start with an overview) with his prior theories of student learning and motivation (give them tiny bits) led Awles to devote an entire hour to the procedure of drawing a cross-section, with almost no references to content.

Ms. Jibson's line of thinking included similarly incompatible ideas. She held a long-standing belief that errors were embarrassing and should be covered up. Then she acquired the idea that students in mathematics classes should be encouraged to make conjectures during their whole-group discussions. This combination of ideas led her to encourage students to guess what she was thinking and to quickly dismiss the guesses that were wrong. She gave students no substantive basis for guessing and no substantive basis for evaluating their ideas as right or wrong.

In both of these cases, the introduction of a reform idea may have made matters worse. In Awles's case, the reform idea was to focus on more important content, but the resulting lesson, involving drawing the ocean, included almost no content. In Jibson's case, the reform idea was to increase intellectual engagement with mathematical ideas by having students make conjectures, but Jibson implemented the idea in a way that reduced intellectual engagement by converting conjectural thinking into a guessing game. In both cases, the new idea was changed as it was filtered through the teacher's prior beliefs about student learning.

In only one case did a new idea motivate a major change in practice. Ms. Toklisch (grade 6 math, 10 years' experience) revised most of her standing beliefs and values and substantially altered her teaching practices in response to the ideas she acquired in a professional development program. This dramatic effect is unique in the set of 45 teachers. Toklisch described moments of tears as she wrenched herself from her prior beliefs and began the slow process of developing a new practice based on a different set of ideas.

The clear resistance of most teachers' lines of thinking to new ideas provides support for the hypothesis that reform ideals are often thwarted by teachers' own beliefs and values. Even though 7 of the 10 teachers acquired new ideas, and even though many of the ideas they acquired were from reform initiatives, the ultimate influence of these new ideas depended heavily on their relation to prior beliefs and values. In the two cases in which the new idea introduced a conflict, it did not improve teachers' practices, although it may later as the teachers wrestle with the contradictions within their own lines of thinking. At the very least, these 10 examples yield a very mixed picture of the potential for new knowledge to improve teaching practices.

Evidence of Learning in Teachers' Examinations of Their Experience

Learning from experience is largely a process of adapting to the circumstances of teaching. Michael Huberman (1983) called experiential knowledge "craft knowledge" and argued that it was largely idiosyncratic, nontheoretical, and derived more from continual tinkering than from systematic analysis. Craft knowledge reflects the myriad adjustments and adaptations teachers make to their situations. Of interest to us here is what kinds of changes teachers make as they adapt, and to what extent these changes resemble the kinds of changes reformers seek.

We routinely asked teachers whether specific practices had changed over time, and if so, what motivated those changes. Even though our question usually referred to the specific practices we had observed, teachers tended to respond by describing broader and more general changes. A teacher might say, for instance, that she had gradually increased the amount of structure in her classroom or that she had gradually developed more hands-on activities. The change described was very general, and the process was very gradual. Many of these changes had to do with becoming more self-assured, learning to maintain a professional distance from students, or becoming comfortable enough to be less rigid and controlling. Sometimes teachers mentioned becoming more aware of students—either knowing what to expect from them or becoming more attuned to them. Teachers also mentioned finding ways to coordinate their lessons better and developing specific techniques for handling specific types of situations. The changes appeared to represent the outcome of continual tinkering as Huberman described it.

Ms. Aires presents a good example of the kinds of changes teachers devise as they try to better respond to their experiences. Recall from Chapter 3 that Aires had developed dozens of routines for handling a wide range of problems, from changing the date on the board from Spanish to English in the afternoon, to using a dinner bell to call students to attention. Aires was a relatively new teacher and was probably still adapting to her situation and its many demands. Apparently these routines were an important part of that adjustment.

However, the improvements that she and others described are very different from the types of improvements reformers seek. Reformers don't tend to talk about the amount of structure in the classroom or about teachers' personae. Yet teachers' ability to meet reformers' ideals depends on their ability to develop reliable systems, routines, and personae that are comfortable for both them and their students. Observers who watch well-functioning classrooms may be unaware of all these aspects that contribute to it, and may think that it all came about "naturally"; but when teachers' discuss changes, they reveal that what appear to be smooth classrooms and "natural" teaching have actually evolved gradually, through years of tinkering, adjusting, and modifying.

These adjustments don't necessarily move teachers toward reform ideals, but they do help teachers accommodate the circumstances of teaching. When a teacher said she needed more structure, something in her situation—perhaps the large number of students in a small space—demanded more structure. Similarly, when a teacher said she had to stop trying to be friends with students, something in her situation was telling her that it is not possible for teachers to befriend students and also accomplish other instructional tasks. It is the circumstances of teaching that compel the daily changes, not the persuasiveness of reformers' ideas.

The problem is that teachers' references to learning from experience were so general that it is hard to learn what features of their situations actually compelled these changes. The learning had occurred in the past, and had occurred gradually over time. However, it is possible to learn more about the role of experience by examining teachers' responses to their own lessons when they saw our videotapes. When we asked teachers to view the tapes and to select episodes to talk about, we stated that our interest was in how teachers made their moment-to-moment decisions, and we asked them to select moments during which they were especially aware of their own thoughts. Our instruction said:

> In preparation for the interview, try to select a couple of episodes that were interesting or important to you. These might be times when
>
> something unexpected happened;
>
> you suddenly had an insight about what was going on;
>
> you were unsure about what to do next; or
>
> you realize something now, in retrospect, that you didn't think of at the time.

Despite this guidance, most of the episodes teachers nominated for discussion reflected their *evaluative judgments* about the success or failure of their practices rather than their awareness of their own in-the-moment deliberations. Teachers volunteered that they had spent too long on one segment, had failed to see a student whose hand was raised, or were glad they had remembered to attend to a particular detail. The prevalence of these evaluative judgments suggests that teachers do routinely review and critique their own practices. Perhaps this process of daily review is the mechanism that leads to changes in practice. As teachers notice these problems, they try to devise solutions for them. To see if this might be so, I examined these self-critiques more closely.

Teachers nominated 44 episodes that they were dissatisfied with, but only 16 that they were pleased with. This is a ratio of almost 3:1. If teachers routinely examine the practices they are dissatisfied with, and use these experiences to generate new ideas for how to handle these situations in the future, then a great deal of learning might follow from the process of self-critique. I examined the self-critiques to see whether they led to new ideas or instead were simply criticisms. In about half the cases, teacher mainly criticized, with no effort to rethink the problem. Some criticisms yielded a conclusion about what to expect from students, and a few yielded ideas for change, as the following passages demonstrate. Notice that both of these teachers have extensive experience but are still learning from it.

> One of the kids says here, "What did you want us to do?" or something that made it clear to me that they didn't understand what I was asking them to look for in these words. But I was using the word "syllable." Now some of them didn't—it's been a summer [this lesson occurred in early fall] and they didn't hear that word, probably. So maybe they didn't remember what that meant or whatever. But sometimes I think we use language with kids and we assume they know what we're talking about, and I don't think they knew what I was talking about. Or some of them might have, but some of them didn't. [Ms. Lafayette, grade 5–6 language arts, 28 years' experience]

> I felt it would've probably been more farsighted to have used an overhead in explaining this business with enlargement. I hadn't anticipated how difficult it was going to be or how I probably needed to do more of the lead-in to it when I realized that I was going around and having to talk to so many people individually. . . . I wondered afterwards if I had started out with an overhead and I had started out by describing what the lines meant that were around the seal if people would understand better what all those lines meant if it didn't look confusing to them or if they

didn't need some practice in advance of that. . . . [Ms. Snyder, grade 4–5 art, 32 years' experience]

Only two teachers mentioned that they intended to think about the problem they had noticed and to try to develop a better approach. Ms. Awkler (grade 5 math, 9 years' experience) was one: "I didn't feel like the transition was smooth. And I wanted—If every time I take three, four minutes to move into something, then by the end of the day, you know, it's 30 minutes that I've wasted changing. And as I watched it I just wondered how I could do that more smoothly. A lot of it is the group of kids that I have, but maybe I need to figure out a new way to transition them from one activity to the next."

The things teachers were changing involved very small details of their practice. Such incremental changes are characteristic of learning from experience. A process of making hundreds of small adjustments over time leads to finely tuned and coordinated systems of instruction. In contrast to their depictions of change as broad and somewhat vague, their self-critiques suggest that these broad changes result from numerous very specific adjustments.

These findings tell us three important things about the role of experience as a guide to practice. First, learning from experience is more a matter of adjusting to the circumstances of teaching than a matter of striving for more rigorous instruction. When teachers described the kinds of changes they had made in their practices over time, and when they critiqued their videotaped practice, they focused more on lesson momentum, efficiency, and accommodating students than on the quality of the content, students' intellectual engagement, or universal access to content. Second, learning from experience yields a multitude of tiny adjustments rather than a handful of substantial changes. Third, improvements appear to be motivated mainly by dissatisfactions with how things went, not by satisfaction; if teachers are satisfied with their practice, they are unlikely to learn much from it. The potential to learn from experience, therefore, may be limited to episodes with which teachers are dissatisfied rather than satisfied, to concerns arising from the circumstances of teaching rather than from reform ideals. And even in these cases, less than half of all such dissatisfactions lead to explicit statements of new ideas.

Evidence of Learning in Changes in Practice

Neither of the analyses above provides much support for the idea that new knowledge can substantially alter teachers' practices or move them toward reform ideals. Yet knowledge is the main resource that reformers can offer. Consequently, it is important to search every avenue for evidence regarding the role of new knowledge. The analysis tied to Table 10 above focused on a sample of teachers whose lines of thinking had been examined earlier. But many other teachers mentioned new ideas that had motivated changes in their practice. These new ideas came from a wide variety of sources: not only obvious sources such as professional development courses, but also less obvious sources such as advice from husbands or brothers, newspaper articles, and therapy.

The sources of these new ideas fall into three broad categories. First there are *informal sources.* Experience, for instance, is an informal source for ideas, as are chats with friends and relatives, articles in the daily newspapers, and so forth. Next are *institutional sources,* which tend to provide guidance on curriculum, desirable learning outcomes, and desirable teaching practices. Finally there are *knowledge-vending sources,* such as professional development programs, college and university courses, research articles, journals, and professional associations.

We examined the role of experience above. The other two sources are of particular interest now, for they represent explicit efforts by reformers to move practice toward reform ideals. But these two sources of knowledge, institutions and knowledge vendors, provide very different kinds of knowledge. Institutions tend to offer prescriptions. Their guidelines include numerous "should" and "ought" statements. Their knowledge tends to be highly codified, sometimes captured in manuals and rule books, and is rarely theoretical or abstract. Knowledge vendors, on the other hand, tend to offer knowledge that is quite theoretical and abstract and that often focuses on the underlying dynamics of teaching and learning—things like how students learn, what ideas they are likely to misunderstand, or how group processes influence student motivation. Many professional development courses are also designed to address teachers' prior beliefs and values and to offer them alternative theories of student learning or student motivation, and even alternative theories about the nature of subject matter itself.

Table 11 summarizes the range of sources for new ideas that teachers mentioned, grouped according to the three broad categories. The

Table 11   Sources of all new ideas mentioned

Type of source	Number of mentions
Informal sources	
Experience as a teacher	40
Colleagues	15
Spontaneous ideas	14
Experience as a child	12
Experience as a parent	10
Empathy	10
Own materials	9
Fads	8
Misc. other sources	16
Total references to informal sources	134
Institutional sources	
Tests and accountability systems	33
Curriculum standards and guides	23
Specific textbooks	24
School building requirements	13
Other policies	24
Total references to institutional sources	117
Knowledge-vending sources	
Professional development programs	60
University courses	9
Research findings	8
Professional associations	3
NBPTS	5
Total references to knowledge-vending sources	85

Note: NBPTS = National Board for Professional Teaching Standards.

table shows that teachers made more references to informal sources than to either of the other two, perhaps reflecting the fact that learning from experience tends to consist of numerous small changes rather than a few large ones. Indeed, one problem with examining frequencies in this way is that they do not indicate the *importance* of the influence. Some references to a particular source of knowledge were offered with a shrug, suggesting that it was a relatively minor influence, while others were mentioned as life-changing experiences. We need more than a tally to ascertain the relative contributions of these different sources of ideas.

One way to sort out the importance of these influences is to examine the types of issues teachers were concerned with when they sought out or acquired new ideas. For instance, one new idea might have been adopted in order to satisfy a teacher's personal need for quiet time, another might have been valued as a way to nurture a sense of community in the classroom, and still a third might have been acquired to improve lesson momentum. Table 12 cross-tabulates the sources of teachers' new ideas with the areas of concern that they addressed.

The table shows that teachers cited informal sources of ideas in the context of several areas of concern, but primarily those of student willingness to participate, lesson momentum, and fostering student learning. In contrast, they relied on institutional sources for help mostly with decisions about content coverage and fostering student

Table 12 Percent of references to sources of ideas, by area of concern

Area of concern	Source of ideas		
	Informal	Institutional	Knowledge vendors
Defining learning outcomes	3	38	10
Fostering student learning	22	32	63
Maintaining lesson momentum	25	15	3
Fostering student willingness to participate	28	9	7
Establishing the classroom as a community	16	3	10
Attending to personal needs	6	3	7
Total	100	100	100

learning, and they relied on knowledge vendors for help mainly in the area of fostering student learning. This pattern suggests that each source of knowledge may offer its own unique benefits to teachers. But the pattern also suggests that institutional and knowledge-vendor sources are more relevant to reform ideals than informal sources are, for these two sources directly address the issues of content coverage and student learning.

Institutional Guidelines

When referring to institutional guidelines as a source, teachers cited tests and accountability systems, curriculum standards and guidelines, specific textbooks, and building policies. That they mentioned these sources so frequently when concerned about content coverage and learning outcomes provides a ray of hope for reformers, for it suggests that teachers do respond to policy guidelines regarding content.

Though most teachers accepted testing and accountability systems as appropriate and useful guidelines for learning outcomes, most also described ways in which their practices deviated from these prescriptions (Ms. Lachamy, for example, redefined her state writing standard to focus mainly on organization), and several also described their frustration at the pressure that accountability systems introduced. And in some cases the institutional prescriptions themselves were not productive. Thus Ms. Todd skipped over a unit on division with decimals because she believed that the mandated curriculum could not all be taught within a single school year. Consequently, she omitted units that she thought were less important.

The tenor of teachers' comments about institutional guidelines also suggests that teachers felt a strong sense of *obligation* to ensure that their students learned the things their districts or states had outlined. They understood that they functioned within larger instructional systems, that their students came to them from someone else's classroom and would eventually enter yet another teachers' classroom. They wanted to make sure that their own contributions fitted into this larger system.

At the same time, teachers perceived institutional guidance as transient. They often contrasted their current school with another where they had worked earlier in their career, or they compared recent policies in this school with earlier policies in the same school. Sometimes these comparisons were accompanied by statements that they preferred the old way or the new way better, but often they described them simply as different ways of doing things. For instance, Ms. Awkler had this to say: "So we have a new textbook adopted this year, which does things in an entirely different order. And this year the county's doing our local diagnostic in a little bit of a different order. So we have a new math curriculum, and they have a time line for that curriculum. And we've looked at that time line as a grade level (there's five of us), and we decided at the beginning of the year, even though it goes, it's a little different from the way we've taught things, to follow that time line and just to see if we like it better, to see if it, to see how it works." Thus, although teachers' remarks suggest that they feel obligated to cooperate with the larger systems in which they function, they aren't really *learning* from prescriptions in the sense that they are gaining new knowledge or capabilities, but instead are merely adjusting to them in the way that a driver adjusts his route to accommodate construction along the highway. Teachers perceived these prescriptions only as current guides, expecting that they would change at some point in the future.

Knowledge Vendors

Though knowledge venders were mentioned less often than other sources, professional development programs were the single most frequently mentioned *specific* source of ideas. The changes teachers described following professional development were more substantial than the numerous tiny adjustments that came from experience, and they were more enduring than those that arose from institutional guidelines. Many teachers referred to programs they had participated in years earlier, or in other school contexts, that they continued to use because they continued to believe they were good ideas. Moreover, when teachers talked about these programs, they were more emotionally committed to what they had learned than they were when they talked about ideas from either institutions or informal sources. One of the most dramatic stories of change motivated by a professional development program was told by Ms. Toklisch, who had been teaching for four years when she enrolled in a summer workshop on teaching a particular mathematics curriculum. After the workshop a mentor from the program came into her classroom to observe her teaching and to help her change her practice. One day the students were learning to measure. They were measuring their own heights, but instead of holding the rulers against a wall, they moved them right up against their bodies, jagging them in and out of curves and lumps in their clothing. Toklisch saw that their measurements would be wrong and tried to correct the students, showing them how to hold the rulers, when her mentor stopped her. The mentor took her out into the hall and firmly insisted that she let the students figure this out for themselves. Then the mentor took over the class and finished the lesson herself. Toklisch watched as the students reported out their findings.

> Somebody said, "Well I'm the same height as you, but your measurement says you are 20 inches taller than me. That can't be right." And so Mary [the mentor] said, "Well, why don't you show the way you measured?" And they showed the way. And the kids went running over and said, "But look what's happening when you're going up and over your hips and up over you shoulders . . . you're adding a whole bunch of extra." And "Oohhhhhhh," they said. And that was so much more powerful than what I did. So much more. Because she just let them make mistakes, and then they saw the mistakes themselves. And then they started to question each other. It was so much more powerful. I think that was the day I think I went home and cried. I went, "Oh my gosh. This is bigger than I thought it was. This is a major change.

Professional development programs have the potential to make powerful and lasting changes in teaching practice. They can genuinely alter teachers' knowledge and capabilities and even their beliefs and values. Several teachers described their earlier skepticism about ideas they had acquired through professional development, only to embrace these new ideas wholeheartedly later.

All of this is good news for reformers who subscribe to the knowledge hypothesis. Professional development is one of the few tools they have to influence teaching practices. In addition, reformers tend to rely on vendors to impart knowledge about how to foster student learning, and teachers mentioned concerns about fostering student learning more often than any other concerns when they mentioned the influence of professional development.

However, the knowledge provided by these vendors is extremely various and uneven, and much of it does not move teachers toward reformers' ideals. The ideas teachers got from professional development were wildly different. Some programs promoted "effective teaching" while others promoted "constructive teaching." Some focused on curriculum, others on pedagogy, and still others on classroom management. Not all were oriented toward reform ideals, and not all represented validated knowledge about teaching and learning. Some advocated fads and unsupported ideas.

Another problem with vendor-provided knowledge is that teachers do not seek it out to solve specific problems. They seek informal sources when they want to improve small disturbances in their lessons, and they seek institutional guidance when they want to ensure that their lessons fit into the larger instructional system. But they appeared to enroll in professional development programs for casual reasons: a friend recommended the program, they needed to fulfill a continuing-education credit requirement, or the location and schedule were convenient. These programs have the potential to exert big effects on teachers' knowledge, their beliefs and values, and their practices, but there was a sense of capriciousness in teachers' participation in professional development. This capriciousness, when combined with the uneven quality and content of the programs themselves, makes knowledge vendors a very unreliable source for moving teaching practices toward reform ideals.

Yet a third problem with vendor-provided knowledge is that its influences are still uneven. Even though there were many references to strong and lasting influences, there were also cases in which vendors had very little influence. For example, one district had required all teachers to take a professional development course to learn a new spelling curriculum, thus combining professional development with institutional guidance. Yet teachers' responses to it varied. Ms. Temple (grade 5 language arts, 15 years' experience was ambivalent about this new program:

> Sometimes I worry that the repetitiveness is not making it automatic, but just a little bit silly. I do like that the kids learn to spell by the spelling rules so they can apply those. What we're having a hard time finding is, them applying it. So this year we decided to put the language arts with the spelling so that these same kids won't have a spelling problem [because] I will know exactly what types of things they should be able to spell, when I look at their reading. So I can hold them accountable. So I think that will help a lot. I like that. It can be a little frustrating, because we group the kids by where they tested at. I like the ideas of it, the rules and things. I'm not sure I like the flow of it. . . . We also fill in with other things as well. . . . We add in, so it's not just the rules, but they will be getting some other things. I think that because it's a schoolwide program it's not fair for me to say, "Well I don't like it, so I'm not going to do it." And then it puts the kids at a disadvantage as they move on from here to sixth grade.

Ms. Lafayette, on the other hand, was very committed to the program. It came up in our interview relatively early, when she discovered that one of her students was unfamiliar with the program routine.

> [So why did you pick this moment?] Because it was a moment of revelation to me. That people throughout the school are not using this program all in the same ways, people are kind of choosing parts of it they're going to do or won't do or whatever. And that concerns me on some levels because I feel like we're trying to

use an approach with kids that will increase their word segmentation skills and their— knowledge and that kind of stuff. . . . I have to decide now how much time I'll need to spend with them, getting them up to speed with this quick drill, or whether we're going to not really emphasize that. I'll have to decide that.

Later, in response to a question about establishing her learning outcomes for a lesson, Lafayette again embraced this spelling program:

[How do you get to "this is more important, that's less important?"] I probably for 15 or more years before I came upon [this program] I was trying to develop my own set of phonetic sequences and my own set of materials and pulling from different sources and that kind of stuff. And then when I went to this training, I was like "here's somebody that's done it!" What I've been trying to figure out, what do you teach after you teach this, and what's critical for kids to know before you can teach this, and all that stuff. And [the author of this program] had organized it and sequenced it and given me ways to check if kids are ready to move on to the next step or not, ready to move on to the next step.

The new phonics program was a godsend for Ms. Lafayette, who already embraced its principles and so was quick to adopt its strategies. But for Ms. Temple, the program was something that required cursory compliance at best.

Evaluating the Three Sources of Knowledge

Virtually every teacher we talked to described ways in which their practices had improved over time, and most teachers had acquired new ideas from all three sources of knowledge. Some were tiny ideas, as when Ms. Aires' brother suggested that she use a bell to get students' attention so that she wouldn't have to raise her voice. Others were big ideas, as when Ms. Toklisch encountered a completely different way of teaching mathematics. Some ideas were resented, as when Mr. Kimberly complained about having to teach everything in the big white notebook; and others were accepted, as when numerous teachers in one school all referred to their "standard course of study." All these ideas led to changes in practice that teachers believed were important. And many of them led to changes that were consistent with reform ideals.

Each source makes unique and important contributions to the improvement of teaching, and none would be adequate by itself. While teachers mentioned informal sources of knowledge more often than other as an impetus for changing their practice, the changes that result from informal sources tend to be smaller and less consequential individually. Moreover, over half of teachers' self-criticisms did not lead to new ideas, a problem that suggests the contributions of experience to learning may be haphazard. Conversely, there was evidence that teachers responded more directly and rapidly to institutional guidelines than to other sources of knowledge, but also that they perceived these guidelines as transient and sometimes interpreted them with remarkable latitude. Finally, although professional development seemed to have provided the most dramatic changes in teaching practices, the professional development programs that teachers described were remarkably various and appeared to have had similarly various effects.

Table 13 summarizes the contributions and drawbacks of each source of knowledge. It shows that teachers benefit from all these sources, that each provides its own unique contribution, and that each has important limitations. Yet teachers routinely improve their practice by combining these different kinds of knowledge, as comments such as these suggest:

> When I started out I right away knew that I needed to learn more about teaching reading. Then I realized as time went on that reading wasn't very fun or it wasn't very interesting, as it was happening back, say, in the 1960s or the 1970s. As time went on, I got little tricks here and little things there, but one of the things that helped me more than anything else was when I got my coun-

Table 13 Contributions and drawbacks of different sources of knowledge

Defining features	Sources of knowledge		
	Informal sources (e.g., experience)	Institutional sources (e.g., guidelines)	Knowledge-vendor sources (e.g., professional development programs)
Relevant hypothesis	Teaching practices reflect circumstances of teaching	Teachers lack knowledge of what to teach	Teachers lack knowledge about how to teach and also have incompatible beliefs
Characteristics of knowledge provided	Idiosyncratic, intuitive	Prescriptive, certain, assertive	Conceptual, theoretical, analytic
Area of concern most often addressed	Lesson momentum, student willingness to participate	Content coverage and learning outcomes	Methods of fostering student learning
Chief motive for acquisition	Dissatisfaction with specific episodes	Sense of responsibility to students and community	Casual interest, convenience, hearsay, sometimes requirements
Impact on teacher	Incremental, cumulative	Transient	Ranges from trivial to dramatic, often enduring

seling credential, because I think it really did reinforce some of the things that I knew already about learning periods and learning problems and what you can't just tune out or what you can't dismiss as far as the things that need to be taken care of before you can get into the story or into a math lesson or anything else. [Ms. Snyder, grade 4–5 art]

I participated in a group about inquiry science, I think I mentioned before, and we talked a lot about scaffolding, and we talked a lot about the powerful questions. I think of it as the hook to get the kids started to question and to think. In the process of doing all that, I've developed [ideas] of how to question. Because it's an ongoing thing. It's not something that you just learn how to do. You just sort of practice and continually practice. [Ms. Chalmers, K–2 science, 22 years' experience]

Implications for Reform

Most reformers believe they need to provide teachers with more knowledge. Some believe that the key to improving teaching practice lies in giving teachers stronger and clearer institutional guidance regarding what content they should teach or what learning outcomes they should seek. Others aim to provide teachers with knowledge about how students learn, and they want to change teachers' beliefs and attitudes on these issues. They rely on knowledge vendors. Meantime, teachers themselves rely mainly on informal sources to accommodate the circumstances of teaching.

None of these sources of ideas is guaranteed to move teaching practices closer to reform ideals. Informal sources of learning mainly help teachers to adapt to the circumstances of teaching, not to move their practices toward reform ideals. Institutional guidance can direct teachers toward more important content, but teachers regard such guidance as transient, and they adjust it to suit their own beliefs and values. Knowledge vendors can help teachers learn practices that can increase content saturation and increase intellectual engagement, but not all of their products and programs even aim for these goals, and among those that do, not all teachers respond as intended.

The changes examined in this chapter suggest that sources of knowledge outside the classroom, such as professional development programs and institutional policies, *can* have very strong and powerful influences on practice, even though they often don't. Their influences are uneven, either because they are transient or because they are inconsistently and unevenly communicated to teachers.

8. The Problem of Reform

Two major questions have motivated this book: Why, when American teachers are well educated, motivated, and provided with numerous resources and professional development opportunities, are both they and reformers so often dissatisfied with their teaching practices? And why, when reformers have been laboring for decades to improve practice, have they been largely unsuccessful?

I began this study with the suspicion that "the reform problem" lay in reformers' relatively narrow lens. I suspected that teachers had a much broader range of concerns than reformers did and that the reform ideals represented a small subset of many things teachers were trying to accomplish. And indeed, the results of these 45 interviews indicate that this is the case. But differences in intentions do not account for all the reasons these teachers were unable to achieve reform ideals. Throughout this book I have examined several hypotheses about this phenomenon:

> Teachers need more knowledge, capabilities, or guidance in order to alter their practices.
>
> Teachers hold beliefs and values that differ from reformers' and that justify current practices.

Teachers have dispositions that interfere with their ability to implement reforms.

The circumstances of teaching prevent teachers from altering their practices.

The reform ideals themselves may be unreachable or may actually impede good practice.

Below I review the arguments for each.

 ## The Importance of Knowledge

The first hypothesis is that teachers lack important knowledge or guidelines needed to achieve reform ideals. This is the hypothesis most frequently subscribed to by reformers, in part because it is easier to address. In fact, teachers' knowledge is addressed every year in thousands of large and small professional development programs throughout the country. However, the knowledge they provide teachers is too diffuse, too unreliable, and too unpredictable in its influence. Teachers pick up some ideas but rarely acquire enough to provoke substantial change in their practice. Sometimes new ideas are combined with existing ideas to yield unexpected conclusions about practice. At the same time, there were a handful of episodes in which teachers' lack of knowledge seemed relevant. Here is a review of evidence supporting the knowledge hypothesis.

1. Some teachers did appear to lack content knowledge. Some lessons were content-deprived because the teachers lacked sufficient grasp of the ideas. Some teachers conceded that their content knowledge was thin; others demonstrated a lack of content knowledge by avoiding discussions of difficult substantive ideas. However, these cases were rare; content knowledge was not noticeably absent in very many of the lessons we observed.

2. Many more teachers appeared to lack the capacity to manage high intellectual engagement with ideas. Teachers frequently discouraged intellectual engagement because they were unable to manage that engagement once it arose. Teachers did not want their students *disen-*

gaged, of course, but they also felt a need to contain student engagement within the limits of their own tolerance for ambiguity and their own ability to respond quickly to unexpected questions and comments. Active and engaged students, who are also novice thinkers, are likely to generate unusual ideas as they try to make sense of the content. These ideas can distract the teacher from her own line of thinking, confuse other students, introduce an issue the teacher would prefer not to address, and in general disrupt the direction of the lesson. Spontaneous and half-formed ideas perplex teachers who want to keep the class moving along, maintain the attention of the rest of the class, and finish the lesson on time. Teachers often resolved these dilemmas by reducing the likelihood that students would generate unexpected ideas. To the extent that managing these dilemmas depends on knowledge, the pervasiveness of this problem is evidence for the knowledge hypothesis. However, it is not clear that *content* knowledge would solve this problem, since it often has to do with how to achieve a balance among competing concerns when such ideas arise, rather than with how to evaluate the student's idea itself.

3. *Teachers generally accepted institutional guidelines regarding content coverage and learning outcomes.* The most visible knowledge offered to teachers consisted of content coverage guidelines provided by states and districts in the form of tests, textbooks, and curriculum standards. These appear to be useful vehicles for communicating to teachers about school content. Teachers based their decisions about what to teach on these guidelines and often based their decisions about how to teach on teachers' manuals and other resource materials provided by their institutions. Institutional guidelines, then, can make an important difference in classroom practice and have the potential to increase the quantity and quality of content that is taught, provided that the guidance itself meets reform ideals.

4. *Teachers experienced enduring and sometimes dramatic benefits from professional development programs.* Teachers who described improvements in their practice over time often referred to ideas they had acquired in professional development programs. Sometimes they had participated in these programs years earlier, but continued

to incorporate the ideas into their current lessons. Sometimes, too, the changes they experienced were substantial, altering their theories of student learning, student motivation, or group processes in the classroom.

These findings suggest that greater knowledge and capabilities could help teachers move their practices toward reform ideals. Reformers already provide a lot of knowledge to teachers, both through institutional guidelines and through professional development programs; but they could do better and they could do more. For example, sometimes institutional guidelines themselves are flawed. This is an important problem precisely because teachers do attend to institutional guidelines. If curriculum guidelines are unrealistic, requiring teachers to cover far more content than they can meaningfully cover within an academic year, teachers are likely to make their own decisions about what to cut. Similarly, textbooks that suggest unworkable learning activities can confuse students and interfere with learning as often as they facilitate it. Institutional guidance that is offered before it has been tested may hinder teaching as often as it improves it.

Professional development programs also appear to have the potential to substantially influence teaching practices. Not only do they provide lasting changes in knowledge; they also change teachers' beliefs and values. However, some of these programs supply poorly designed curriculum materials and lesson suggestions, untested theories of student learning, and untested pedagogies. Policymakers could enhance teaching a great deal by seeking more supporting evidence about the value of knowledge vendors' programs before adopting them.

Finally, reformers could strive to target their professional development directly toward problems associated with achieving reform ideals. For instance, one of the most visible problems teachers had was responding to off-script student comments. Many teachers seemed unable or unwilling to take on these challenges and consequently tried to contain active intellectual engagement. They need assistance with this problem. Reformers might consider offering more professional development on the specific problem of responding to unexpected ideas in ways that move the lesson forward without discouraging intellectual engagement. Such assistance might help teachers stretch the limits of intellectual engagement that they are able to manage, and it might also help them achieve other desirable outcomes such as maintaining lesson momentum and covering content within available time limits.

 The Importance of Beliefs and Values

The second hypothesis for why reform initiatives so often fail is that teachers' values and beliefs differ from those of reformers. This divergence may occur because teachers care about different things, or it may occur because even when they care about the same thing, they conceive of the issue in slightly different ways. If either version of this hypothesis is true, then reformers may need to find ways to confront these differences directly. Several findings support this hypothesis.

1. Teachers hold multiple and conflicting intentions. My examination of teachers' intentions suggests that they are both numerous and varied. They can be roughly grouped into six broad areas of concern, and when they are, we can see that teachers want, simultaneously, to (1) avoid distractions and maintain momentum, (2) cover required content, (3) increase student willingness to participate, often by providing unwavering positive support, (4) foster student learning, (5) ensure that all students participate equally, and (6) ensure that their own personal needs are met. Though reform ideals are often included in this array of concerns, they are barely visible among all the other things that teachers hope to achieve. Moreover, when these intentions conflict, and when teachers are forced to choose one over another, teachers usually pursue the first intention: *avoid distractions and maintain momentum.* This fact alone can lead them away from reform ideals.

2. Teachers' versions of reform ideals are slightly different from reformers' versions. Teachers' interviews suggested that nearly all of them had some interest in reform ideals. However, their expressions of these ideals were slightly different from reformers' expressions. Instead of focusing on content that was inherently important, they focused on content that fitted sequentially into the larger curricular system. Instead of intellectual engagement, they sought *any* kind of engagement, a subtle difference that can lead to activities that are fun and keep students busy, even if not *intellectually* busy. Finally, instead of talking about universal access to knowledge, they tended to talk about universal *participation* in classroom activities.

3. Teachers often interpreted institutional guidelines to suit their own beliefs and values. Though teachers frequently mentioned institutional guidelines when they accounted for their practices, they often reinterpreted those guidelines to fit better into the landscape of their own beliefs and values. They ignored some guidelines, tilted others, and embraced still others, in a pattern that suggested that beliefs and values strongly influence teachers' decisions.

4. Some teachers held unproductive or dysfunctional beliefs about how students learn. I found some cases in which teachers' beliefs about how students learn or about how to motivate students interfered with their ability to achieve reform ideals. Teachers who believed that students needed unrelenting praise, for instance, sometimes kept their questions at lower levels so that students would experience nothing but success. Teachers who believed that students needed to be given explicit instructions about what to do tended to focus on procedures rather than on content. These beliefs led to lessons that were not content-rich or intellectually engaging.

These findings provide evidence for the "beliefs and values" hypothesis. Beliefs influence teachers' interpretations of virtually all their experiences, their interpretations of institutional guidelines, and the construction of nearly all their teaching practices. Moreover, beliefs appear to be both resilient and resistant to change. However, we also found many cases in which teachers' theories of teaching, learning, and motivation had been altered by vendor-supplied professional development programs. The programs that appeared to have the greatest influence on teachers' practices were those that provided teachers with new ideas about how students learn, especially how they learn complicated ideas and difficult content, and programs that provided concrete pedagogical strategies that were consistent with these theories. Therefore, reformers might want to consider investing more in vendor-provided professional development programs that directly address theories of teaching and learning.

 The Importance of Dispositions

The third hypothesis, that teachers lack the dispositions needed to meet reform ideals, is difficult to test because dispositions are simply tendencies to respond to events in particular ways. Thus, when an outsider observes a teacher becoming impatient with students or anxious about time constraints, it is difficult to discern whether the response reflects a general tendency toward this type of response or whether, instead, it reflects a particular response to the situation itself. Still, there were some findings that support this hypothesis.

1. Two or three teachers seemed unusually disorganized, rigid, or disgruntled, to the point that they probably could not implement reform ideals.

2. Two or three teachers seemed unusually calm and unafraid of distractions, even distractions arising from unusual student ideas. These teachers seemed better able than most to respond to reform ideals.

Numerous teachers expressed anxiety over distractions and expressed fear that they might lose their lesson momentum or lose their students' willingness to participate, but the very pervasiveness of these fears suggests that these emotions did not reflect dispositions in the teachers, but instead reflected the circumstances of their teaching situations. On the whole, I found only a handful of classrooms in which teachers' practices appeared to reflect general dispositions and where their practices were hindered by those dispositions. The proportion may be similar to the proportion of dysfunctional employees in any other line of work. But these problems are nonetheless severe when they occur, and reformers could develop better procedures for screening such teachers out of the profession before they attain tenure.

The Importance of the Circumstances of Teaching

The fourth hypothesis for the repeated failure of reform is that the circumstances of teaching themselves prohibit the achievement of these ideals. Here are the findings relevant to this hypothesis.

1. Teachers experienced numerous disruptions and distractions. Repeated distractions can have many effects on teachers. Teachers who expect to be distracted may avoid teaching difficult content to begin with, so that nothing is lost when distractions occur. Teachers who do try to promote intellectual engagement may find it lost when their lessons are disrupted. To the extent that these distractions are more consequential for students who have difficulty learning, they may also interfere with the reform ideal of universal access to knowledge. I found that lessons were interrupted by other teachers, by students coming and going, by public address systems, by telephones, and so forth. Ironically, some of the distractions teachers experienced were side effects of other well-meaning reform initiatives.

2. Teachers were often constrained while preparing and organizing their work. Teachers appeared to have very little time to prepare their lessons and were often pulled from one thing to another. They worked at home in the evenings and forgot to bring their work products with them in the morning. They monitored students in the hallway and then hurried to class without time to compose themselves before teaching. They misplaced needed materials. Their hurriedness and confusion, combined with various unexpected distractions, give the impression that educational institutions do not provide tranquil or reliable working environments for either teachers or students.

3. Teachers had difficulty managing complicated lessons and faulty props. Reformers frequently advocate more complicated learning activities for students. They want experiments and group projects rather than individual seat work. But these kinds of activities are very difficult to coordinate and often actually reduce attention to the lesson's most important ideas. Content gets lost in the commotion, or gets lost as teachers try to explain to students what they are supposed to *do*. Faulty lesson props also frequently distracted either teachers or students. Many of the props we saw were homemade, but even those provided by textbook publishers frequently didn't work as expected, so that both teachers and students became confused. These logistical complications often hindered everyone's ability to focus on important ideas.

These three findings suggest that the circumstances of teaching can be important impediments to reform. Many of these circumstances could be improved. For instance, reformers could improve local school administration so that it provides better support for teaching and learning. The many interruptions we witnessed could have been contained or eliminated. School policies could be altered to prohibit interruptions during class, reroute telephones, cut off public address systems, and the like. In addition, teachers' schedules and workspaces could be enhanced to provide them with time and space in which to plan their lessons and keep their materials together. Schools could also develop systems to help teachers gather and store high-quality instructional materials. In virtually every classroom we visited, lesson props were abundant. Walls were covered with posters that showed diagrams, listed main points from earlier lessons, behavior admonitions, and so forth; and teachers had many physical demonstrations readily accessible. I neither saw nor heard any evidence that schools were helping teachers in either the production or archiving of these materials. The plethora of file cabinets and storage cupboards in most classrooms suggests that teachers generally managed their own supplies. Given the limits on teachers' time, how much of that time appears to be spent making props, and how frequently those props didn't work as intended, it seems reasonable to ask their institutions to provide some support for this work.

The Problem of the Reform Ideals Themselves

The fifth hypothesis suggests that the failure of reform efforts stems from the reform impulse itself. Support for this hypothesis comes in part from support for all the others, for the combination of them all makes the likelihood of reform success even more remote. But even apart from these other hypotheses, there are reasons to believe that reform ideals are unrealistic. They sometimes conflict with one another, forcing teachers to choose between, say, universal access and intellectual engagement. And they can conflict with other things teachers that care about, such as lesson momentum and covering content within scheduling constraints. Moreover, even though some of the distracting conditions of teaching could be removed by reformers, the general level of distraction that is inherent in classroom teaching, and the complications in the task itself, cannot. These features of teaching must be accommodated by any reform theory: teaching requires a large number of students to occupy a small space; students are novice thinkers and are highly likely to veer off in unanticipated directions; and children are physically active, quickly bored, and frequently restless. These are the nonnegotiable circumstances of teaching that can thwart even the most zealous reformer.

Further evidence that the reform ideals themselves are unreasonable comes from past reform initiatives. Histories of these efforts suggest that they were able to enlist teachers to invest heavily in these movements, often devoting long hours over evenings, weekends, and summers to reform efforts. However, the evidence also suggests that these efforts exhausted teachers and ultimately discouraged them from continuing. The teachers we interviewed often referred to time spent in the evenings making materials and planning lessons, a pattern suggesting that overtime is needed just to sustain an ordinary practice, without aiming for an ideal practice.

Reformers could make their ideals more attainable by fitting them into the full range of concerns that teachers care about. Reformers tend to think only about their own concerns, but teachers must think about a much broader array of concerns. They cannot sustain a practice if they don't create classroom communities in which students share, take turns, and are generally respectful to one another. Nor can they sustain a practice if they work night and day to create content-rich and engaging lessons but wear themselves out in the process. Nor can they sustain a practice if they can't complete their lessons each day and move students through the curriculum.

Reformers must adapt their ideals to these realities. They can do this in two ways. On one side, they can find ways to support teachers by removing distractions and disturbances that now thwart good teaching, by organizing teachers' time so that they have more opportunities to concentrate, and by helping them organize their teaching materials and props. On the other, they can find ways to address the new complications that their own ideals introduce. For their vision itself requires serious trade-offs. Intellectual engagement invites numerous enthusiastic, but unrelated, ideas from students as they try to make sense of new content. Orchestrating such conversations and ensuring that they arrive at timely and appropriate conclusions are not easy tasks. Complex learning activities also create problems. They divert attention away from substance and toward logistical details, and they increase the chances that something will go wrong, thus further distracting everyone. Even content itself can introduce problems if it is unrelated to the content that precedes and follows it and does not fit within the larger curriculum. Such drop-in units, even if important and engaging, can increase intellectual incoherence and ultimately hinder learning. These trade-offs all need attention. Reformers have tended to focus mainly on their ideals. They overlook the complications teachers already struggle with, and they overlook the new complexities they themselves are introducing. Until they address these complications, they are unlikely to achieve their dream.

Appendix on Method

This appendix describes the procedures used in each step of the design and conduct of this study: selecting sites, selecting individual teachers and lessons at each site, videotaping the classrooms, interviewing teachers, and coding and analyzing the data.

Selecting Sites

I had several goals for site selection. First, I wanted to maximize efficiency of data collection by visiting clusters of teachers instead of individual teachers. It would be more efficient to visit 10 teachers in one school, or in one vicinity, than it would be to visit 10 teachers in 10 unrelated regions of the country. So my team and I sought collections of teachers, either in individual schools or in clusters of schools in a region. Second, I wanted sites that were geographically diverse. Third, I preferred states that were actively promoting policies that they thought would achieve reform ideals. I did *not* want schools that were widely recognized for their reform activity, for such schools tend to be heavily visited, and staff are very self-conscious about their practices. Rather, I wanted schools that were ordinary in most respects but that lay in the target territory of a reform initiative. My fourth goal was to ensure some variation in the nature of these reform initiatives, thereby increasing variation in the types of messages teachers had been exposed to. The eventual goal was to visit and interview 10–12 teachers in each school, with each school responding to a different reform initiative, and with the initiatives themselves varying from one school to the next, knowing that the teachers themselves, as individuals, would also have had different degrees of exposure to the initiative.

Though there are several hypotheses for why teachers tend not to respond to reformers' pressures, most reform initiatives tend to assume that the problem is one of knowledge; accordingly, they devise various strategies for giving more or better knowledge to teachers. They may do this by providing guidance about what should be taught or what students should be learning, by sponsoring professional development programs that aim at strengthening teachers' knowledge of content or of pedagogy, or by encouraging or rewarding teachers who obtain advanced degrees or advanced certification. To ensure a varied sample, we sought a strong example of each of these approaches to communicating reformers' intentions.

Guidance on Student Learning Outcomes

Several states have recently launched new student assessments, and these assessments differ in the extent to which teachers are privy to their content. We focused on Vermont because students there are evaluated through a portfolio of products that they produce as part of their regular school work. Teachers must therefore enable their students to produce the kinds of products the state requires, and they are also actively involved in scoring student products (Koretz et al., 1994). In fact one goal of the Vermont assessment was to improve teaching practice by alerting teachers to the kinds of products students should be producing in school and to criteria for evaluating student work.

The Vermont school we selected serves a town of about 17,000 people, most of whom have a high school education or less. Median family income is around $40,000; 8 percent of households receive financial assistance, and 20 percent of students receive free or reduced-cost school lunches. The district spends around $800 per pupil. The school we visited served more than 700 children and had an average class size of 20. On its fourth-grade math assessment, 60 percent of students had met the math skills standard, 30 percent had met the concepts standard, and 20 percent had met the problem-solving standard. In language arts, the percentages ranged from 37 percent (writing effectiveness) to 74 percent (basic understanding in reading).

Guidance on Content Coverage

Another strategy used by reformers to convey their ideals is to provide curriculum guidance. Such guidance, though not common in states even a decade ago, is now relatively widespread. After examining a variety of systems relying on curricular guidance to influence teachers, we decided to visit an Edison School. The Edison Corporation is a private company that manages schools in many states and school districts. Its management style looks more like that of a private company than a public agency. In particular, and most relevant to us, is its very specific curriculum. The Edison Corporation selected the curricula it would use in each subject and each grade level, and it expects teachers to abide by these decisions.

The school we visited serves a city of about 150,000. Average household income is around $42,000. The city is the center of a larger metropolitan area of around 450,000. The school district has 31 elementary schools; their population is about 53 percent black and 30 percent white. The Edison school we visited is a charter school. It was considered to be a part of the public school system but was a school of choice within that system. According to the principal, most parents who requested that their children be enrolled at the Edison school did so because they felt that their children were not succeeding in their neighborhood school.

Encouraging Advanced Certification

Another way reformers convey their ideals to teachers is through special recognition of outstanding teaching. Some states and many school districts have devised systems for documenting and assessing teachers' practices. Among the teacher evaluation systems we examined, the National Board for Professional Teaching Standards (NBPTS) seemed to have the most potential to influence teaching because it was the most labor-intensive and time-consuming system designed to date. Moreover, there was anecdotal evidence that teachers believed they learned something about teaching simply by going through this process of seeking certification. We wanted to visit teachers who sought certification on their own as well as teachers who sought certification in a school that encouraged it. For the independent teachers, we searched Michigan Web sites to find nearby board-certified teachers. Unfortunately, a combination of influenza outbreaks and scheduled school breaks meant that we were able to interview only one teacher who had independently sought certification. For teachers who sought certification within a school community, we went to North Carolina, where the state and many districts actively encouraged teachers to seek board certification. Since the decision to seek board certification was voluntary, and is available only to experienced teachers, we did not expect all teachers in this school to have participated in this process.

The school we visited in North Carolina was part of a county system serving a total population of 145,000, grouped around eight small towns. It is about 85 percent white and 15 percent black. Median household income is around $40,000, with 9 percent of the population classified as below the poverty line. The school system serves 24,000 students and spends about $1,300 per pupil. The school we visited serves over 700 students, of whom 16 percent are eligible for free or reduced-cost school lunches. Student achievement appears to be within the bounds of the state's expected growth rates.

Enhancing Teacher Capacity

Another approach to communicating reform ideals to teachers is through professional development programs. This approach differs from the others in that it does not necessarily provide guidance to teachers on what the student outcomes, teaching practices, or curriculum *should* be (though most professional development programs have clear ideas about these issues) but instead tries to enhance teachers' knowledge of subject matter, pedagogy, or student learning in ways that will enhance their own decision making. We visited two examples of this approach. One was a cluster of professional development schools in which teachers had had a long relationship with university professors and in which professional development appeared to address all aspects of teaching—teaching practices, learning outcomes, and curriculum content. Though geographically close, these schools represented a variety of demographic settings. Most were urban and relatively low-income.

The second professional development program we looked at was a standards-based professional development program in California. The state of California sponsors a series of projects aimed at increasing teachers' knowledge of subject matter and of the state's subject-matter standards. Most projects are housed in universities and include academics in specific disciplines as well as in education departments. The program we visited was one of about 20 science-oriented projects in the state. The program aims not only to enhance teachers' knowledge of science, but also to provide them with science curriculum units that it believes meet reform ideals.

We visited a collection of schools associated with this program, all of which served a rural agricultural region. The city center has a population just under 150,000 and is just an hour's drive from a much wealthier coastal city. Median household income is around $42,000. About 38 percent of the population is non-Hispanic white, and 16 percent Hispanic white. Twenty-eight percent of the population are immigrants. In the schools we visited, it appeared that the great majority of students were Hispanic. Many teachers were bilingual, and many classes were labeled as bilingual classes.

Table A1 summarizes the final sample of sites we selected and the number of participating teachers at each site. Though the specific reform initiatives at these sites were sometimes different from what we expected, the overall package of policy contexts served our purposes: the mix of sites provided a variety of reform initiatives and a variety of regional cultures, and ensured that our findings would not be distorted by anomalies associated with one particular district or state. In addition, the sample met the standard for "ordinariness," in that none of the schools was widely recognized as a seat of reform or innovation. Moreover, very few of the schools served well-educated or

Table A1 Final sample of schools and teachers

Reform ideal	Type of reform initiative	Specific initiative	Number of schools visited	Demographic context	Number of participating teachers	Number who could have been influenced by this initiative[a]
More important content	Provide guidance on learning outcomes	Vermont portfolio assessment	1	Rural low-income white	12	6
	Provide guidance on curriculum content	Edison School (charter)	1	Urban low-income black	5	4
		California science project	6	Rural Hispanic	11	4
More intellectual engagement	Enhance professional knowledge and judgment	Professional development schools in Michigan	6	Mixed urban and suburban	6	3

All three ideals	NBPTS certification with state encouragement (North Carolina)	1	Rural low-income white	10	4
Reward professional knowledge and judgment	NBPTS certification without state support (Michigan)	1	Suburban upper-middle-income white	1	1

a. Potential influence was determined as follows: First, teachers in their first or second year are considered unlikely to be influenced, because they are novices. Second, the subject matter of the lesson we observed had to match the subject of the reform initiative. In California, for instance, only 4 of the 11 teachers we visited chose to have us observe a science lesson. In the case of the NBPTS, we specifically asked if the teachers had applied for board certification.

Note: NBPTS = National Board for Professional Teaching Standards.

wealthy populations. In the entire sample of 45 teachers, only 3 worked in schools serving professional communities. The rest served working-class communities that did not provide large tax bases of support. With respect to ethnicity, the students and teachers across the sample were mostly white, with the proportions of black teachers and students substantially higher in the Edison school, and the proportion of Hispanic teachers and students substantially higher in the California cluster of schools, which served a primarily rural Hispanic area.

Despite this detailed description of the types of reform initiatives and local contexts of the sample of schools, I provide little information in the text about the school in which any given teacher worked. Research of this sort has a small-town quality. All the teachers in the participating schools know one another and know who participated in our study. If I described a teacher as, say, a male sixth-grade teacher with 15 years of experience in the Vermont school, everyone in that school would know who that teacher was. There are times in individual stories when more contextual information is revealed because it is essential to the story, but otherwise I treat the teachers as if they came from the sample as a whole, rather than from a specific school context or a specific reform initiative. I have also tried to assign pseudonyms to teachers that reflect their ethnic backgrounds, and I have given students ethnically appropriate pseudonyms to help readers grasp the social dynamics of these episodes.

Comparative Value of This Sample

The presence in the sample of different approaches to reform creates a temptation to try to compare them, to see which strategies have the greatest effect on teachers' ideas and practices. Such a comparison could be very valuable, helping us understand the best way to package our messages for teachers. However, such a comparison is risky when sample sizes are small. Moreover, even if a dozen teachers had been sampled from a particular reform context, not all of them would necessarily have been influenced by that initiative. Table A1 shows that the initial number of teachers in each setting was small, and that the number in each group who might have been influenced by the particular initiative was even smaller.

Another reason comparisons would not be wise here is that purposive sampling strategies rarely work out in the way expected. Some schools didn't show much evidence of the policy initiative that we expected to appear there, and some showed evidence of initiatives that we had not expected. One school we visited, for instance, showed almost no evidence of any influence from the reform initiative that interested us, but was heavily influenced by other policy initiatives, including a number of "pull-out" programs which resulted in students coming and going regularly from teachers' classrooms, and an inclusion program that added handicapped students to most teachers' classrooms. In addition, many teachers in that school had participated in a common professional development program, and we saw the influence of that program in the terminology they used and in some of the rationales they used for their practices. So while we were able to see evidence that teachers were influenced by particular institutional policies and by particular professional development programs, these policies and programs were unrelated to the initiative that motivated our visit in the first place.

Similarly, our choice of North Carolina as a place to study the NBPTS also exposed us to a site that was influenced by several other reform initiatives, for the state of North Carolina had numerous such initiatives. Teachers there were aware of the National Board, but they were also aware of state curriculum guidelines, student assessment programs, and so forth. And the Vermont portfolio assessment addressed only mathematics and writing, and occurred only in grades 4 and 8. We therefore could not expect many teachers in our sample to have been directly involved in the professional development associated with this assessment, though they may have encountered the ideas second hand.

Finally, although we selected the California site on the grounds that its orientation was toward building teacher capacity, we discovered that its professional development program also had a strong curriculum component and in fact was quite prescriptive about teaching specific science topics. In addition, many teachers we visited chose to show us a lesson in a subject other than science, where we would not necessarily see evidence of the effects of this program.

These numerous complications are nothing more than normal school life. Schools are routinely either beneficiaries or victims of a variety of reform initiatives, with the specific initiatives changing over time and competing with one another for teachers' attention. The value of a heterogeneous sample, then, lies not in its potential to compare one reform initiative with another, but in its potential to ensure that patterns of influence on teachers do not reflect site-specific idiosyncrasies. This diverse collection of schools achieves this goal admirably well.

Selecting Teachers and Lessons

The typical strategy for soliciting teachers was to present our study to a gathering of teachers, such as an afterschool faculty meeting. At this meeting we explained the purpose of the study, the procedures we would use, and the amount of time we would need from them. Participation was entirely voluntary. We also gave teachers a say in what happened to the videotapes once we had completed our interviews. If teachers were uncomfortable with the tape, we would destroy it. If they wanted a copy for themselves, we would provide it. If they allowed us to retain a copy but did not want us to show it to anyone else, we abided by their wishes.

At most sites, about half of the teachers we solicited volunteered to participate. This is a lower participation rate than I have experienced in other studies that demanded comparable amounts of time and offered comparable reimbursements. But those studies were not as invasive, in that they did not involve videotaping the teachers' practice. I suspect that the videotaping aspect of this study made teachers more self-conscious about participating. In fact few of these teachers had ever seen themselves on tape, even after teaching for 30 years or more.

Knowing that a videotape is a more invasive form of data collection than an audiotape, we offered teachers the opportunity to select the lesson they would have us observe. In general, teachers appeared to select lessons that were logistically most practical rather than lessons they thought they would do better with. For example, many teachers asked us to observe their first lesson in the morning or just after lunch because we needed time to enter the room and set up our equipment beforehand and created less distraction if we arrived while the students were away for recess or lunch. Teachers often mentioned other complications as well, such as test schedules and assemblies, which they needed to work around.

Our initial plan was to focus mainly on upper elementary teachers, and on the basic academic subjects of language arts, mathematics, science, and social studies. But because our response rates were lower than we had hoped for, we occasionally accepted a teacher who either taught a lower grade or a different subject. The final sample of lessons is shown in Table A2.

Recording the Lessons

The general idea for the study was to observe and videotape teachers as they taught a lesson of their choice, and then to interview them about that lesson after they had had a chance to look at the tape. We also asked teachers to complete a brief questionnaire so that we would have some background information on them.

During the lesson, we simultaneously made two copies of the tape, one in the video camera and a second in an attached video recorder. The amount of paraphernalia associated with the camera, microphones, and second recorder required the observer to be stationary throughout the lesson. After the lesson we gave our second copy of the tape to the teacher to review before the interview. Between the observation and the interview, both the teacher and the researcher reviewed the tape and selected episodes to discuss.

Table A2   Number of lessons observed

Grade level	Language arts[a]	Math	Science	Social studies	Other	Total in grade
K–2	0	2	1	0	0	3
3	2	2	1	0	1 (Spanish)	6
4	2	3	3	1	0	9
4–5	1	0	1	1	0	3
5	3	4	1	1	1 (drama)	10
5–6	1	1	0	0	0	2
6	3	5	4	0	0	12
Total in subject	12	17	11	3	2	45

a. Includes reading, spelling, writing, and literature discussion.

Videotaping Procedures

We used two general rules for videotaping. First, the camera was always located in the back of the room, so that it could follow the teacher's movements around the front of the room. Second, it had its back or side to the window so that the bright light from the window would not throw the classroom into darkness. In many classrooms it was not obvious where the "back" was. Student desks were arranged in clusters, blackboards appeared on more than one wall, and posters and displays appeared on all walls. In these cases we asked the teacher where she normally stood, and located the camera accordingly.

With respect to the focus of the camera, we followed Stigler and others' (1999) guideline, which was to focus either on the teacher or on whatever an attentive student would be looking at. Thus, if the teacher put a problem on the board or showed a display on the overhead projector, the camera would focus on that display to establish a record of what the teacher was showing the students. If the teacher was moving about the room, the camera followed the teacher.

We did not rely on professional videographers. The cameras and microphones were operated by me and my research assistants. Occasionally the pictures or sound were not as clear as we would have wanted. Young children have amazingly small voices in the classroom, and our audio equipment often couldn't pick up their comments. On the other side, our equipment was remarkably good at picking up ambient noise such as chairs scraping the floor and pencil sharpeners.

It is difficult to gauge the influence of our presence on the behaviors of teachers and students. Certainly there were instances of children posing and making silly faces in front of the camera, and there were times when they would leave their seats, ostensibly to get something from the back of the room or to sharpen a pencil, and would use this opportunity to peak into the viewfinder and see what their classroom looked like through the camera lens. Only one teacher was visibly nervous throughout the lesson we videotaped. In the main, it did not appear that the meat of the lesson or the substantive interactions between teachers and students were altered by the presence of the camera. Most of the giggling and curiosity passed within the first few minutes, and once the lesson got under way, students appeared to attend to it rather than to us.

Instructions to Teachers

After the lesson, teachers were given a copy of their videotape along with a small tape recorder and sheet of instructions. The instructions read as follows:

> Viewing the tape
>
> When viewing the videotape, be sure to have a pencil and paper handy for notes, and be sure to have the tape counter showing so that you can write down the counter times associated with your notes or thoughts. (Press the "display" button in the upper left corner of the control panel).
>
> In preparation for the interview, try to select a couple of episodes that were interesting or important to you. These might be times when

- something unexpected happened
- you suddenly had an insight about what was going on
- you realize something now, in retrospect, that you didn't think of at the time

In the meantime, I will also watch the tape and will select some episodes to ask you about. Mine may be harder for you to talk about because they may refer to actions that were more automatic or that seemed obvious to you.

Expect the interview to last up to two hours, so that we have ample time to talk about both of our lists of events.

Teachers also completed a brief questionnaire, usually at the time they agreed to participate, about their college preparation and professional development experiences, whether there were school subjects they especially liked to teach or didn't like to teach, and how long they had been teaching. The questionnaire was not designed to obtain any "meaningful" information about teachers. That is, it did not ask about their reasons for becoming teachers, their current attitude toward their work, and the like, but instead simply asked for some basic demographic information. At the time, we thought we might need this to make sense of the interviews, but in practice we relied very little on the questionnaire.

Interviewing Teachers

The interview strategy we used is often called "stimulated recall," since it relied on the videotape to stimulate the teachers' recall of specific events. The strategy is relatively common in educational research, but is not without controversy. In particular, some researchers have doubted the validity of teachers' recollections after the fact, and wondered about the extent to which these recollections are dressed up to impress the interviewer. The most highly articulated argument against stimulated recall, however, comes from researchers who seek not to learn their subjects' reasoning, but instead to observe the thought process itself (Ericcson and Simon, 1993). These authors argue that thought processes are fleeting, and that cognitive details can be lost from memory even moments later. They advocate a procedure called "think aloud," in which research subjects try to speak their thoughts as they occur and before they can be forgotten. But such a strategy is obviously not possible in teaching situations. Moreover, since I was not concerned with teachers' thought processes themselves, but only with their conclusions, this objection did not overly concern me.

This is not to say, of course, that teachers were entirely honest with us. No doubt they did try to put their actions in the best possible light. However, what constituted the "best light" differed substantially from one teacher to another, so that we were still able to capture the values that teachers embraced.

Interview Strategy

Three ideas guided our interviewing strategy. First, we wanted to keep ourselves out of the conversation; we didn't want teachers to account for their practices by using ideas they got from us or ideas they thought we would approve of or agree with. Interviews are not merely information exchanges. They are social events, and when people are interviewed about what they just did, as our teachers were, they are motivated to come up with defensible reasons, to look good, or to appear thoughtful. This is not to say that we could not laugh at a joke or express sympathy over a sad story; but we worked hard not to articulate our own perceptions of the events we saw in a way that might influence teachers' thinking. Instead of saying, for instance, "I notice that you scolded Jimmy when he talked out of turn," we would ask, "What was that interaction with Jimmy about?" Or instead of referring to it with any words at all, we sometimes replayed the episode on the videotape and asked the teacher to talk about "what happened there." This strategy did not prevent us from probing teachers' comments. Each interviewer was free to pursue as much as possible the line of thinking that a teacher laid out, asking for more detail, asking why that mattered, asking "what if" questions to clarify the thinking, and so forth.

The second idea governing our interviews was to focus on specific events as a way to avoid broad platitudes. Instead of asking about general patterns of practice, we wanted to ask about very specific episodes of practice. I knew from other research that teachers often define their own practices in ways that differ from researchers' perceptions. Researchers from the 1960s (e.g., Hoetker and Ahlbrand, 1969) to the 1990s (e.g., Cohen, 1990; Applebee, 1991) have noticed that teachers tend to describe their own practices as more "reform oriented" than observers do. Apparently, teachers learn the lingo of reform and apply it to their ongoing practices. These findings made me leery of any discussions about general patterns of practice or about general reform ideas, and motivated me to focus instead on very specific events. I hoped, in so doing, to avoid rationales that referred to platitudes and relied on popular jargon and to learn instead about rationales that connected directly to real events. In addition, I suspected that the reasoning that stands behind specific practices may be quite different from the reasoning that stands behind broad, general ideas about education.

The third idea is related to the second. We didn't want to ask directly about the influence of reform initiatives because we didn't want teachers to invent "influences" that weren't really there, simply to help us. Questions about reform can introduce two problems into data analysis: they can artificially inflate the number of references to policy influences, and they can move the conversation away from a specific episode to a very general policy initiative. We wanted our discussions to remain in the concrete world of the classroom. Instead of asking about policy influences, as most researchers do, and asking teachers to generate examples of practices that had been influenced, we focused on practice to see what kinds of influences came up naturally in the context of these specific events.

This interview strategy therefore differs from many policy analyses that rely exclusively on interviews outside the classroom. Such studies often ask teachers directly about reform initiatives or about how these initiatives influence their practices, but because they ask about generalities, I suspected that the practices teachers describe may reflect their general aspirations, whereas questions about the specific practices we *see* are likely to reflect a more complex mosaic of ideas. Our aim was to learn teachers' theories in use rather than their espoused theories (Argyris and Schön, 1996).

Interview Structure

The structure of the interview also presented challenges. We wanted to cover roughly the same territory within each lesson and within each episode, yet the lessons and episodes would be various. We needed a standardized strategy for selecting episodes to discuss, and a roughly standard way of interrogating each episode.

Selecting Episodes

Although teachers could select any episode they wanted, we had a set of guidelines for selecting episodes. To the extent possible, we tried to ensure that each interview covered the following:

> At least one instance of the teacher portraying subject matter to students. This could be a formal demonstration of some idea or phenomenon, with pictures or models; it could be a minilecture, or it could be a series of questions aimed at introducing a new issue.

> At least one instance of a learning activity for students. A learning activity is any activity students engage in that requires them to interact with the content, including conducting an experiment, filling in a worksheet, calculating an area, measuring a circumference, debating an idea, putting on a play, or reciting phonemic sounds.

> At least one instance of a question-and-answer sequence. Virtually every elementary classroom includes a sequence of interactions between teachers and students in which teachers pose questions, students respond to them, and teachers then respond to the students.

At least one instance of a student saying something that is unexpected in the situation that requires the teacher to decide immediately how to respond.

At least one instance of what appears to represent a classroom routine, such as a standard way of calling on students, grouping students, or distributing and collecting materials.

At least one question about the lesson as a whole and its purpose.

The hope was to discuss more than one of some of these categories—for instance, two or more occasions when a student said something unexpected, or two or more learning activities—but the actual number necessarily depended on what actually occurred during the lesson.

Interview Sequence

All interviews were audiotaped and later transcribed. The interview began with an orientation to our interviewing procedures, which covered the following points in as conversational a manner as possible:

We need to describe events for the audiotape, because the data analysis will be based on the interviews, and we won't always have the videotapes on hand when we study the interviews. Sometimes, just reading an interview, it is hard to imagine what you are talking about without a verbal description of it.

If we decide to look at portions of the tape again during the interview, I will stop the audiotape so that the sound of it won't interfere with the interview. I will also ask you to hold back on your comments until I turn the audiotape back on.

I will probably ask you things that seem obvious to you, but I want to make sure I am not inserting my own ideas into your thinking.

I will be asking about the pros and cons of some teaching practices, sometimes playing "devil's advocate." This is not because I think there is a problem, but to make sure I have understood all of your thinking on these things.

Sometimes I may ask about something that you really hadn't thought about. If so, it is okay to say that you hadn't really thought about it. I'd rather you say that than feel that you have to invent something just to satisfy the interview.

I would like to reserve the last 10 minutes of our interview time to check over my notes and make sure I haven't missed anything, and I also want to review your answers to the questionnaire to make sure I understand them. So let's stop at __[time] to take stock of where we are.

The general outline of the interview was to start with this orientation, then ask an ice-breaking question, usually something like "How did it feel to see yourself on tape?" Next we asked the teacher to discuss the episodes she had selected. Then we asked about the episodes we had identified, and at the end reviewed the questionnaire to make sure we understood the responses to it.

We also considered the sequence in which different types of episodes should be discussed. For instance, we always waited until late in the interview to ask about the lesson as a whole and about the central learning activity, because we didn't want to force a logic onto teachers' thinking that wasn't actually there. That is, if we first asked about the purpose of the lesson as a whole, then asked about the rationale for their initial presentation of content, then asked about the main learning activity, teachers might realize through this sequence that we expected the reasoning behind each episode to follow from the reasoning of the previous episodes. To prevent the possibility that we might impose an artificial rational consistency across the set of episodes, we tried to ask about them in reverse order to their centrality in the lesson. We asked first about relatively smaller events, such as those in which a student said or asked something unexpected, and last about the lesson as a whole.

A typical interview lasted about an hour and a half and covered about 11 episodes.

Interrogating the Episodes

Since the episodes themselves would each be unique, we could not ask a standard set of questions about each episode. We first identified a small set of things we wanted to know about each episode:

What teachers saw or how they understood the situation

Why they responded as they did

Whether their practice for this particular type of task had changed over time

If it had changed, what prompted the change

For each of these general questions, we developed a family of possible interview questions that could be used interchangeably to pursue this issue.

How they understood the situation. In asking teachers what they saw during an episode or how they construed the situation as it unfolded, we wanted to avoid questions that seemed artificial. This was highly likely to happen when asking teachers what happened during an episode because both the researcher and the teacher had already witnessed the episode, so both knew full well what had happened. One advantage of audiotaping interviews was that we could ask teachers to describe what happened "for the tape." And indeed, much of the data analysis was based solely on interview transcripts when the videotapes were not immediately accessible.

We also were careful not to inadvertently interpret the episode while asking about it. For instance, we could ask, "I notice that you cut off Juan when he tried to offer an unrelated idea here." This question would predispose the teacher either to use the same interpretation we had used or to feel defensive because of our interpretation. In either case, such phrasing would decrease the probability of learning how the teacher would have interpreted the episode if we had not already saturated it with our own interpretation.

To prevent the problem of artificiality and the problem of leading questions, we tried to refer directly to the videotape and then to ask questions that did not require us to depict the events:

> Describe for the tape [in this case, the audiotape] what happened.
>
> Tell me what just happened there.
>
> What did you make of that?
>
> Did that surprise you?
>
> Now tell the tape what you did then.
>
> What did you *see* that motivated you to do that?

This strategy did not work for classroom routines, because routines are patterns of repeated behaviors. When asking about routines, we wanted teachers to address the fact that they relied on a repeating practice without having to show them each occurrence on the tape. So we had to describe the pattern that we perceived to be a routine. For these, we tried to be as behavioral as possible, not using any interpretive language of our own. For instance, we might say, "I noticed that whenever multiple students raised their hands, it looked as though you chose someone by pulling sticks from a jar on your desk. Can you explain that practice to me?" The question described the pattern of practice without also describing its apparent rationale. We did not say, for instance, "I notice that you have developed a strategy for ensuring that everyone has an equal chance to be called on" or "I notice that you have developed a strategy that keeps everyone on their toes." These interpretations of the pattern include an assumed rationale as well as a description of the practice itself.

Finally, when an episode had been nominated by the teacher, we often asked question such as these:

Why was that important to you?

What made this event stand out in your mind?

How did you decide to pick this event to talk about?

Rationale for action. The next family of questions was designed to learn why teachers did what they did. Included in this family were straightforward questions about why they did what they did, as well as questions designed to learn how committed they were to their actions:

How did you arrive at that response?

Did you have any reservations about what you did in this case?

Does this practice ever create problems for you?

Are there other ways you could have handled this situation?

We were concerned in this portion of the interview that teachers might not fully disclose all their reasons for doing something. Much of human behavior occurs unreflectively, so we needed questions that would push teachers to elaborate on their thinking about these practices. At the same time, it was not socially possible to be overly persistent in asking teachers to justify their actions, for an aggressive pursuit of rationale could ultimately make the interviewee resistant. We developed two special categories of questions to help us challenge teachers' rationales without seeming to be hostile: the *constraint eliminator* question and the *devil's advocate* question.

Constraint eliminator. In earlier research, I had noticed that teachers have a tendency to attribute their actions to extant policies—for instance, to say that they teach this content because it is in the curriculum, that they chose this learning activity because it was in the textbook, or that they did something because they knew they were running out of time. So we developed a collection of "constraint eliminators." These questions essentially tried to get teachers to say *what else* they considered. When teachers attributed their actions to some external sources or external constraints, we would ask questions like these:

> Do you always teach everything that is in the text?
>
> Do you always comply with school policies?
>
> Do you always teach everything that is in the state curriculum [or on the test]?
>
> Do you always capitulate to the clock?

Nearly always, the answer to these questions was "no," and that allowed us to then ask why they did so on this particular occasion. Similarly, when they attributed their practices to other constraints such as the clock or the need to coordinate with someone else, we could ask what they might have done had that constraint not been there.

Devil's advocate. The devil's advocate question was designed to ask teachers to consider an alternative strategy for handling the same type of situation. If, for instance, a teacher presented a new concept using a diagram, we might ask about the possibility of using a three-dimensional representation. These were difficult to devise, of course, and nearly always had to be constructed before the interview. That is, the interviewer would first select episodes to ask about, and then think of alternatives that could plausibly have been used in the same situations. The lead to the devil's advocate question usually took one of these forms:

> Some teachers say it is a good idea to. . . . What do you think of that idea?
>
> Last week I happened to see another teacher in a situation like this and she. . . . What do you think about that idea?

Changes in practice. The third family of questions was designed to learn more about how outside influences such as state policies, professional development programs, and the like might have influenced teachers' practices. This is an extremely difficult area to ask about, because few people realize whether or how much any particular ideas may have influenced them. It is also difficult to ask about because any direct question about a policy alerts teachers that the interviewer is "looking for" the influence of that particular policy, so they will try to help out by generating an influence.

Instead of asking whether their practice had been influenced by a particular policy, we decided to ask how their practice had changed. Then, if a change was established, we could ask what had motivated that change. If it was relevant, they would bring up the policy or professional development program that had originally motivated us to visit that school. The questions we devised were:

> Was there a time earlier in your career when you would have
> handled this situation differently?
>
> What brought about that change?

These open-ended questions allowed teachers to identify both when a change had occurred and why it had occurred. And indeed, responses to this question were quite various. One teacher might say, for instance, that she had changed her strategy when she changed the grade level she was teaching, another that she had changed her strategy when she moved to a different school, and a third might say that she had changed after taking a professional development course or after the state introduced a new policy.

Coding and Analyzing Teachers' Responses

In qualitative data analysis, it is impossible to compute means or standard deviations, and it is difficult to justify statements to the effect that something happened frequently, rarely, or typically. Moreover, before any kind of "analysis" can occur, the data must be sorted, categorized, coded, and classified—all activities that are heavily analytic and interpretive in themselves.

For this study, I used a software program called N-Vivo. This was the first time I had relied on computer software to perform an analysis, and the program both helped and hindered analysis.

Stage 1: Marking off Episodes

The first step in most qualitative studies is to mark off segments of transcripts that address particular issues. I wanted to segment interviews according to the types of episodes they addressed:

Teacher-nominated moments

Unexpected student questions or ideas

Representations of subject matter

Question-and-answer routines

Classroom routines

Learning activities

Lesson topic

Using N-Vivo for this task first requires that all the interview transcripts be imported into the program, where they become listed as a set of documents. Though there are certain types of formatting codes that N-Vivo cannot accept, it does allow documents to be imported with formatted headings, and we took advantage of that feature. Before the transcripts were imported, researchers went through each transcript and entered headings indicating what the next portion of the interview was about. N-Vivo is designed to allow automatic coding of sections of text according to these headings, but this feature did not work for our transcripts. I think there were two problems: first, we had multiple sections with the same heading (e.g., three sections of the interview all labeled "teacher-nominated moment"). Second, the sequence of these sections changed from one interview to the next. Ms. A. might have been asked first about an unexpected student move, then about a classroom routine, and then a Q&A routine, while Ms. B. might have been asked about a Q&A routine first, then two unexpected student moves, and then a classroom routine.

This autocoding feature in N-Vivo appears to be designed for interviews that are very structured, where the interview always moves through a specified list of topics in a specified order and addresses each topic only once.

Still, with the headings in place, manually segmenting the interviews was not difficult. The documents in N-Vivo can be viewed and easily segmented on the screen. It is simply a matter of blocking a portion of text and then clicking on the relevant label for that segment. In this case, each passage was coded as a type of episode (portrayal of content, learning activity, etc.) and as a type of question (interpretation of situation, rationale for action, change in practice, etc.). There were 45 interviews, each represented as a document, there were seven categories of episodes, and there was a small set of questions or issues that had been discussed in the context of each episodes. N-Vivo allows all these distinctions to be marked off for quick future reference.

Using a computer program to do these tasks offers an important advantage over doing a markup by hand. Qualitative researchers routinely struggle with the problem of how to physically sort out evidence pertaining to one or another issue while keeping their original transcripts intact. With N-Vivo, the original documents are always clean and readable. At the same time, it is possible to ask N-Vivo to pull out all the "clippings" from those documents that refer to a particular topic or type of episode or both.

Stage 2: Conceptualizing Themes and Main Ideas

Sorting, segmenting, and categorizing do not require a great deal of interpretive judgment. The more difficult task was to capture what people actually said about these topics and issues. The second stage of qualitative work was to go through the transcripts and identify common themes and ideas that came up in them. This part of data analysis is highly judgmental, and it tends to be done through an iterative process rather than a systematic process with a priori categories. For instance, when I wanted to ascertain all the intentions that teachers mentioned for the things they did, I began by identifying all the passages that described intentions and marking them as such. N-Vivo allowed me to gather all these passages, pulled from the original transcripts, so that I could read them together and begin thinking about what they said. I then identified specific categories and developed a new coding system that sorted all of these intentions into their types. This approach to sorting intentions tends to be iterative. The alternative is a systematic process of coding, in which the researcher defines a list of a priori categories of intentions and then reviews the data, placing each stated intention into one of the categories. Most qualitative researchers prefer iterative approaches.

There are several iterative approaches. One is to code intentions into dozens of categories, resisting the temptation to form a few broader ones. Under this approach, each discrete intention could constitute its own category if necessary. This approach prevents the analyst from force-fitting an intention too quickly into a label that he or she may not want to use later on. N-Vivo allows this method, as it places no limits on the number of categories that can be used. So if 45 people list 85 intentions, it would be possible to have 85 categories for these intentions. Of course, this may not be particularly helpful analytically, but once a long list of such categories is available, it is possible to reexamine those that sound similar to see if indeed they can be merged to form a more comprehensive category.

This was the approach I used to outline the various sources of influence on teachers' thinking. Table 11 lists the full array of sources that teachers mentioned. When I first went through the data I grouped these influences into some 20–30 categories; then I gathered them into three very broad categories. This approach enabled me to see what I had included in each of the larger categories and to reconsider the groupings if necessary. N-Vivo allows these incremental and continuing adjustments to the codes in several ways. It allows the analyst to change the contents of categories by merging them, making one a subset of the other, or making two or more categories into parallel subcategories of another broader category. It also allows the categories to be renamed as their contents change. Finally, it allows the analyst to relabel portions of text so that they belong to a different category from the one originally assigned to them.

The second iterative approach to analysis is to develop an a priori set of tentative categories as a way of getting started. Then, once a collection of passages has been identified as belonging to a particular category, the analyst can browse through this set of passages to see if they indeed form a homogeneous group. This approach was useful to me when I realized how many references teachers made to avoiding off-task behaviors. Some teachers mentioned a fear of chaos, others a need to stick with the plan, others a personal need for order. There were numerous passages on this broad theme, but they were so various that it was difficult to sort them into specific subcategories and to see what the dominating concern really was in all these comments. Pulling them into one broad category allowed me to read all the passages together and get a feeling for the emotional and intellectual issues that was being addressed.

I used both of these approaches at different times during the conceptual phase of analysis. Though the computer program facilitated the physical processes of sorting and grouping passages, and made it easier to read subsets of passages that had been labeled with common codes, it did not facilitate the heart of the analysis, which is necessarily judgmental. Any approach to conceptualizing prominent themes and ideas in a large body of text is slow, iterative, interpretive, judgmental, and filled with trial and error. Two forces are at work concurrently during this process. One is that the category system itself is becoming more refined; in particular, the differences among categories are becoming clearer. This occurs through a vetting process, wherein the viability and validity of the categories are tested by examining the collection of passages that fit or don't fit into them. Second, the analyst's thinking is becoming clearer and his or her understanding of the issues is growing deeper. As new insights emerge, so do new ideas for clarifying category definitions, and these go through a new vetting process before their viability is established.

The two steps I have described so far are not necessarily steps that all qualitative researchers would go through. They were important steps for me because my analytic focus was on the categories of ideas that teachers drew on to make their decisions. For the type of study I was doing, N-Vivo proved to be a very useful tool.

Stage 3: Defining Patterns

Once transcripts have been sorted and segmented, and once a set of ideas and themes has been conceptualized, the researcher is in a position to search for patterns. One way of finding patterns, which we could call the "qualitative" way, is to read through all the passages that have been identified as representing a particular idea, and then develop an overarching and nuanced portrait of what that theme or idea really is all about. This approach to analysis is interpretive, and aims to give readers a deeper understanding of the meanings attached to certain types of events or concepts. I used this approach to understand the concept of "maintaining momentum." Within this broad area of concern were numerous themes, such as not losing students, avoiding chaos, keeping everyone on the same page. Though these ideas were related, teachers talked about them in very different ways, and seemed to link them causally in different ways. For instance, keeping everyone on the same page can be a way of avoiding chaos, and losing students may or may not be the inverse of keeping them all on one page. Reading a collection of related passages together, and repeatedly, is the only way to get a grasp of the nuances of the concept as a whole.

The other way to find patterns is quantitative. That is, the analyst tallies up how often one idea is mentioned in comparison to another. This is a pattern of *frequencies* rather than of *meanings*. In my case, simple tallies of relevant passages were often helpful. I used simple tallies to show how frequently teachers mentioned different intentions, and I used them to show how frequently teachers mentioned different sources for new ideas. These are easily generated with N-Vivo. It routinely reports, for any given category, how many passages have been labeled with that category, how many characters are in these passages (which gives a sense of how much text people devoted to these ideas), and how many documents contain passages that fall into that category. If anything, the ease of generating such tallies encourages researchers to tally things even when they are not very theoretically interesting.

N-Vivo also allows researchers to look for combinations of ideas. For instance, I could find out how many teachers mentioned an intention of maintaining momentum in the context of a learning activity as opposed to the context of a question-and-answer routine, or I could compare how frequently different types of intentions were mentioned in relationship to different types of episodes. Because these analyses are so easy to generate, they may have the unusual disadvantage of encouraging overuse and of looking at relationships even when there is no good reason to do so.

One problem with automated categorical analyses is that errors in the way passages were marked off can lead to errors in later analyses. A single character may be counted as a "passage" that has been coded in one category but not in another. Although it is easy to use N-Vivo to generate quantitative cross-tabulations, the researcher needs to check *each resulting instance* to verify that it really is a valid instance of a "passage."

Stage 4: Narratives

The first three stages of analysis enabled me to sort passages according to their content and to conceptualize the themes and ideas that seemed to dominate teachers' thinking. Making all of this come to life for readers, however, requires the development of narratives, stories that summarize what happened and why. I used two types of narratives. One was the line of thinking that summarized the entire set of ideas that a particular teacher described when explaining her reasoning for a particular episode. The second kind of narrative included more detail about how events unfolded in the classroom, as well as what the teacher was thinking as these events unfolded. These narratives often entailed going back to the original video and sometimes even transcribing it, to create an accurate record of events, and then overlaying the video transcript with annotations from the teacher's interview that explained her hopes or fears as events unfolded.

These stories breathe life into the themes and categories of ideas, but they also threaten the validity of the report because they are so easy to digest. While narratives are central to qualitative reporting, they can also distort findings. It would be easy to mislead readers by presenting one particularly poignant story, even if that story was an anomaly in the context of study as a whole. Because each story is internally consistent and plausible, readers are inclined to believe they represent larger truths—even to generate their own morals to the stories. For this reason, I tried to balance stories with tallies of frequencies and with extracts from multiple teachers. The stories bring the findings to life, but the tallies and tables provide a sense of how typical or representative the story is. Without these other tools, the representativeness, and consequently the morals to the stories, would all be suspect.

Notes

1. ## The Mysterious Gap between Reform Ideals and Everyday Teaching

   1. Because most teachers in this sample are females, I refer to teachers in general as "she."
   2. Since my focus is on what teachers are doing in their classrooms, I do not address the plethora of reform proposals related to textbooks, course offerings, or school organization.
   3. The eight-year study was a large-scale effort during the 1930s to encourage secondary schools to adopt more progressive curricula. As part of this effort, colleges and universities agreed to suspend their traditional admissions criteria so that participating students would not be denied access to colleges of their choice.
   4. I define context in terms of the operative reform initiatives. Another researcher might focus on other aspects of context, such as the community's economic status or its ethnic or religious composition. I chose this focus because I was interested in the influence of these reform initiatives. However, knowing that teachers might respond to other issues, I left the interview questions open enough that teachers could mention any aspects of their teaching context that were relevant to the specific practices we were discussing.
   5. The same person who observed the lesson interviewed the teacher. However, since the study involved multiple interviewers, for rhetorical simplicity I routinely refer to the interviewer as "we."

2. ## How Teachers Think about Their Practices

   1. Details of the interview strategy are provided in the appendix.
   2. Because we can never know the truthfulness of teachers' rationales for their practices, I refer to these lines of thinking as *accounts* of practices. My reliance on teacher accounts stems in part from the lack of any alternative strategy for learning how teachers reason in situ, and in part from the wide range of ideas teachers presented in these lines of thinking. If the rationales they presented reflect their notions of what is socially acceptable, then teachers perceive tremendously different things as socially ac-

ceptable. The sheer variety of ideas presented therefore suggests that they have at least some merit in teachers' minds.

3. All the ideas mentioned in the line of reasoning come directly from the interview. They are paraphrased here for the sake of brevity, but nothing is imputed.

4. Throughout this chapter, I refer to the number of times an idea was mentioned by teachers. To arrive at these tallies I did not include single-line or single-sentence references but instead tallied ideas only when the teacher provided a longer discussion. That is, if a teacher mentioned a goal or a constraint in passing I did not include it. The tallies I refer to here were places in the interviews where teachers discussed a particular goal, constraint, or concern that was important to them.

3.   Creating a Tranquil Environment

1. As mentioned in Chapter 2, Buford was working on her persona because one of her students was overly excitable.

References

Aguirre, J., and N. M. Speer. 1999. Examining the relationship between beliefs and goals in teacher practice. *Journal of Mathematical Behavior* 18(3): 327–356.

American Association for the Advancement of Science. 1989. *Science for All Americans: A Project 2061 Report on Literacy Goals in Science, Mathematics, and Technology.* Washington, D.C.

Applebee, A. N. 1991. Informal reasoning and writing instruction. In J. F. Voss, D. N. Perkins, and J. W. Segal, eds., *Informal Reasoning and Education,* pp. 225–246. Hillsdale, N.J.: Erlbaum.

Argyris, C., and D. A. Schön. 1996. *Organizational Learning II.* New York: Addison-Wesley.

Artiles, A. J., M. P. Mostert, and M. Tankersley. 1994. Assessing the links between teacher cognitions, teacher behaviors, and pupil responses to lessons. *Teaching and Teacher Education* 10(5): 465–481.

Ball, D. L. 1991. Teaching mathematics for understanding: What do teachers need to know about the subject matter? In M. M. Kennedy, ed., *Teaching Academic Subjects to Diverse Learners,* pp. 63–83. New York: Teachers College Press.

Berlak, A., and H. Berlak. 1981. *Dilemmas of Schooling: Teaching and Social Change.* London: Methuen.

Borko, H., and R. Putnam. 1996. Learning to teach. In D. C. Berliner and R. Calfee, eds., *Handbook of Educational Psychology,* pp. 673–708. New York: Macmillan.

Bransford, J. D., A. L. Brown, and R. R. Cocking. 1999. *How People Learn: Brain, Mind, Experience, and School.* Washington, D.C.: National Aacademy Press.

Brophy, J. 1999. Classroom management as socializing students into clearly articulated roles. *Journal of Classroom Interaction* 33(1): 1–4.

Brophy, J., and T. L. Good. 1986. Teacher behavior and student achievement. In M. C. Wittrock, ed., *Handbook of Research on Teaching,* 3d ed. pp. 328–375. New York: Macmillan.

Bruner, J. S. 1996. *The Culture of Education.* Cambridge, Mass.: Harvard University Press.

Bussis, A., E. Chittenden, and M. Amarel. 1976. *Beyond Surface Curriculum.* Boulder: Westview.

Carlsen, W. S. 1987. Why do you ask? Effects of science teacher subject matter knowledge on teacher questioning and classroom discourse. Paper presented at the March meeting of the American Educational Research Association, New Orleans.

———. 1997. Never ask a question if you don't know the answer: The tension in teaching between modeling scientific argument and maintaining law and order. *Journal of classroom interaction, 32*(2), 14–23.

Cazden, C., and H. Mehen. 1990. Principles from sociology and anthropology: Context, code, classroom, and culture. In M. C. Reynolds, ed., *The Knowledge Base for Beginning Teachers*, pp. 47–57. New York: Pergamon.

Chall, J. S. 2000. *The Academic Achievement Challenge: What Really Works in the Classroom?* New York: Guildford.

Cohen, D. K. 1988. Plus ça change. In P. Jackson, ed., *Contribution to Educational Change: Perspectives on Research in Practice Issues,* pp. 27–84. Berkeley: McCutchan.

———. 1990. A revolution in one classroom: The case of Mrs. Oublier. *Educational Evaluation and Policy Analysis* 12(3): 311–329.

Cohen, D. K., and D. L. Ball. 1998. *Instruction, Capacity, and Improvement.* Philadelphia: University of Pennsylvania Center for Policy Research in Education.

Corrie, L. 1997. The interaction between teachers' knowledge and skills when managing a troublesome classroom behavior. *Cambridge Journal of Education* 27(1): 93–105.

Cremin, L. 1990. *Popular Education and Its Discontents.* New York: Harper and Row.

Cronbach, L. J., and P. Suppes, eds. 1969. *Research for Tomorrow's Schools: Disciplined Inquiry for Education.* New York: National Academy of Education and Macmillan.

Cuban, L. 1984. *How Teachers Taught: Constancy and Change in American Classrooms, 1890–1980.* White Plains, N.Y.: Longman.

———. 1990. Reforming again, again, and again. *Educational Researcher* 19(1): 3–13.

Cusick, P. A. 1983. *The Egalitarian Ideal and the American High School: Studies of Three Schools.* New York: Longman.

Doyle, W. 1983. Academic work. *Review of Educational Research* 53(2): 159–199.

———. 1986. Content representation in teachers' definitions of academic work. *Journal of Curriculum Studies* 18(4): 365–379.

Doyle, W., and K. Carter. 1984. Academic tasks in classrooms. *Curriculum Inquiry* 14: 129–149.

Edwards, A. D., and D. P. G. Westgate. 1994. *Investigating Classroom Talk.* London: Falmer.

Egan, K. 1997. *The Educated Mind: How Cognitive Tools Shape Our Understanding.* Chicago: University of Chicago Press.

———. 2001. Why education is so difficult and contentious. *Teachers College Record* 103(6): 923–941.

Elmore, R. F., and D. Burney. 1999. Investing in teacher learning: Staff development and instructional improvement. In L. Darling-Hammond and G. Sykes, eds., *Teaching as the Learning Profession: Handbook of Policy and Practice,* pp. 263–291. San Francisco: Jossey-Bass.

Ericcson, K. A., and H. A. Simon. 1993. *Protocol Analysis: Verbal Reports as Data.* Rev. ed. Cambridge, Mass.: MIT Press.

Fenwick, D. T. 1998. Managing space, energy, and self: Junior high teachers' experiences of classroom management. *Teaching and Teacher Education* 14(6): 619–631.

Gall, M. D. 1970. The use of questioning in teaching. *Review of Educational Research* 40: 707–721.

Gallagher, M. C. 2001. Lessons from the Sputnik-era curriculum reform movement: The institutions we need for educational reform. In S. Stotsky, ed., *What's at Stake in the K-12 Standards Wars,* pp. 281–312. New York: Peter Lang.

Gamoran, A., W. G. Secada, and C. B. Marrett. 2000. The organizational context of teaching and learning: Changing theoretical perspectives. In M. T. Hallinan, ed., *Handbook of the Sociology of Education,* pp. 37–63. New York: Kluwer Academic.

Gold, B. A. 1999. Punctuated legitimacy: A theory of educational change. *Teachers College Record* 101(2): 192–219.

Goodson, I. 1994. Studying the teacher's life and work. *Teaching and Teacher Education* 10(1): 29–37.

Hammer, D. 1997. Discovery learning and discovery teaching. *Cognition and Instruction* 15(4): 485–529.

Hargreaves, A. 1996. Revisiting Voice. *Educational Researcher* 25(1): 12–19.

Hoetker, J., and W. P. Ahlbrand Jr. 1969. The persistence of the recitation. *American Educational Research Journal* 6: 145–167.

Huberman, M. 1983. Recipes for busy kitchens. *Knowledge: Creation, Diffusion, Utilization* 4(4): 478–510.

———. 1994. *The Lives of Teachers.* New York: Teachers College Press.

Hunt, T. C. 2003. *The Impossible Dream: Education and the Search for Panaceas.* New York: Peter Lang.

Ingersoll, R. M. 2003. *Who Controls Teachers' Work? Power and Accountability in America's Schools.* Cambridge, Mass.: Harvard University Press.

Jackson, P. W. 1968. *Life in Classrooms.* New York: Holt, Rinehart and Winston.

Johnson, S. M. 1990. *Teachers at Work: Achieving Success in Our Schools.* Boston: Basic Books.

Kagan, D. M. 1992. Implications of research on teacher belief. *Educational Psychologist* 27(1): 65–90.

Kahneman, D., and A. Tversky. 1986. Choices, values and frames. In H. R. Arkes and K. R. Hammond, eds., *Judgment and Decision Making: An Interdisciplinary Reader,* pp. 194–210. New York: Cambridge University Press.

Kennedy, M. M. 1991. Merging subjects and students into teaching knowledge.

In M. M. Kennedy, ed., *Teaching Academic Subjects to Diverse Learners,* pp. 273–284. New York: Teachers College Press.

Kilpatrick, W. H. 1918. The project method. *Teachers College Record* 19(4): 319–335.

Koretz, D., B. Stecher, S. Klein, and D. McCaffrey. 1994. The Vermont Portfolio Assessment. *Educational Measurement Issues and Practice* 13(30): 5–16.

Kounin, J. 1970. *Discipline and Group Management in Classrooms.* New York: Holt, Rinehart and Winston.

Labaree, D. F. 2000. On the nature of teaching and teacher education: Difficult practices that look easy. *Journal of Teacher Education* 51(3): 228–233.

Lampert, M. 1985. How do teachers manage to teach? Perspectives on the problems of practice. *Harvard Educational Review* 55: 178–194.

Leinhardt, G., C. Weidman, and K. M. Hammond. 1987. Introduction and integration of classroom routines by expert teachers. *Curriculum Inquiry* 17(2): 135–176.

Lortie, D. C. 1975. *Schoolteacher: A Sociological Study.* Chicago: University of Chicago Press.

Lumpe, A. T., J. J. Haney, and C. M. Czerniak. 1998. Science teachers' beliefs and intentions regarding the use of cooperative learning. *School Science and Mathematics* 98(3): 123–135.

McLaughlin, M. W., and I. Oberman. 1996. *Teacher Learning: New Policies, New Practices.* New York: Teachers College Press.

McNeil, L. M. 1985. *Contradictions of Control: School Structure and School Knowledge.* London: Routledge and Kegan Paul.

Mehan, H. 1979. *Learning lessons: Social Organization in the Classroom.* Cambridge, Mass.: Harvard University Press.

Metz, M. 1993. Teachers' ultimate dependence on their students. In J. Little and M. McLaughlin, eds., *Teachers' Work: Individuals, Colleagues, and Context.* New York: Teachers College Press.

National Commission on Excellence in Education. 1983. *A Nation at Risk.* Washington, D.C.: U.S. Department of Education.

National Council of Teachers of Mathematics. 2000. *Principles and Standards for School Mathematics.* Reston, Va.

Nisbett, R. E., and L. Ross. 1991. *The Person and the Situation: Perspectives of Social Psychology.* New York: McGraw-Hill.

Oliver, W. A. 1953. Teachers' educational beliefs versus their classroom practices. *Journal of Educational Research* 48(1): 47–55.

Pajares, M. F. 1992. Teachers' beliefs and educational research: Cleaning up a messy construct. *Review of Educational Research* 62(3): 307–332.

Porter, A. C. 1989. A curriculum out of balance: The case of elementary school mathematics. *Educational Researcher* 18(5): 9–15.

Porter, A. C., et al. 1989. Content determinants in elementary school mathematics. In D. A. Grouws, T. J. Cooney, and D. Jones, eds., *Effective Mathematics*

Teaching, pp. 96–113. Reston, Va.: National Council of Teachers of Mathematics.

Pressley, M., J. Rankin, and L. Yokoi. 1996. A survey of instructional practices of primary teachers nominated as effective in promoting literacy. *Elementary School Journal* 96(4): 363–384.

Ravitch, D. 2000. *Left Back: A Century of Battles over School Reform.* New York: Touchstone.

Richardson, V. A. 1996. The role of attitudes and beliefs in learning to teach. In J. Sikula and T. Buttery and E. Guyton, eds., *Handbook of Research on Teacher Education,* pp. 102–119. New York: Macmillan.

Rowan, B. 1996. Standards as teacher motivation for instructional reform. In S. H. Fuhrman and J. A. O'Day, eds., *Rewards and Reform: Creating Educational Teacher Motivation That Works,* pp. 195–225. San Francisco: Jossey-Bass.

Ryans, D. 1960. *Characteristics of Teachers.* Washington, D.C.: American Council on Education.

Schmidt, W. H., C. C. McKnight, and S. A. Raizen, eds. 1997. *A Splintered Vision: An Investigation of U.S. Science and Mathematics Education.* London: Kluwer Academic.

Schoenfeld, A. H. 1999a. Toward a theory of teaching-in-context. University of California at Berkeley. Retrieved in March 2001 from www.gse.berkeley.edu/aschoenfeld/TeachinginContext/tic.html.

———. 1999b. Models of the teaching process. *Journal of Mathematical Behavior* 18(3): 243–261.

Schwab, J. J. 1978. The "impossible" role of the teacher in progressive education. In I. Westbury and N. J. Wilkoff, eds., *Science, Curriculum, and Liberal Education: Selected Essays,* pp. 167–183. Chicago: University of Chicago Press.

Schwille, J. R., et al. 1983. Teachers as policy brokers in the content of elementary school mathematics. In L. S. Shulman and G. Sykes, eds., *Handbook of Teaching and Policy,* pp. 370–391. New York: Longman.

Sedlak, M., C. Wheeler, D. C. Pullin, and P. A. Cusick. 1986. *Selling Students Short: Classroom Bargains and Academic Reform in the American High School.* New York: Teachers College Press.

Shavelson, R. J. 1983. Review of research on teachers' pedagogical judgments, plans, and decisions. *Elementary School Journal* 83(4): 392–413.

Smith, B. 2000. Quantity matters: Annual instructional time in an urban school system. *Educational Administration Quarterly* 36(5): 652–682.

Spillane, J. P. 1999. External reform initiatives and teachers' efforts to reconstruct their practice: The mediating role of the teachers' zones of enactment. *Journal of Curriculum Studies* 31(2): 143–175.

Stevenson, H. W., and J. W. Stigler. 1992. *The Learning Gap: Why Our Schools Are Failing and What We Can Learn from Japanese and Chinese Education.* New York: Summit.

Stigler, J. W., and J. Hiebert. 1999. Teaching is a cultural ectivity. *American Educator* 22(4): 4–11.

Stigler, J. W., and H. W. Stevenson. 1991. How Asian teachers polish each lesson to perfection. *American Educator,* spring, 12–48.

Stigler, J. W., et al. 1999. *The TIMSS Videotape Classroom Study.* Washington DC: National Institute for Education Statistics.

Stodolsky, S. S. 1988. *The Subject Matters: Classroom Activity in Math and Social Studies.* Chicago: University of Chicago Press.

Stoel, C. F., and T.-S. Thant. 2002. *Teachers' Professional Lives: A View from Nine Industrialized Countries.* Washington, D.C.: Council for Basic Education.

Tyack, D., and L. Cuban. 1995. *Tinkering toward Utopia: A Century of Public School Reform.* Cambridge, Mass.: Harvard University Press.

van den Berg, B. 2002. Teachers' meanings regarding educational practice. *Review of Educational Research* 72(4): 577–625.

Wagner, A. C. 1987. "Knots" in teachers' thinking. In J. Calderhead, ed., *Exploring Teacher Thinking,* pp. 161–178. London: Cassell.

Waller, W. 1932/1961. *The Sociology of Teaching.* New York: Russell and Russell.

Index